OLDMAN'S

BRAVE NEW WORLD

OF WINE

ALSO BY MARK OLDMAN

Oldman's Guide to Outsmarting Wine,
winner of the Georges Duboeuf Wine Book of the Year Award

W. W. NORTON & COMPANY NEW YORK · LONDON

OLDMAN'S
BRAVE NEW WORLD
OF WINE

Pleasure,
Value, and Adventure
Beyond Wine's Usual Suspects

MARK OLDMAN

For information about permission to reproduce selections from this book,
write to Permissions, W. W. Norton & Company, Inc.,
500 Fifth Avenue, New York, NY 10110

For information about special discounts for bulk purchases, please contact
W. W. Norton Special Sales at specialsales@wwnorton.com or 800-233-4830

Manufacturing by Courier Westford
Book design by Chris Welch
Illustrations by Josh Cochran
Production manager: Devon Zahn
Digital production by Adrian Kitzinger and Sue Carlson

ISBN 978-0-393-33484-5

W. W. Norton & Company, Inc.
500 Fifth Avenue, New York, N.Y. 10110
www.wwnorton.com

W. W. Norton & Company Ltd.
Castle House, 75/76 Wells Street, London W1T 3QT

1 2 3 4 5 6 7 8 9 0

"Drink bravely, old boy . . . for nothing is
so dear and precious as time. . . ."

—*François Rabelais,*
Gargantua and Pantagruel, *Book V (1564)*

CONTENTS

BUBBLY

DESSERT WINES

THREE FOR THE ROAD

APPENDICES

OLDMAN'S
BRAVE NEW WORLD
OF WINE

INTRODUCTION

Is there no greater godsend than a savvy soul who can tip you off to a city's best eateries? Before a trip, I am indebted immeasurably to an in-the-know friend who can help me navigate streets of endless choice, steering me away from the same old standards and tourist traps in favor of new finds and estimable rediscoveries. I want to know the worthiest five-stars and falafel counters for sure, but I'm mostly lusting for that holy grail of gastronauts: less familiar gems where costs are moderate and insiders hang their hats.

And so it is with wine: never before in the history of fermented grape juice have there been so many tempting choices, and, accordingly, never before has there been such need for a carefully curated guide to wines worth your while. With a yearning to inspire new taste sensations and a fiercely consumerist eye, I offer you this guide to our brave new world of wine. My mission, pure and simple, is to fast track you to a world of pleasure, value, and adventure beyond wine's usual suspects. In a phrase: I want to inspire you to *drink bravely*.

Why Should Insiders Have All the Fun?

The brainstorm for this book seized me a few years ago at a gathering of wine pros. Sommeliers and importers were darting back and forth, offering each other tastes with the giddy joy and competitive zeal of parents brandishing baby photos. Bonhomie filled the room, rising out of the dozens of opened bottles before us. Glasses clinked, place mats disintegrated, and the thrill of discovery and a good buzz was reflected in the room's ratcheting din.

As I soaked up the scene at this bring-your-own-bottle gathering of wine pros, I marveled at how elated these folks were to be sharing wine discoveries with each other.

"You *have* to taste the texture of this Oregon Pinot," said one, magnum in hand.

"Can you believe this Bordeaux is only fourteen dollars?" asked another.

"This Grüner would sing with shellfish," remarked a third.

The sheer volume of wine knowledge being exchanged, I thought, could have filled the (wine-saturated) pages of a small encyclopedia. And then it occurred to me: *why* should the insiders have all the fun? Why should *they* be privy to the wines that bring the ooh's and aah's while the rest of us make do with the same old usual suspects? It was high time to bring what they know to everyone else.

The Golden Age of Wine Choice

The time is indeed opportune as we venture further into what has become a golden age of wine choice, one in which an ambitious new generation of winemakers and improved winemaking technology are revitalizing forgotten grapes and revamping wine regions throughout the world. Whereas just a generation ago there wasn't much choice beyond the classics of Bordeaux, Burgundy, and California, now you can trot the globe from the comfort of your own dinner table, sampling a new region or grape every night of the month if you so desire. The diversity of wines and their quality and affordability has never been greater.

Now your local wine merchant or beverage superstore not only stocks mainstream pours but offers wine from nontraditional grapes such as Torrontés, Moschofilero, and Petite Sirah and from regions as far-flung as New Zealand, Portugal, and Greece. And if your neighborhood store doesn't have exactly what you want, the Internet has made it possible to search the world's inventory of wine and have specific bottles sent to you in time for lunch the next day.

Similarly, wine bars and wine-themed restaurants have sprouted up in every city, offering everything from Albariño to Vinho Verde on their increasingly varied lists. Sommeliers and wine directors have become the new gastronomic rock stars, profiled, with Windsor knots a-bulge, in magazines and blogs, becoming almost as renowned as the chefs with whom they work.

Coinciding with the dawn of this new era of wine choice has been a rocketing of popular interest in gastronomy. The Food Network, the cult of celebrity chefs, and television franchises like *Top Chef* are now part of our cultural fabric. The American palate has broadened to the point where hummus is a refrigerator staple, vast swaths of eaters have learned to pronounce "chipotle," and even Wrigley Field makes a mean spicy tuna roll. This increasing culinary sophistication has permeated winedom, too, from the "Anything but Chardonnay" adherents who inveigh against leaden styles of that grape to the growing ranks of bloggers who routinely call for wines of personality and integrity over monochromatic, industrial quaffs.

Mired in a Merlot Morass

Yet so many drinkers remain mired in a Merlot morass, falling back on the same old standards with exasperated resignation, clinging to the coastline of familiarity like anxious castaways. Who can blame them, given the sundry impediments to experimentation, from restaurants' vertiginous markups to the fetishists who'd have you believe that wine appreciation requires a slavish devotion to ratings, florid language, and pricey gadgets? Compounding this problem is the relative opacity of wine knowledge itself, replete as it is with bedeviling pronunciations and obfuscatory terminology.

A similar inaccessibility plagues art appreciation. Unless one makes a personal study of art or grows up in a family that collects it, most of us never get beyond Picasso, Monet, Warhol, and other museum staples that, however distinguished, prove limiting if that's all you know. Like in wine, connoisseurs of art have their own code of less familiar options that remain concealed from curious outsiders. It wasn't until I met my friend Andrea, an art consultant with an uncanny ability of making the insular art world knowable and unintimidating, that my eyes were opened to the works of Walton Ford, Jules de Balincourt, Walead Beshty, and a host of other exhilarating but less obvious artists.

The Brave New Pours

So my mandate crystallized: it was time to build a bridge of knowledge from the insiders to everyone else, revealing wines that so electrify me and my fellow wine pros—opening the curtain on what I call the "Brave New Pours."

When I touched upon a few of these less familiar wines in the "Secret Alternatives" section of my last book, *Oldman's Guide to Outsmarting Wine*, readers wrote me that they couldn't get enough of them. I heard similar enthusiasm from the students of my "Wines to Devastate Your Friends" classes at New York University and from the attendees of my seminars at the Aspen Food & Wine Classic and at the South Beach Wine & Food Festival. Everyone, it seemed, wanted to imbibe like an insider.

So what qualified as a Brave New Pour? With apologies to those yearning to discover Gaglioppo, Mavrodaphne, or the wines of Turkmenistan, I resolutely avoided covering the hopelessly obscure, because if you can't actually get your claws on a wine, what use is it? I'm besotted with a white wine from Austria called Zierfandler, for instance, but there isn't yet enough of it available in the United States to make it a chapter. I focused instead on less obvious types that are nevertheless obtainable, most locally and others with a few clicks of your mouse. These range from twists on the classics (not Chardonnay but *low or no oak* Chardonnay; not any Merlot but *good* Merlot; Riesling not from Germany but from Austria and Australia) to the almost famous (e.g., Malbec, Grüner Veltliner, Gewürztraminer) to the not yet popular.

This last category was the largest, populated by types ranging from the Reputationally Ascendant (Reds from Portugal) to the Dogged-by-a-Checkered-Past (Lambrusco); from the Delicately Feminine (Rosé Champagne) to the Medievally Masculine (Cahors); from the Excessively Disdained (Box Wine) to the

Unnecessarily Intimidating (Old Wine); from the Prime-Time Ready (Moschofilero) to the Lovably Eccentric (Sparkling Shiraz); from the Humbly Understated (Muscadet) to the Unapologetically Flamboyant (Big Bottles); from the Next Big Thing (Torrontés) to the Forever Overlooked (Bargain Bordeaux). Moreover, while many of the Brave New Pours are cutting-edge discoveries, a sprinkling of them are old friends worthy of rediscovery—Côtes du Rhône, to name one.

Not only are the Brave New Pours insider picks, they also share the common attribute of being exemplars of economy. Many of them average under $20 a bottle, including rosé, *cru* Beaujolais, and Prosecco. Others such as Vinho Verde, Muscadet, Nero d'Avola can be outright steals at $10 or less. And even when they aren't inexpensive per se, they typically offer compelling quality for their price—with picks such as grower Champagne, reds from Washington State, and Aglianico significantly less costly than their more famous equivalents. It is an open secret in the wine world that the more popular a wine is, the more likely consumers must pay extra for that demand. Usual suspects like Pinot Grigio and Cabernet Sauvignon are like a Sony camera or Nike sneakers: they command a comfort premium. In contrast, the unfamiliar—and especially the unfamiliar *and* hard-to-pronounce—are not as coveted and thus typically a better value.

Striving for the Satisfyingly Diverse

Any grouping like the Brave New Pours is, of course, subjective. This book is not meant to be inclusive of all possible insider wines, but instead to offer a compelling and satisfyingly diverse assortment of wine types that have resonated with my wine pro friends and my students. If your favorite new discovery is not represented, rest assured that it's probably on deck for my next book.

I have nevertheless labored mightily to assemble here a rich tapestry of stimulating wine types—mostly affordable pours but also a few special-occasion picks like rosé Champagne and Madeira. In doing so, I hope to demonstrate that our new world of wine choice liberates us from traditional conceptions of what it means to be a connoisseur and that the casual and the upscale can and should co-exist in one's vinous repertoire. As in art, fashion, and virtually every other endeavor involving good taste, there is much to be gained from embracing both the high and the low—of learning that there are times to appreciate box wine and situations that call for splurging on a Serpico Aglianico.

The benefits of broad-mindedness and a well-considered eclecticism are recurring themes in this book—from the wines I choose and how their information is presented to the types of wine lovers I quote and their sometimes surprising preferences. It is a relief to read that some of the world's most exalted palates aren't embarrassed about committing such seeming sins as adding ice to wine, pairing red Burgundy wine with pepperoni pizza, and even mixing red wine with Coke. The message is this: a slavish adherence to rules has never mattered less in wine appreciation.

Relevance to All Levels of Knowledge

Just as this book embraces the mighty and the modest, it also caters to enthusiasts of all levels. Novices will find that the chapters, taken together, are meant to provide easy on-ramps into our burgeoning universe of options, furnishing just enough information for beginners to start to identify new styles that suit their tastes. In doing so, they will realize that neither sommelier credentials nor a foreign tongue is necessary to experience the thrill of discovery and economy that comes with drinking like an insider.

For those with intermediate knowledge, this book is designed to provide more bullets for their vinous belt, illuminating new and reborn regions as well as fresh twists on certain classics. Because even aficionados tend to limit themselves to just a handful of regions or grapes that they happened to encounter early in their wine journeys, I aim to help them shatter their vinous complacency. The book provides escape hatches for enthusiasts caught in a Stockholm-Syndrome-like dependence on mainstream wine types. Those who rely solely on Pinot Grigio for summertime sipping, for example, will learn that Rueda from Spain and Vermentino from Italy are tempting alternatives.

For wine professionals, collectors, and other experts, this book is designed to fill in the gaps, reinforce the newly learned, and help choose among the stars in a constellation of worthy wine types. Even the most adventurous and knowledgeable grape-nuts have to work at staying abreast of the latest and greatest. If you are already a black-diamond imbiber, chances are that some of the more exotic Brave New Pours, such as Sparkling Shiraz, Txakoli, or Austrian Riesling, have remained below your radar.

Practicality and Interactivity

Whatever your level of knowledge, I have constructed each chapter to emphasize the practical. As I did in my last book, I have concentrated on what you really need to know and spared you lengthy elaborations on geology, chemistry, and history. My passion is to provide easily implementable nuggets of wine wisdom, focusing on how a wine typically tastes, as well as its cost, availability, best food matches, and other useful information. And because if you can't pronounce a wine you're probably not going to give it much of a chance, I made sure to include hundreds of tricky pronunciations.

I also want to inspire you to interact heartily with each Brave New Pour. Readers of my last book wrote me about how useful it was to attack each new wine chapter by chapter, some even dedicating an evening to trying different producers of one particular wine type. Others hosted tasting parties for a particular category or created their own wine-flights in restaurants and wine bars. Nothing pleased me more than to learn of these adventures, as the easiest way to broaden your vinous horizons is to spend time interacting with a new discovery. If you spend a night focusing solely on Madeira or Viognier, you're more likely to remember it. We thus have the "Spend the Night Together" section of each entry, where I propose ways of deepening your familiarity with each Brave New Pour.

Inspiration and Memorableness

Because I personally gain inspiration from hearing about what others like to drink, I interviewed and surveyed 146 insiders and wine lovers—my "Bravehearts"—about their vinous preferences. Peppered through the book, their insights are meant to stoke your appetite for experimentation. My Bravehearts comprise a stable of wine-passionate luminaries as diverse as the Brave New Pours themselves: rock stars and their culinary equivalent as well as actors, writers, athletes, vintners, sommeliers, importers, consultants, and others happily infected by oenophilia. It is a prodigiously varied group of cool cats, ranging from the Metropolitan Opera's concertmaster to master rapper Busta Rhymes; from wine-rhapsodic Virginia Madsen of *Sideways* to woman-rhapsodic Antonio Banderas of *Zorro*; from Ariane Daguin, a legendary purveyor of high-end meat, to the carnivorously named Kevin Bacon; from acclaimed young winemakers such as Beringer's Laurie Hook to the late, great pioneer Robert Mondavi.

Finally, every moment I spent writing this book has been animated with the desire to make expanding your wine knowledge as memorable and engaging as possible. I don't want you to just read about how Aglianico tastes; I want you to associate it with the macho aesthetics of George Clooney's hypothetical study. When you think about American sparkling wine, I want you to visualize my ritual of the Pre-Hotel Bubbly Run. When you see Vermentino, I want you to picture my pouring it into a Sprite bottle for the purposes of clandestine imbibing at movie theaters. My greatest wish is for you to be in a restaurant or wine store and turn to your beloved and say, "Honey, I do believe this was the wine that got medieval on Mark's tongue" (Cahors). For me, visual associations are a key to painless learning and retention and they're even more effective when they are lighthearted and vivid, or, to paraphrase Mark Twain, when they are presented in a way that never lets schooling interfere with your education.

May that education be adventurous and your wine bravely drunk.

EXPANDING VINOUS HORIZONS

"The world of wine types keeps expanding for the consumer. There are fantastic Cabernets from South Africa, Pinots from New Zealand, even cider from the city of Hardanger in Norway. Ask your local wine shop, 'What do you got that's exciting for me?'"

—*Marcus Samuelsson, chef and co-owner, Aquavit, New York, NY*

"We can get stuck in a rut, buying the same wine over and over again. If you find yourself always going for a Cab or a Shiraz, why not explore the world of Sauvignon Blanc? Why, you ask? To surprise your senses and open up your mind. It's kind of like having a party or better yet, a new lover.

"As with most wine lovers, my palate is always changing, evolving, to evoke the *Sideways* reference. We too are forever evolving, just as wine itself."

—*Virginia Madsen, actress and star of* Sideways

"To limit yourself to one or two wine types would be ridiculous."

—*Drew Bledsoe, football great*

"Open yourself to a broad spectrum of wine styles and experiences. Don't get stuck!"
—*Brian Duncan, owner and wine director, BIN 36, Chicago, IL*

"The wine world is completely different now—do not listen to those who say you have to spend a hundred dollars and buy Bordeaux to get a good bottle. There are very good wines at very reasonable prices now."

—*Lidia Bastianich, chef and host, PBS's* Lidia's Italy

"I love wine's diversity and so I'm constantly falling in love with new wines from new regions. There must be a thousand wines that have captured me at any given time: some expensive, some rare, but many have been neither expensive nor rare."
—*Doug Frost, master sommelier and master of wine*

"Force yourself to hang your control-freakishness on a hook and embark on a journey of experimentation."
—*Paul Grieco, wine director and co-owner, Hearth, New York, NY*

"I went through every wine phase. I was the Bordeaux King in the '70s; I had my Vega Sicilia phase, then Pinot. Now it's Barolo and Chianti."
—*Sammy Hagar, vocalist, Chickenfoot, former vocalist, Van Halen*

"My advice is to sample widely—such as Rhône reds, Alsatian whites. Find something besides chocolate-cakey Cabernets."
—*David Chan, concertmaster and violinist, Metropolitan Opera Orchestra, NY*

"Although I used to collect mostly Bordeaux and Burgundy, my cellar is more broadly based now. I get crushes on things: white Bordeaux, Rhône, Alsatian Gewürztraminer, Italian wine, and others."
—*Al Stewart, folk-rock musician, "Year of the Cat"*

"The overall sophistication of wine drinkers has gotten much greater. People are experimenting with different varietals. They will ask for wine that's higher in acidity or fermented in stainless steel."
—*Todd English, chef and restaurateur, Olives, Charlestown, MA*

"Wines from New Zealand, South Africa, Australia, and California are terrific—the price-to-quality there is amazing. A good inexpensive wine from there can be as satisfying as a Bordeaux or Burgundy from the best year."
—*Julio Iglesias, music legend*

"When I was presenting my wine at a Costco store, I met this young married couple. I told them, 'Be careful, don't store the wine in your car.' And they said, 'No, Mr. Fleetwood, we have a cellar.' People's knowledge of wine has so changed."
—*Mick Fleetwood, drummer and namesake, Fleetwood Mac*

KEY

Adventure & Price at a Glance

Plots out each wine type by how much daring (i.e., Adventure) and how much money (i.e., Price) is required of the drinker. While virtually all of the wines in this book are meant to provide new taste sensations, some types offer more adventure than others. The Adventure rating takes into account such factors as how unusual the wine typically tastes, how much contemplation is required to fully appreciate it, how difficult it is to pronounce, and how scarce it is. The Price rating provides an approximation of the retail price you are most likely to encounter, not including exceptional cases on both ends of the pricing continuum.

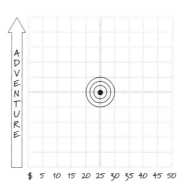

You'll notice that the majority of the wine types in this book appear in the lower-left quadrant of the grid—meaning that they are affordably priced and especially "safe" for everyday drinking, large parties, and other times where cost and user-friendliness are paramount. At the same time, if you are stalking a special gift or an indulgent or celebratory experience, you might try a selection from the upper-right quadrant.

Brave New Pour

Refers to a wine type beyond the usual suspects. The Brave New Pours range from twists on the classics such as low or no oak

Chardonnay to almost famous types such as Grüner Veltliner to less familiar gems like Priorat. "Brave" stands for having the courage to embrace the new or different. "New" refers to not so much wine types that are new to the market—though those are well represented—but regions and grapes that are unfamiliar to a drinker's typically limited range of preferences. "Pour" reflects that these new taste sensations are only a cork pull or cap twist away.

←→ Audacious Alternative To

Lists a few usual suspects that a Brave New Pour most closely resembles. Usual suspects include the classic "Big Six" grapes (Chardonnay, Sauvignon Blanc, Riesling, Cabernet Sauvigon, Merlot, Pinot Noir) in their most general manifestations, as well as other familiar types, as detailed below.

Usual Suspects
(*White*)
Chardonnay (the overall category, *but* we cover low and no oak
    Chardonnay)
Pinot Grigio
Riesling from Germany (*but* we cover Riesling from Australia
    and Austria)
Sauvignon Blanc (the overall category, *but* we cover Sauvignon
    Blanc from New Zealand)

(*Red*)
Beaujolais (the overall category) or Beaujolais Nouveau (*but* we
    cover *cru* Beaujolais)
Bordeaux (the overall category, *but* we cover bargain Bordeaux)
Burgundy (the overall category, *but* we cover bargain Burgundy)
Cabernet Sauvignon (the overall category, *but* we cover classic
    Cabernet and reds from Washington State)

Chianti

Merlot (the overall category, *but* we cover *good* Merlot and it is
   included in reds from Washington State)

Shiraz from Australia

Syrah

Zinfandel

(Other)

Beer

Box wine (the overall category, *but* we cover premium box wine)

Champagne

Gin/Vodka and Tonic

Port (the overall category, *but* we cover Tawny Port)

White Zinfandel

 Enthusiasts Also Like

To help expand your vinous repertoire, you will discover which
of the other Brave New Pours tend to appeal to people who
like the featured wine. Many will be simi-
lar in weight, aroma, and taste (e.g., Txakoli
and Vinho Verde), but rarely exact matches.
Some, in fact, share a distinguishing trait—
e.g., a floral quality—but differ in important
ways such as body; Torrontés and Viognier are
grouped together for their floral aroma, but
the former shades toward lighter weight while
the latter typically displays more heft. Moreover, some wines are joined less by similar
personalities and more by situational appro-
priateness. Occasions that call for casual,
unpretentious Prosecco often also fit box wine, while places
where Madeira is served tend to also welcome big bottles.

> "There's always a very
> close alternative to a
> more expensive and
> famous wine type.
> You're not going to
> get the full monty,
> but you can get
> close."
>
> —*Richard Brierley, former
> head of North American
> wine sales, Christie's*

Weight

(Light, Light-to-Medium, Medium, Medium-to-Full, Full Bodied)

Indicates the body (i.e., mouthfeel) of a Brave New Pour relative to other wines of its color. With wine being subject to the variables of winemaker influence and the weather of a particular vintage year, styles within a particular category can differ widely, so the Weight rating is only an approximation of the style you are most likely to see in the marketplace.

 Price

Represents the retail price range you're most likely to encounter, again with the caveat that prices vary by such factors as geographic market and merchant prerogative. Exceptional cases are typically found above and below the price range. With white wines, "Low" refers to a price of less than $20, "Medium" is $20 to $35, and "High" is above $35.

> "I want to taste the wine before I know the price of it. I don't want to have built up expectations."
> —*Guy Fieri, chef and television host*

 Cheat Sheet

Provides a pithy overview of a Brave New Pour.

 Label Logic

Indicates whether a Brave New Pour is named for its grape or region.

 Bravely Said

Supplies pronounications, often a chief stumbling block to diversifying your vinous portfolio.

Mark's Picks

Reflects a sampling of producers that I have found notable for their excellence, reliability, and availability. The Internet is an invaluable way to track down these wines. Use Internet databases such as Wine-Searcher.com to discover which merchants stock a particular wine. You are encouraged to also email the winery itself, as many will gladly help locate their wine in your area.

 Poosh It!

My homegrown term for broadening your vinous horizons through different wine types, deeper knowledge, and memorable experiences. In the chapter boxes, "Poosh It!" refers specifically to an extra nugget of knowledge about a Brave New Pour that is illuminating or entertaining. In wine, as well as in life, endeavor always to "poosh it."

> "To remember the wines you like at a restaurant, save the cork. Then use the Internet to find out which stores have it. Call a store and see if they'll offer a better price if you buy a case or two."
>
> —Courtney Taylor-Taylor, lead singer and guitarist, The Dandy Warhols

Culinary Sweet Spot Because food and wine pairing primarily involves matching the weight of a wine with the weight of its accompanying food (so that one doesn't obscure the other), the Culinary Sweet Spot charts each wine's ideal range in terms of the richness of the accompanying meal. It is meant merely as general guidance, and your personal preferences should always reign supreme. If you prefer Txakoli with steak au poivre or a brawny Portuguese red with poached sablefish, then your taste buds should have the final word.

> "I consider myself a 'kitchen table family' type of person. Wine combined with food and people creates an unequalled experience. After discovering wine paired with food, I became even more of a 'foodie.'"
> —*Hilary Swank, actress*

> "When working with Greek food, no complement is more simple than maintaining the cultural profile and drinking Greek wine."
> —*Michael Psilakis, chef and co-owner, Anthos, New York, NY*

> "I'm a big believer in pairing the local. I was in Oregon and just loved eating the local salmon with Pinot Noir from the Willamette Valley.
> —*Guy Fieri, chef and television host*

 A Lovable Feast

Provides a list of food matches that tend to flatter the featured wine. They are meant to inspire and broaden your thinking about culinary possibilities—to provide food for thought, literally.

 Locally Lusty

Zeroes in on regional food pairings, true to the adage that "what grows together goes together" and modern gastronomy's embrace of the local.

 Spend the Night Together

To make learning more interactive and memorable, I suggest different ways of deepening your familiarity with a particular Brave New Pour.

> "I'm a big fan of pairing wine and food from a particular region. Certain wines just go with certain dishes, such as a white Rioja with the Spanish-influenced white anchovy sandwich (with salsa verde and egg) at my sandwich shop 'wichcraft."
> —*Tom Colicchio, chef and restaurateur, Craft, New York, NY*

THE
BRAVE NEW POURS

PRIMING THE PALATE

"Every *single* night of my life I drink wine—it makes me feel *alive*. Wine makes me a much better person—it makes me friends. As soon as I pour a good wine: to see just the color, my blood immediately gets running."

—*Julio Iglesias, music legend*

"Eating without wine on the table is not eating completely."

—*Lidia Bastianich, chef and host, PBS's* Lidia's Italy

"I enjoy a good bottle, but I'm no label shaver."　　—*Bill Nye, PBS's "Science Guy"*

"You should take the time to engage all of your senses with wine. Use good glassware. Look at the label. Take the time to swirl and taste it. Treat it with love."

—*Guy Fieri, chef and television host*

"Occasionally I'll drink wine when I'm reading—I'll smell it, leave it in my mouth, savor it.

　"Wine, like movies, is about personal taste. First and foremost, you have to *like* the wine. I like velvety wines—not ones that are too acidic. Wine shouldn't hit you in your stomach."

—*Antonio Banderas, actor*

"While sniffing and drinking a great wine, I'll sometimes think to myself, 'I'll spend any amount of money to get drunk to this smell.'"

—*Courtney Taylor-Taylor, lead singer and guitarist, The Dandy Warhols*

"My stepmother is Malaysian, and in her home country 'How are you?' means 'Have you eaten yet?' That kind of communality is what I love about wine and sharing it with friends."

—*Gavin Rossdale, solo artist and former vocalist and guitarist,* Bush

"Just picking the wine for dinner is an event in itself. You go down to the cellar with your guests, we talk about regions—'I had this bottle, you that one.' Selecting the night's wine is a pre-appetizer—it whets your appetite.

"Wine to me is life."

—*Chazz Palminteri, actor and writer,* A Bronx Tale

WHITES

WHITES: ADVENTURE & PRICE AT A GLANCE

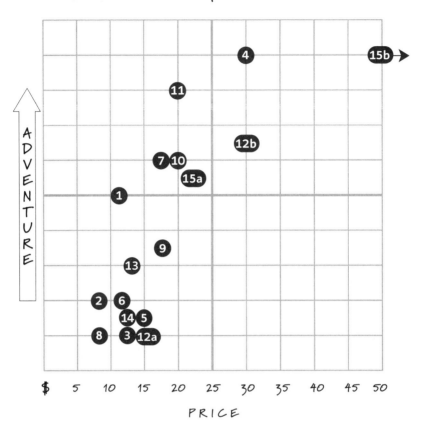

PRICE

1. Moschofilero
2. Muscadet
3. Riesling from Australia
4. Riesling from Austria
5. Sauvignon Blanc from New Zealand
6. Torrontés
7. Txakoli
8. Vinho Verde
9. Albariño

10. Gewürztraminer
11. Grüner Veltliner
12a. Low/No Oak Chardonnay
12b. Chablis
13. Rueda
14. Vermentino
15a. Viognier
15b. Condrieu

1 MOSCHOFILERO

Down with da Mosko?

Dear Greek Winemakers:

   Allow me to suggest a revenue enhancer for these troubled times. As an ardent admirer of Moschofilero, I am convinced that it could achieve Pinot Grigio—like popularity here in the States if you would just make these two adjustments to your marketing:

   1) Label each bottle as "Resin Free": It doesn't matter that Moschofilero never had resin in the first place. Many casual drinkers assume that all Greek wine tastes like retsina, the traditional Greek wine flavored with pine resin. You might see retsina as festive and nostalgic—but to some it tastes more like something that could imperil the ozone layer than a fine wine.

   2) Truncate: Even my second-grade speech therapist, the gloriously Goldie Hawnish Mrs. Bunker, wouldn't have been able to get its name (Mo-sko-FEE-leh-ro) to roll off her tongue. Grüner Veltliner is shortened to "GruVe." Gewürztraminer gets by with "Gewürz." How about dubbing Moschofilero "The Mosko"? Couldn't you just see Snoop Dogg mug for the camera and twist up his fingers, querying the viewer: "Yo, yo, yo—you down with da Mosko?"

Until this happens, Moschofilero will just have to remain an insiders' secret, which is fine by me, since you and I will have more of this exotic refresher. One of the primary grapes in a country notorious for hundreds of unpronounceable varieties, Moschofilero hails from the Peloponnese region of southern Greece, where it prospers in the hills of an area called Mantinia, a name you'll often see on labels. The grape's pinkish hue sometimes imparts a slight blush to the wine itself, which is the perfect foreshadowing of its understated nose of peaches and flowers, not unlike wine from the Muscat grape. But Moschofilero keeps it clean with tangy notes of lime and kiwi, providing the landlocked drinker a summertime plunge into the Ionian Sea.

Speaking of summer, this is the season when Moschofilero shines like a whitewashed wall against the cerulean sky. Its generous acidity makes it a reflexive pick with the brininess of shellfish and the verve of goat cheese and well-dressed salads, not to mention gazpacho and other tomato-based creations common to the summertime table. You don't need Dionysian powers to sense how well Moschofilero matches with lighter Greek fare, from the salty pink spread called *taramosalata* to the tangy feta triangles that are spanakopita. Don't spare the hot sauce, either, as Moschofilero's subtle peachiness and low alcohol can handle the occasional drizzle of heat.

While Moschofilero isn't going win any awards for ubiquity, neither a divining rod nor an Onassian allowance is required to secure a bottle. A quick Internet search shows it to be in stock at dozens of wine shops across the country, with the average price $12 and the most common producer Boutari, the 130-year-old powerhouse that has done much to raise the profile of Greek wines in the last decade. While they have a long way to go before it becomes a household name, the Mosko could be their breakout wine, especially if they dared to call it that.

BRAVEHEARTS ON *Moschofilero*

"I have poured Moschofilero by the glass in many of my restaurants. Beyond being one of the most readily available Greek wines on the market in the U.S., it's a great blend of fresh flavors that suit a beautiful seafood meal.

"For people who like Pinot Grigio or Sauvignon Blanc, Moschofilero can offer a similar flavor while also being a little different, with hints of orange blossom or fresh peach."

—*Michael Psilakis, chef and co-owner, Anthos, New York, NY*

"Moschofilero has a wonderfully floral aromatic profile with hints of citrus that together with great acidity gives you balanced wines without extremes or angles."

—*Yiannis Voyatzis, chief winemaker, Boutari, Naoussa, Greece*

"If you normally drink Pinot Grigio, Moschofilero offers a similar taste profile but often with slightly more aromatics like a bit of flowers or honey.

"You're tasting wine from an ancient region, so Moschofilero offers adventure, but it is so inexpensive and consistent that you can experiment without worrying about getting burned from a bad bottle." —*Fred Dexheimer, master sommelier and wine consultant, New York, NY*

"When I first arrived in the region of Mantinia in 1979, you couldn't find a single Moschofilero. Thirty years later, we have established the region as one of the most successful in Greece and an ambassador of Greek wine abroad."

—*Yiannis Tselepos, winemaker and co-owner, Domaine Tselepos, Mantinia , Greece*

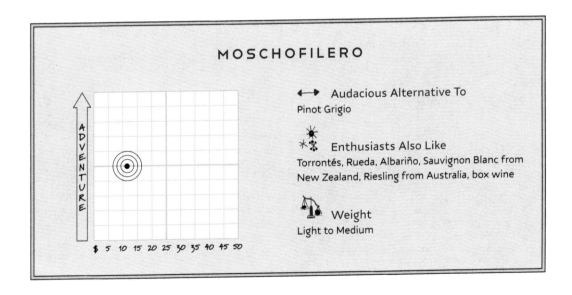

MOSCHOFILERO

⬅➡ **Audacious Alternative To** Pinot Grigio

✳❄ **Enthusiasts Also Like** Torrontés, Rueda, Albariño, Sauvignon Blanc from New Zealand, Riesling from Australia, box wine

⚖ **Weight** Light to Medium

ADVENTURE

$ 5 10 15 20 25 30 35 40 45 50

$ Price

Low

Cheat Sheet

A world away from the resinous, Pine-Sol-with-a-cork many folks still associate with Greek wine, Moschofilero delights with its delicate body, peach-and-flowers aromatics, and mouthwatering crispness.

Label Logic

Moschofilero is a grape. It comes from the Mantinia area of Greece's Peloponnese region.

Bravely Said

Assyrtiko	Ah-SEER-tee-ko
Moschofilero	Mo-sko-FEE-leh-ro
Mantinia	Man-tuh-NEE-uh

Mark's Picks

Antonopoulos	An-toh-NOP-uh-los
Boutari	Boo-TAH-ree
Domaine Sigalas	See-gah-LAH
Gaia Estate	GUY-uh
Nasiakos	Nah-see-AH-kos
Olympus Hellas	
Semeli	Sem-UH-lee
Skouras	SVOOR-us
Tselepos	Tze-LEP-pos

Poosh It!

Another Greek white that enchants insiders is Assyrtiko a steely, lemony pour that is best from the island of Santorini. Among its many admirers is Laurie Hook, chief winemaker at Napa's Beringer Vineyards, who told me that she is partial to the versions from Domaine Sigalas and Gaia Estate.

CULINARY SWEET SPOT

Lightest ▲ Heaviest

A Lovable Feast

As an aperitif or with shellfish like scallops and lighter fish such as sea bass, sea bream; vegetables, especially ones with slight bitterness such as eggplant and zucchini; olives; lemony sauces; brothy soups; spicy fare; tangy and soft cheeses

Locally Lusty

Grilled octopus; mezedes (appetizers) such as dolmades (stuffed grape leaves), tzatziki (yogurt-cucumber dip); spanakopita (spinach and feta cheese wrapped in phyllo pastry), *taramosalata* (creamy fish roe spread); Greek salad

Spend the Night Together

To imbibe as they did in ancient Greece, host a *symposium*, or wine drinking party, where each participant drinks in sequence from *kraters* or vases (you can use glass pitchers or flower vases). Fill each of three with a different Moschofilero, and label them as Dionysus was said to have recommended: one for health, another for love and pleasure, and the third for sleep.

2 MUSCADET

Modest, Minerally, and Made for Mollusks

AFFLICTED WITH THE lingering effects of childhood food squeamishness, I used to avoid oysters at all costs, relegating myself to the ignominy of oyster wallflower while others seemed to be relishing them with orgasmic zeal. Then, on a trip to Virginia's Northern Neck, I reluctantly slurped a few raw Chincoteagues and everything changed. The oceanic salinity of these bivalves surged through me like a slow-motion shiver, a life force that launched what would become an ongoing and obsessive oyster odyssey. With much practice, I have gone from nibbling Kumamotos with a fork and cocktail sauce to shooting Skookums *au naturale*.

What wine has ridden shotgun with me during my oyster explorations? Why, of course, it is the famously mollusk-ready Muscadet, which is so briny and minerally that it sometimes seems as if it too were a creation of the seas. Reared in the westernmost district of France's Loire Valley, Muscadet is less about vivid fruit—though a faint lemony or appley scent is often detectable—and more concerned with simple, cleansing refreshment by way of its light body, ample acidity, and geology-class aroma of wet stones.

The best bottles of Muscadet come from the subregion of Sèvre et Maine, so look for that appellation on the label. Another marker of quality is Muscadet made *sur lie*, or aged on its dead yeast cells. While "dead" and "yeast" don't immediately sound like virtues, contact with sediment will often impart to the wine a slightly creamy texture, a faint yeastiness, and a lively dose of spritz—all of which compensates for the Muscadet grape's relatively neutral character.

I suspect that this somewhat bland flavor, combined with Muscadet's sober-looking, critter-free labels, account for why the grape is overlooked by most drinkers, even as there's no shortage of insiders extolling Muscadet's cleansing, salty powers. If critical praise doesn't put Muscadet on your short list, its easy availability and bargain-bin pricing should. It typically inhabits the rare and wonderful realm of the single digit, and in restaurants you'll find it sitting pretty on a wine list's low end along with Vinho Verde (Chapter 8), Vermentino (Chapter 14), *cru* Beaujolais (Chapter 17), and other vinous steals. It would be hard to find a more impressive $13 gift than the Muscadet from Domaine de la Pépière, which is reliably invigorating and elegantly attired with a traditional cursive that would pass muster at Buckingham Palace.

I tell my students that light-and-zippy Muscadet is a hydraulic pump for the appetite, making your salivary glands anticipate a coming meal like the ringing of a Pavlovian bell. Being such an easy partner with shellfish—even with the infamous steeliness of Belon oysters—and also a staple of brasserie menus, it deserves to be anointed the "Official Wine of *Fruits de Mer* platters." Its tangy, minerally charms are a pitch-perfect accent and affordable counterpoint to the towering, extravagant troughs of ice-laden sea creatures you find in restaurants like New York's Balthazar and Au Pied de Cochon in Paris.

BRAVEHEARTS ON *Muscadet*

"I always like Muscadet because it's clean tasting, not oaky, and good with almost any food except red meat."

—David Chan, concertmaster and violinist, Metropolitan Opera Orchestra, New York, NY

"I strongly recommend tasting Muscadet in the raw bar context rather than trying it alone. It's a wine that's all about understatement, a wine that steps out of the way to shine the spotlight on succulent morsels of fresh seafood instead."

—Marnie Old, author, Wine Secrets, and wine educator

"Muscadet tastes like nothing that would ever come from the U.S. It's for when you feel like taking a trip to the coast of France, at low cost."

—Heather Willens, importer and owner, HW Wines, Buenos Aires, Argentina

"You tend to know it in the first few moments if a diner is knowledgeable about wine. If they say something like, 'Wow, I haven't seen a Luneau-Papin Muscadet on the list in years,' then it's evident that they are in the know."

—Christopher Ycaza, wine director and general manager, Galatoire's, New Orleans, LA

"My wife and I were having a celebratory dinner with the late Win Wilson, co-founder of the wine marketing firm Wilson Daniels. I figured that I needed to bring a bottle of my best white Burgundy and California Chardonnay to the dinner. He brought a $7 bottle of Muscadet. I couldn't believe it. But guess which of three paired best with the oysters?"

—Bart Araujo, owner, Araujo Estate Wines, Napa, CA

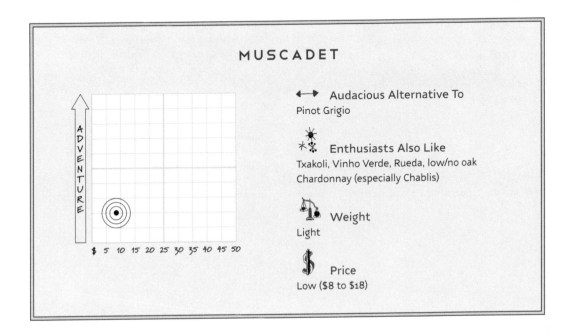

MUSCADET

ADVENTURE

$ 5 10 15 20 25 30 35 40 45 50

↔ **Audacious Alternative To**
Pinot Grigio

✳☘ **Enthusiasts Also Like**
Txakoli, Vinho Verde, Rueda, low/no oak Chardonnay (especially Chablis)

⚖ **Weight**
Light

$ **Price**
Low ($8 to $18)

Cheat Sheet

Understated but uplifting, Muscadet offers clean beams of citrus and sea salt for a price that barely lightens your wallet.

Label Logic

Muscadet is a grape, also known as Melon de Bourgogne. It is grown in France's Loire Valley.

Bravely Said

Fruits de mer	*Frweed MEHR*
Loire	*Luh-wahr*
Melon de Bourgogne	*Muh-lon duh Boor-goh-nyuh*
Muscadet	*Moose-cah-DAY*
Sèvre et Maine	*Sev-ruh ay Men*

Mark's Picks

Chéreau-Carré	*Chay-roh Cahr-ey*
Comte de Malestroit	*Comp-tuh duh Mal-ay-twa*
Domaine de la Pépière (Marc Ollivier)	*Payp-YEHR*
Domaine de la Tormaline	
Domaine des Dorices	*Doh-rees*
Guy Bossard	*Bo-sahr*
Joseph Landron	
Luneau-Papin	*Loo-no Pah-pehn*
Marquis de Goulaine	*Mar-key duh Gou-lane*
Michel Delhommeau	*Mee-shel Del-oh-moh*
Sauvion & Fils	*So-vee-on ay Fees*

Poosh It!

The tradition of *sur lie* is said to originate from the special barrel that a French winemaker would set aside when his daughter announced plans to get married. Aged for months on its yeast cells, the wine in these wedding barrels, or *barriques de noce*, would take on rich, lively flavors, inspiring many Muscadet winemakers to make *sur lie* a standard part of their wine production.

 CULINARY SWEET SPOT

Lightest ▲ Heaviest

A Lovable Feast

As an aperitif or with bivalves of all kinds, especially oysters, clams, or steamed mussels; poached salmon and other light fish preparations; salads; chicken, pork, and other white meats; salty snacks; crepes; creamy fare such as potato salad and risotto; steamed snowpeas and other mild-flavored vegetables

Locally Lusty

Raw oysters, especially the Vendée Atlantic variety; mussels à la marinière (mussels cooked in wine, olive oil, and garlic); fish in beurre blanc (white butter sauce); dishes with lentils

Spend the Night Together

To better grasp what tasters mean by minerality in Muscadet and similar wines, drop a tablet of Alka-Seltzer in a glass of water, let it fizz a bit, and then dab a bit on your tongue.

3 RIESLING FROM AUSTRALIA

Orchard Fresh and Dependably Dry

THE LEGIONS WHO write off Riesling because they mistakenly assume that it is always sweet remind me of those who dismiss Indian food because they don't like curry. Not only does the offending quality (i.e., sweetness in Riesling, curry in Indian food) come in many manifestations—some quite likable if rendered with finesse—but that characteristic hardly defines the entire category. Just as many fine Indian creations contain not one grain of curry powder, some renditions of Riesling have little, if any, sweetness—including two of my favorites—Riesling from Austria (Chapter 4) and Riesling from Australia.

While Aussies' plush Shirazes and fruit-forward Chardonnays have long been box office draws, their splendid Rieslings have been relegated to the shadows when they really deserve a throne of their own. Of light-to-medium weight, they are gloriously floral on the nose and tinglingly limey on the palate, imbued with a river-rocks minerality that can be less pronounced than it is in Rieslings from Europe. You may also detect cantaloupe or some stone fruits such as nectarines, but the overriding taste is likely to be a burst of puckery citrus, like chomping down on a green apple or kumquat. One of a microscopic group of white wines capable of improving with age, the finest Australian Rieslings can gradually transform from orchard fresh and brisk to gently honeyed and petrol tinged.

Although Riesling is planted in cooler climes throughout Oz, the two key regions to know are the Clare and Eden Valleys of South Australia. The Riesling kingpin of the Clare Valley, and perhaps of the entire country, is Grosset, a small producer with a big reputation for complex, ageworthy wines that shade toward the steely, as is typical of Clare Rieslings. Grosset's offerings can ring up in the $20 to $40 range, but a long march of Australian Rieslings limbo under $20, with nice grouping of those ducking the $10 mark. Jacob's Creek, Alice White, and Lindeman's are among those delivering quality at the lower end of the price curve. At all levels, Australian Riesling is one of the more consistent wine types, with abject Tasmanian Devils mercifully few and far between.

When mealtime comes, inspiration lies no farther than the beginning of this entry: Riesling and Indian food—as well as other moderately spicy Asian cuisine—are natural complements, as the wine's svelte and floral character, absence of oaky onerousness, and moderate alcohol do an admirable job of taming exotic fires. The wine's vibrant acidity also makes it a toothsome candidate for oysters and shellfish of all kinds, simple fish preparations, tangy cheeses like feta and chèvre, and salads and salad dressings—especially those with the apple and citrus flavors that the wine echoes.

BRAVEHEARTS ON *Riesling from Australia*

"Australian Riesling is truer to the Riesling grape than anything else. They have their own personality—they have their own way."
—*Richard Geoffroy, chief winemaker, Dom Pérignon, Champagne, France*

"It is more pure than water."
—*Reid Bosward, winemaker, Kaesler Vineyards, Barossa Valley, Australia*

"There is no hiding behind oak or other winemaking methods—Australian Riesling is a pure expression of its origin and variety.

"In the same way that Coopers beer is the winemaker's beer, then Riesling is definitely the winemaker's white."
—*Tom Newton, Group Chief White Winemaker, Constellation Wines Australia*

"Riesling from Australia can have raging, off-the-charts acidity. It is bone dry, crisp, with notes of Granny Smith apple . . . incredible with food." —*Paul Grieco, wine director and co-owner, Hearth, New York, NY*

"I'm an unoaked white kind of girl and Australian Riesling is my favorite underdog wine . . . Americans are so convinced that 'Riesling' means sticky-sweet that they walk right past these sleek and stylish whites. Australians eat a lot of seafood and grow very little Sauvignon Blanc or Pinot Grigio, so they like their Riesling dry and crisp. They're seriously underpriced and even mega-labels such as Jacob's Creek Reserve are often good." —*Marnie Old, author, Wine Secrets, and wine educator*

"Young and zesty Australian Rieslings are delicious with delicate pan-fried fish fillets served with a squeeze of fresh lime juice and salt and pepper, a cold cucumber soup on a hot day, and Asian cuisine such as Thai green chicken curry. Aged Rieslings pair with rich meats such as duck and roast pork, as well as heavier soups such as cauliflower, chowder, and potato and leek."

—*Andrew Holt, owner Poonawatta Estate, Edna Valley, Australia*

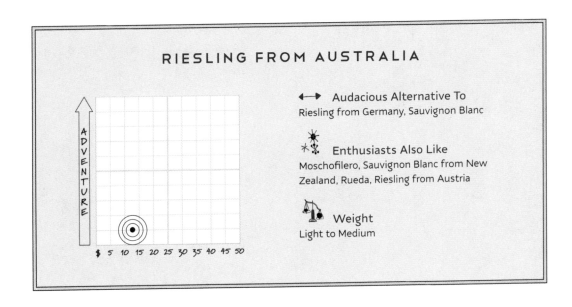

RIESLING FROM AUSTRALIA

ADVENTURE

$ 5 10 15 20 25 30 35 40 45 50

←→ Audacious Alternative To
Riesling from Germany, Sauvignon Blanc

Enthusiasts Also Like
Moschofilero, Sauvignon Blanc from New Zealand, Rueda, Riesling from Austria

Weight
Light to Medium

Price

Low ($8 to $25+)

 Cheat Sheet

With its dependable dryness, gentle pricing, and uncomplicated, non-Germanic labeling, Riesling from Australia is a lovable crossing of limey brightness with spring flowers.

 Label Logic

Riesling is a grape.

 Mark's Picks

Alice White	Jim Barry
Annie's Lane	Leasingham
Banrock Station	Lindeman's
Grosset	McWilliam's
Jacob's Creek	Penfolds

 Poosh It!

A major factor keeping Riesling prices low is that it doesn't require expensive oak barrels for fermentation or aging.

 CULINARY SWEET SPOT

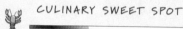

Lightest ▲ Heaviest

 A Lovable Feast

As an aperitif or with Indian, Chinese, Thai, and other spicy cuisines; oysters, clams, scallops, and other shellfish; fish of all kinds, especially trout and other freshwater varities, prepared simply (e.g., poached or lightly sautéed); lighter chicken dishes; baked ham; feta, goat, and other tangy cheeses; dishes with lime or lemon juice; salads and salad dressings, especially with apple, citrus, or tropical fruit flavors

Spend the Night Together

Track down a Riesling or two with some bottle age. Compare it to one without. What aromas and flavors are found only in the aged bottled?

4 RIESLING FROM AUSTRIA

The Floral, Flinty Invigorator

UNTIL I CONSULTED with novelist and wine writer Jay McInerney, I must confess that I didn't give Austrian Riesling much of a chance. Why bother with Austria when the world template for Riesling lay in neighboring Germany? Then McInerney stressed to me that Austrian Riesling "may be the ultimate food wine for the way we eat now" and that "even if you think you don't like Riesling you owe it to yourself to try the Austrian stuff."

These were the statements that for me launched a thousand sips and an appreciation for this favorite pick of sommeliers. Whereas German Riesling can be dry, semisweet, or fully sweet, Austrian Riesling is more straightforward in that it is virtually always dry—sometimes so much so that you can feel it in the back of your throat. Moreover, Riesling from Austria typically has some stuffing in its sock, manifesting itself as a wine of medium body and occasionally richer, whereas its German counterpart is often feathery light, which isn't necessarily a negative—just different.

What I love most about Austrian Riesling is what I see as its left-brain-right-brain personality. Its creative side manifests itself with aromas of roses and peaches, vivid as a Cézanne still life, while its analytic side has the kind of austere minerality that will make you think you've stumbled into a storage closet of Rocks-R-Us. At its best, then, Austrian Riesling combines the floral and the flinty, framed by limey acidity, with no oak but perhaps a grind of white pepper on the finish.

While wine merchants won't have a neon sign hawking "Austrian Riesling" in their window, they should be able to at least produce a few examples. The best stuff comes from the steeply terraced hillsides of the country's Wachau region, which is useful to know if only to utter that name in the presence of a persnickety sommelier, its guttural sound aggressive and cathartic like a Bavarian expletive. Prices top out at $70 or so and drift down to about $20, with names like Leth, Domäne Wachau, Schloss Gobelsburg consistently keeping the faith on the low end.

If you find the stony tang of Austrian Riesling a bit off-putting on its own, I implore you to judge it again in the presence of seafood, especially that which is richly sauced. The highlight of a book tour I did in Belgium wasn't the bookstores or the beer, though both were first-rate, but a piercing Austrian Riesling that perfectly complemented a plate of lobster tail and endive in cream sauce.

BRAVEHEARTS ON *Riesling from Austria*

"Austrian Riesling has been the hottest tip among sommeliers for years and it tends to go incredibly well with the lighter and spicier cuisines. The range of flavors—from minerals to tropical fruits—can be breathtaking."

—*Jay McInerney, novelist and wine columnist,* The Wall Street Journal

"Rieslings from Austria are so fantastic because they are bone dry and Riesling is hands-down the most versatile food grape on the planet. Their acidity is a great start to any meal.

"Though Austria shares a language with Germany, they could not be any more different in their lifestyle, energy, and wine. I love German wines, but Austria is where it's at! The people are organized but fun. If Italy and Germany had a baby, it would be Austria."

—*Liz Willette, Willette Wines, New York, NY*

"I don't like big flavor-bombs that do all the work for you. I appreciate wines which speak in an urgent whisper rather than bellow in a testosterone scream." —*Terry Theise, wine importer, Bethesda, MD*

"Great Rieslings, the ones that bring to mind earthy minerality and taste like overripe stone fruits balanced by exhilarating acidity, are the ones I love, and like to pair with just about anything on the plate."
—Anthony Giglio, wine educator and author

"I prefer high-acidity whites—like Riesling, Sauvignon Blanc, and Grüner Veltliner—over a heavy Chardonnay."
—Tom Colicchio, chef and restaurateur, Craft, New York, NY

"Most Austrian whites imported to the U.S. are of pretty damn good quality. A fun thing to do with Austrian Riesling is to serve it to your friends but don't tell them what it is until after they try it. You'll make them believers."
—Lou Amdur, owner, Lou's Wine Bar, Los Angeles, CA

"Compared with the lean, delicate Rieslings you find in Germany, Austrian Rieslings are bigger but not overwrought.

"I'm sick and tired of people equating Riesling with sweetness. I doubt that even 10% of the world's Riesling is sweet. The younger generations are more open to it, but Boomers and above still think of Riesling as the treacly sweet Blue Nun.

"Riesling is the greatest grape on the planet."
—Paul Grieco, wine director and co-owner, Hearth, New York, NY

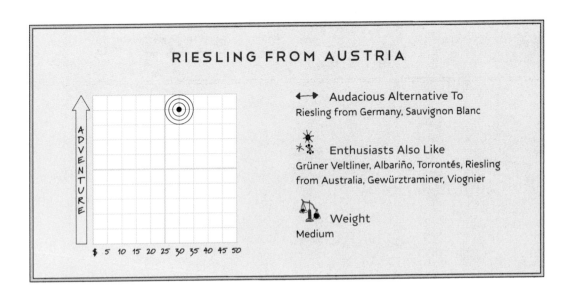

RIESLING FROM AUSTRIA

A D V E N T U R E

$ 5 10 15 20 25 30 35 40 45 50

←→ Audacious Alternative To
Riesling from Germany, Sauvignon Blanc

✳❋ Enthusiasts Also Like
Grüner Veltliner, Albariño, Torrontés, Riesling from Australia, Gewürztraminer, Viognier

⚖ Weight
Medium

Price

Medium to High ($25 to $40+)

 Cheat Sheet

Lightly perfumed yet minerally, markedly dry, and richer than its German counterpart, Riesling from Austria scours the palate with the zest of ripe apples, pears, and white pepper.

 Label Logic

Riesling is a grape.

 Bravely Said

Riesling	REES-ling
Wachau	VOK-ow

 Mark's Picks

Alzinger	AHL-tzin-gehr
Bründlemayer	BRUN-dle-my-er
Domäne Wachau	VOK-ow
Hirtzberger	HEERTS-bur-gur
Leth	
Nikolaihof	NIK-oh-liy-HOFF
Schloss Gobelsburg	Shlos Go-bels-BOORK

 Poosh It!

As with German Riesling, grower Champagne, and Grüner Veltliner, importer Terry Thiese's name on a wine's back label is bankable seal of quality. Do a Web search for his ebullient and eloquent catalog of wines.

CULINARY SWEET SPOT

Lightest   ▲   Heaviest

 A Lovable Feast

Flounder, trout, sole, skate and other mild fish, especially grilled or sautéed; lemon and other citrus sauces; salad and salad dressings; pepper sauces; cream sauces; mustard; chèvre and other tangy cheeses; creamy cheeses; Thai, Chinese, and other spicy Asian cuisine

 Locally Lusty

Wiener schnitzel (fried veal cutlet); *spargel* (white asparagus); sausages; *rindsuppe* (beef soup); *spätzle* (dumplings); pickled vegetables; cow's milk cheeses

 Spend the Night Together

Do a comparative tasting of German and Austrian Rieslings. Do you notice any differences in weight, sweetness, or flavor?

5 SAUVIGNON BLANC FROM NEW ZEALAND

Reliably Fluorescent

SAUVIGNON BLANC FROM New Zealand is like a pizza slice, a back scratch, or an episode of *The Office*: often rewarding, almost never disastrous. In the parlance of investments, it delivers reliable returns with little downside risk. In fact, I'll go so far as to say that I've never had a bottle of it that was an outright horror show—which is more than can be said for many wine types.

New Zealand Sauvignon Blanc's dependability is a case of the right grape grown in the right place by the right people. The Sauvignon Blanc grape flourishes in the intensely sunny days and cool, maritime nights of Kiwi country, particular in the stony soils of the South Island's Marlborough region. The wine benefits from the wealth of winemaking expertise and talent that has emerged there in the last generation. The result is a Brave New Pour of great distinction *and* distinctiveness—a modern classic that, like the band Coldplay or the restaurateur Danny Meyer, has set the standard even for acts that have been at it much longer.

If New Zealand Sauvignon Blanc were a NASCAR driver, its racing suit would be Kelly green and covered with John Deere logos, since it is all about fresh-cut grass—an in-your-face herbaceousness joined by a veritable scimitar of limey, grape-fruity acidity. Add to that notes of passion fruit, guava, or other tropical fruits and it's no wonder that "New Zealand Sauvignon Blanc" has become a global style, not unlike New York pizza, Argentine steak, and—forgive me—Brazilian wax. It is so aggressively green, so glowingly bright, that for me it evinces a kind of fluorescence.

This is not to say that you will not find more muted renditions, especially as a small minority of winemakers like to tame the wine's *sauvage* personality by fermenting or aging it in oak barrels; and occasionally it can want for flavor, a victim of vintners looking to cash in on its popularity by overproducing grapes and rushing dull stuff to market. Furthermore, there's no guarantee that you and your guests will cotton to its brassy intensity: I tell my students to think of it as Pinot Grigio with fangs.

To an increasing numbers of folks, however, a good "Savvie"—as the Kiwis call it—has all the right moves. Bottles are widely available, affordably priced, and almost always topped with a screw cap, which eliminates the scourge of cork taint and allows you to wet your whistle with greater velocity.

Oh, and the gastronomic places it can go: high-acid fare like fresh tomatoes and goat cheese, the normally problematic pairing of salads, vegetarian dishes of all stripes, and shellfish are just a few of its soulmates. Actress Virginia Madsen, famous for rhapsodizing about wine in *Sideways*, recommends trying it with sea bass grilled with fresh basil and even the iconoclastic choice of rare beef with baby asparagus on the "barbie." To those who would disdain pairing a white with red meat, she responds: "Naughty, I know. But it will delight the most snobby palates you know."

Author Eric Arnold, whose book *First Big Crush* detailed his time as an apprentice winemaker in New Zealand, told me that scallops are the best possible match. In fact, he revealed that the locals are fond of drinking it with freshly-caught-and-sautéed scallops on buttered white bread—which, to me, sounds like a feast fit for a Kiwi King.

BRAVEHEARTS ON *Sauvignon Blanc from New Zealand*

"The finish is perfect, like the verbal expression of 'Ahh,' when you drink a refreshing glass of cold water with a squeeze of lime, after a walk through the woods. I wax, I wane, I gush. It's fair to say, I love this wine.

"I've seduced many a Pinot lover with Sauvignon Blanc from New Zealand—wait, that didn't sound right, but you know what I mean. It's a crowd pleaser."

—Virginia Madsen, actress

"For me, New Zealand Sauvignon Blanc passes the bullsh@t test. There aren't as many bad bottles of it as there are of Pinot Grigio and Chardonnay. . . . If I'm coming out of a hot kitchen and I'm thirsty, it's what I drink."

—David Burke, chef and restaurateur, David Burke Townhouse, New York, NY

"It is my favorite—it is power-packed, man. They say that New Zealanders plant strawberries and kiwis, between the rows of vines and I believe it."

—Sammy Hagar, vocalist, Chickenfoot, and former vocalist, Van Halen

"The aromas of the wine are pungent (think a fire hose of passion fruit juice sprayed on a freshly mowed lawn); the flavors are as powerful and unapologetic as they get (think a grapefruit-juice wet-T-shirt contest).

"Trying a Marlborough Sauvignon Blanc against one from California or Sancerre is like putting Roger Federer against kids from your high school tennis team and asking who the better player is."

—Eric Arnold, author of First Big Crush: The Down and Dirty on Making Great Wine Down Under

"I love the passion-fruity, gooseberry qualities in New World Sauvignon Blanc. Nothing against Chardonnay, but I think that my wife and I just drank too much of it in the '80s."

—Ming Tsai, chef and restaurateur, Blue Ginger, Boston, MA

SAUVIGNON BLANC FROM NEW ZEALAND

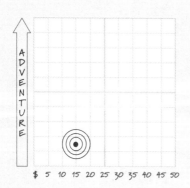

 Audacious Alternative To

Sauvignon Blanc, Pinot Grigio

 Enthusiasts Also Like

Rueda, Moschofilero, Albariño, Riesling from Australia, Grüner Veltliner, Txakoli, Vinho Verde, Vermentino

 Weight

Medium

 Price

Low ($10 to $20)

 Cheat Sheet

A wine so amped that each bottle seems equipped with its own battery pack, Sauvignon Blanc from New Zealand positively glows with grassiness, citrus fruits, and tropical nuances.

Label Logic

Sauvignon Blanc is a grape.

 Bravely Said

Savvie   *SAH-vee*

 Mark's Picks

Babich
Brancott
Cloudy Bay
Dashwood
Huia   *HOO-yah*
Kim Crawford
Matua
Oyster Bay
Palliser
St. Clair
Sauvignon Republic
Stoneleigh
Te Kairanga   *Tee Kigh-runga*
Villa Maria

 Poosh It!

Sauvignon Blanc's unrestrained, tangy-herbal personality inspires wine pros to use equally memorable descriptors for it, including "hay," "paraffin," "lemon verbena," "gunpowder," "narcissus flower," "gooseberries," and "cat's pee" (or, in French, *pipi du chat*).

 CULINARY SWEET SPOT

Lightest   ▲   Heaviest

 A Lovable Feast

Shellfish and other seafood; vegetarian dishes; dishes with "green" tastes, such as green pepper, herbs like dill and tarragon, spinach, asparagus, and pesto; tomatoes and tomato sauces; salads, especially with tart dressings; lighter Mexican fare, including ceviche, salsa, and guacamole; goat, feta, ricotta, and other fresh cheeses

Locally Lusty

Scallops, preferably freshly caught, sautéed, and sandwiched between slices of bread; green-lip mussels; fish and chips, especially with blue cod; whitebait (tiny young fish eaten whole) fritters

 Spend the Night Together

Sip the wine on its own, then try it with a lemon wedge. Notice how the wine gets a bit sweeter? Acidity in food subdues an acidic wine, creating a net effect of sweetness on your palate. This is why Sauvignon Blanc from New Zealand pairs so well with tomatoes, lemon sauces, goat cheese, and other tangy foods.

"LET'S MAKE CHABROT": DAGUIN ON THE PLEASURES OF MIXING WINE AND SOUP

D'Artagnan owner Ariane Daguin revealed to me a fascinating ritual from her native Gascony. Called making "chabrot" (*shah-broh*), it involves pouring a bit of wine into a soup's remaining broth and then drinking the mixture from the bowl. Originally a peasant custom to get diners to clean their own plates, Ariane likes to make Chabrot when she has company over. Here's how it's done:

INGREDIENTS

Bowls of brothy soup (e.g., vegetable, beef consommé)
At least 1 bottle of inexpensive wine

1) Finish all of the solids in your soup, leaving just the broth.
2) Announce to your tablemates, "Let's make chabrot!"
3) Add wine from your glass (about half the amount of the remaining broth).
4) In unison, diners should put their elbows on the table and lift their soup bowls.
5) Everyone should drink simultaneously, being careful not to spill any on themselves.

Ariane explains: "The wine adds acidity, fruitiness, coolness to the broth. It is an acquired taste: weird the first time, but it grows on you really fast."

6 TORRONTÉS

Smells Like Flaah-wehrz

"IT SMELLS LIKE flaah-wehrz," said my friend Adrian for the millionth time in his inimitable accent that channels Ricardo Montalban, Tony Montana, and a cartoon spy on the sly.

Like "bam!," "no soup for you," or "more cowbell," this simple little exclamation eventually became something of a humorous catchphrase among my friends, peppered into conversation to emphasize anything that is unequivocally worthwhile. In the case of the wine Torrontés, the description is doubly true: it is highly pleasurable and, appropriately enough, unmistakably floral.

Although better known for its lush red Malbec (Chapter 27), Argentina is also responsible for Torrontés, which happens to be the country's most popular white, though comparatively little of it leaves its borders. It is gaining a foothold here thanks in part to the growing legions of Malbec maniacs who are now looking to that country for an equally arresting white. More often than not, Torrontés fits the bill, seducing the drinker with the tropical aromatics of Viognier (Chapter 15)—think peaches, apricots, or orange peel—but with the lighter weight and crispness of Pinot Grigio or Sauvignon Blanc. It is the perfect springtime white, floral and alive, like crocuses peeking up through April snow.

When you contemplate when to drink Torrontés, remember this scene. It's May and I'm wedged into the bar at the always bustling Mary's Fish Camp in New York. It's just man and lobster roll, locked in a passionate embrace, joined by a cold tumbler of Torrontés. This is a ménage à trois of maximal pleasure, the wine's faint notes of nectarines harmonizing with the near-sweet chunks of lobster, while its zippy acidity provides lift to the richness of the mayonnaise and buttered roll.

Crustaceans, however, are just one stop on the Torrontés pleasure trip with food: sea dwellers of all kinds are always welcome, as are chicken and pork. Heat seekers find that the wine's peachy character and light body does an admirable job of cooling down hot ethnic food, especially the spices and scorches of chile-centric dishes and soy-and-wasabi soaked pieces of sushi. My friend Heather, a wine importer based in Argentina, reports that locals use Torrontés to wash down empanadas and tamales with the spicy red *putaparió* sauce, whose name is derived from an expletive that probably shouldn't be printed here.

Although you won't see an entire section devoted to Torrontés at your neighborhood wine shop, you'll likely encounter a few representatives, including the Crios de Susana Balbo, which always seems to please like the lick of a puppy's tongue. That bottle rings up at about $15, and you can often find good versions below the $10 waterline. At those prices, there no excuse not to invest in an extra bottle—not only to slake thirst, but also to deliver the fragrance of "flaah-wehrz" directly to your lover's pulse points, without ever having to step foot in Sephora.

BRAVEHEARTS ON *Torrontés*

"Torrontés smells floral and a bit sweet on the nose, but on the palate is much more serious than you thought it would be, and finishes unexpectedly dry and crisp.

"I have great memories of being in a traditional bar in Salta—Torrontés's home city—listening to Saltan folkloric music and eating spicy empanadas. Argentine wine is all about the place it comes from. It's not the most complex wine or the wine with the most *terroir*, but it is just *so* Argentine."

—*Heather Willens, importer and owner, HW Wines, Buenos Aires, Argentina*

"Torrontés is tremendous. I like wines that are inexpensive and extremely accessible. Sometimes you don't want to swirl and *think*— you just want to *drink*."

—*Drew Nieporent, restaurateur, Tribeca Grill and Nobu, New York, NY*

"Torrontés is soft and floral, and there is usually no oak, so you don't get toasty vanilla flavors.

"My sister fell in love with Torrontés when her hairdresser brought her a glass while she was waiting in the beauty salon."

—*Dana Farner, beverage director, CUT: Wolfgang Puck, Los Angeles, CA*

"Floral, with tropical fruit, citrus, and star anise, with hints of spice, this aromatic white is dangerously easy to drink and a perfect segue out of the mass-marketed, big-name Pinot Grigios."

—*Elizabeth Harcourt, sommelier, Corton, New York, NY*

"Torrontés is one of the most interesting whites on the market right now; Tomero, Crios de Susana Balbo and Alta Vista are total favorites and the wine is fabulous with pork loin chops and peach salsa."

—*Inez Ribustello, sommelier and co-owner, On the Square, Tarboro, NC*

"Torrontés is a medium-bodied wine with a fruit basket of aromas, including peach, zesty citrus, and in some cases candied pineapple. Its mouth-watering acidity allows it to pair well with pork and goat, the latter especially when grilled and served with the classic Argentine accoutrement *chimichurri*."

—*Anjoleena Griffin-Holst, wine director, Borgata Hotel Casino & Spa,*
Atlantic City, NJ

TORRONTÉS

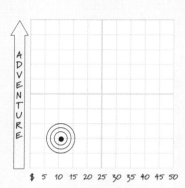

A
D
V
E
N
T
U
R
E

$ 5 10 15 20 25 30 35 40 45 50

 Audacious Alternative To

Pinot Grigio, Riesling

 Enthusiasts Also Like

Moschofilero, Riesling from Australia, Riesling from Austria, Viognier, Gewürztraminer, Moscato d'Asti

 Weight

Light

$ Price

Low ($7 to $15)

 Cheat Sheet

With a nose fit for FTD and a flavor as refreshing as lemonade, Torrontés seduces with ambrosial aromatics, a tangy taste, and a price for the cost conscious.

Label Logic

Torrontés is a grape. It is grown mostly in high-altitude regions of Argentina.

 Bravely Said

Torrontés   Tor-rahn-TEZ

 Mark's Picks

Alamos
Andeluna
Astica   Ahs-TEE-Kah
Bodega Colome   Bo-DAY-gah KOH-loam
Crios de Susana   CREE-os day Soo-ZAH-nah
   Balbo   BAHL-boh
Crisol   Cree-SOL
Jelu   Jay-loo
Koch
Michel Torino   Mee-shel Tor-EE-nyo
   "Don David"   don Da-VEED
Norton "Lo Tengo"
Santa Isabel   SAHN-tah Ee-ZAH-behl

 Poosh It!

The sticklers who would have you avoid Torrontés and similar whites in wintertime have clearly never sat by a roaring fire and luxuriated in the wine's special perfume. Light, pigment-deficient zingers can be a refreshing change of pace in cooler months.

 CULINARY SWEET SPOT

Lightest   ▲   Heaviest

 A Lovable Feast

As an aperitif; oysters; shellfish and other seafood, including lobster rolls; chicken (especially curried chicken) and pork; German potato salad; spicy Asian and Spanish fare; salads and salad dressing; tangy or soft, creamy cheeses; on Valentine's or Mother's Day

Locally Lusty

Lobster or spinach empanadas; salt-crusted chicken; *palmitos* (hearts of palm); sausages with *chimichurri* (spicy green) sauce; grilled vegetables; spicy *putaparió* sauce

 Spend the Night Together

Host a wine tasting where you compare Torrontés with Viognier. Can you detect an overlap in aromatics but a contrast in weight?

7 TXAKOLI

Zingy Like a Downed Power Line

HOLD THE BOTTLE high, the tumbler glass low, and drizzle the wine as if it were a circus clown plunging into a barrel below. If you're lucky, your wine waterfall will hit its mark and the show will go on.

Such is the ritualistic "high pour" performed with gusto by San Sebastian bartenders to intensify the fizz of Txakoli, a semi-sparkling white wine from Spain's Basque country.

While the spelling of Txakoli may strike some as a cruel result of alphabet soup, its pronunciation thankfully doesn't require tongue twisting; it is simply "Choc-OH-lee."

Ordering a tumbler of Txakoli will land you a lightweight pour that is as satisfying as being able to correctly enuciate its name. In addition to teasing your tongue with a gentle effervescence, Txakoli will kick your salivary juices into overdrive, its lemony tang zipping around your mouth like a downed power line. While your palate positively vibrates with excitement, your nose may detect hints of green apples, pears, and limes, along with a chalky minerality—all in all, a spritzy, pleasantly sour rush that will revive you faster than Eskimo-kissing a round of smelling salts. Its refreshment factor, combined with its insider status and pouring ritual, makes me think of it as the Wine Geek's Gatorade.

Though known mostly to wine pros and others with opportunity to conquer its consonants, Txakoli is increasingly finding its way into more adventurous wine shops. A typical bottle will set you back $15 to $20, its relative scarcity preventing it from being the screaming bargain that is the similarly-flavored Vinho Verde (Chapter 8). The producer I see most often is Txomin Etxaniz, a fearsome jumble of letters that spells out Spain's most venerable Txakoli specialist. Its elegant, Gothic-scripted label contrasts mightily with that of another pleaser, Ameztoi, whose gaudy, green-and-gold label sports a curiously Kazakstani font that belies its chalky goodness within.

Txakoli merits the company of seafood the way a budding Einstein deserves an advanced calculus book. New York's always packed Pearl Oyster Bar has been the scene of many a Txakoli-fueled bivalve feast, and French Launderer Thomas Keller is known to marry his signature "Oysters and Pearls" (oysters and caviar on a bed of tapioca) with it. It is, of course, a fast friend to tapas of all kinds, and there is nothing quite like spending a summer evening with good friends, a grill, and a case of Txakoli. A *case*, you ask? At only about 11% alcohol, it is one of the least boozy wines you can buy.

BRAVEHEARTS ON *Txakoli*

"To me, Txakoli is the adult beverage of summer. It is fermented so that it retains a bit of its carbonic gas, and has a tingle that dances on your palate.

"The best Txakoli tastes salty, like seafoam, which suits its geography, because most of the vineyards overlook the sea and have salt crystals on their vines, like someone who's been at the beach all day."
                    —*Kerin Auth, co-owner, Tinto Fino, New York, NY*

"I might have been the first person to serve Txakoli in San Francisco when I was the wine director at EOS Restaurant and Wine Bar. I still serve, sell, and drink it on a regular basis. There is always a bottle in the side door of my refrigerator. "
        —*Debbie Zachareas, co-owner, Ferry Plaza Wine Merchants, San Francisco, CA*

"Having a few friends over for pre-dinner drinks? Txakoli is an absolute must for anyone interested in wine. This dry, salty, citrusy delight has spicy floral components to make it the perfect answer with marcona almonds, charcuterie, a semihard cheese, or Spanish caperberries. It is also fantastic with shrimp or anything briny."

—*Elizabeth Harcourt, sommelier, Corton, New York, NY*

"Txakoli can be aromatic of kiwi, lychee, peach, and kaffir lime and is slightly lower in alcohol and often has a slight prickle, which gives a lift to food. Argentines enjoy it with fresh fish, sheep's milk cheese, and cured meats.

"We were able to offer it to the guests in a playful way by nicknaming it the 'Cha Cha Cha' wine."

—*Anjoleena Griffin-Holst, wine director, Borgata Hotel Casino & Spa, Atlantic City, NJ*

"I love this stuff! When Vinho Verde is too simple, this is the next logical step up."

—*Ross Outon, winner of the first season of* The Winemakers *on PBS and beverage consultant, Austin, TX*

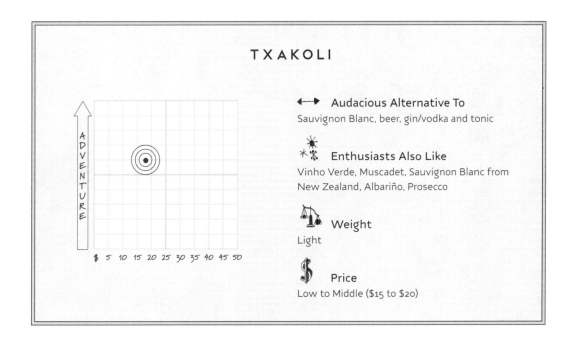

TXAKOLI

ADVENTURE

$ 5 10 15 20 25 30 35 40 45 50

◄──► Audacious Alternative To
Sauvignon Blanc, beer, gin/vodka and tonic

Enthusiasts Also Like
Vinho Verde, Muscadet, Sauvignon Blanc from New Zealand, Albariño, Prosecco

Weight
Light

Price
Low to Middle ($15 to $20)

Cheat Sheet

From the Atlantic regions of Spanish Basque country comes Txakoli, the sea spray in a bottle that is feathery light, super tart, and action packed.

 Label Logic

Txakoli is a region in Basque country. The wine is made from indigenous grapes that aren't important to remember.

 Bravely Said

Bacalao	Bah-cah-LAH
Pinxto	Peen-CHO
Txakoli	Choc-OH-lee

 Mark's Picks

Ameztoi	Ah-mehz-toy
Bodegas Itsas-Mendi	IT-sas MEH-dee
Nicolas Ulacia	Oo-lah-SEE-ah
Talai-Berri	
Txomin Etxaniz	Cho-MEEN Ex-CHAN-ess
Xarmant	Shar-MANT

 Poosh It!

Txakoli is sometimes labeled as "Txakolina" or "Chacoli"; traditionalists like to pour it into tumblers instead of a wineglass because the former provides a deeper, wider target for the "high pour" and helps retain the wine's fizziness; rosé versions exist, but they are harder to find.

 CULINARY SWEET SPOT

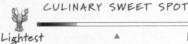

Lightest ▲ Heaviest

 A Lovable Feast

As an aperitif or with seafood of all kinds, especially oysters; chicken, pork, and other white meats; salty snacks such as popcorn; cheeses, especially fresh sheep's milk; with brunch and birthday celebrations

 Locally Lusty

Pintxo (bread and ingredients such as stuffed peppers, cod, anchovy, or baby eels, held together with a toothpick); salted almonds; caperberries; tuna in oil; squid; sardines; and *boquerones* (small, fresh anchovies); *bacalao* (salt cod)

 Spend the Night Together

Using two tumbler glasses, perform your own "high pour"; it will energize the wine with the fizziness of ginger ale.

To make the high pour easier, servers at Spanish wine bars sometimes use a plastic T-shaped spout that pours the Txakoli in a neat stream. A Spanish wine specialist can help you track down one of these rarities.

8 VINHO VERDE

G&T, After a Diet and a Discount

SOME PEOPLE ARE just in the know. On the prowl for superlative chicken kabobs? Cut-rate antique paintings? Dentists generous with nitrous oxide? Marcy—the editor-in-chief of the dot-com I used to run—will know. With ears like radar dishes and eyes perpetually scoping for the next great find, she is a one-woman NORAD for savvy shopping.

So when Marcy raved about Vinho Verde some years ago, I scrambled to track down a few bottles. Once again, Marcy was on to something: this was a zestful little charmer, bracingly fresh and often a touch fizzy, a splash of lemon-lime and green apple that makes the palate resonate like a subwoofer. And, as she had stressed to me, all of that can be yours for less than a ten-spot.

Hailing from the northwest corner of Portugal, not far from Spain's equally verdant Rias Baixas region (Chapter 9), Vinho Verde is Portugal's most popular white. It comes from a blend of up to twenty-five mostly indigenous grape varietals, though sometimes you'll see bottles that comprise mainly one variety, such as Alvarino, the Portuguese name for the Albariño grape.

I think of Vinho Verde as a gin and tonic after a diet and a discount, because not only is it crisp and light, with typically around 10% alcohol, and thus perfect for cocktail hour, but it is also one of the best bargains in all of wine, usually requiring only a single-digit outlay. Quality is good across producers, but you'll never regret reaching for Aveleda, whose Quinta de Aveleda bottling deserves its own flag and anthem for its zesty-goodness, Third-World pricing, and ubiquity.

If I had my way, I'd install a Vinho Verde faucet near every one of the world's hibachis. Light enough to glug, it should be considered as essential for the busy backyard barbecuer as long-handled tongs and a "Kiss the Cook" apron. And never forget that Vinho Verde's lively acidity flatters any light bites that contain zing of their own—such as seafood, salads, yogurt, and ceviche. In August I've made a habit of serving it to friends with Jersey beefsteak tomatoes on slices of freshly-baked sourdough sourced from New York's Union Square Greenmarket.

On the subject of "green," while Vinho Verde translates to "green wine," it is not named for its color but because it should be drunk in its youth, ideally less than a year after production. Not only does its moniker make it an apt alternative to Guinness Draught on Saint Patrick's Day, but its low alcohol and sprightliness makes it one of the best thirst-slakers for the links, so find a caddy to stash a few bottles next to your putter.

BRAVEHEARTS ON *Vinho Verde*

"Vinho Verde is my preferred wine for a hot day."
   —*Heather Willens, importer and owner, HW Wines, Buenos Aires, Argentina*

"Vinho Verde is one of my favorite summertime wines. It is crisp, slightly effervescent, and full of green apples and stones. My favorites include Casal Garcia, Aveleda, Broadbent Selections."
   —*Inez Ribustello, sommelier and co-owner, On the Square, Tarboro, NC*

"Vinho Verde is vastly undervalued by wine consumers because they mistakenly assume that expensive equates with quality. The price is shockingly low, and you get mouth-watering acidity and slatey minerality."   —*Elizabeth Harcourt, sommelier, Corton, New York, NY*

VINHO VERDE

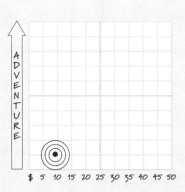

 Mark's Picks

Aveleda	*AVAY-lay-duh*
Broadbent	
Casal Garcia	*Cah-SAL Gar-SEE-yah*
Gazela	*Gah-ZEH-lah*
Anselmo Mendes	*MEN-des*
Quinta de Serrade	*Say-rahd*
Quintas de Melgaço	*KEEN-tas day Mel-GAH-so*

 Audacious Alternative To
Sauvignon Blanc, beer, gin and tonic

 Enthusiasts Also Like
Txakoli, Muscadet, New Zealand Sauvignon Blanc, Tocai, Prosecco and other sparklers

 Weight
Light

 Price
Low ($8 to $15)

 Cheat Sheet
Priced for overindulgence, Vinho Verde is about as far from an oaky Chardonnay as you can get, a spritzy splash of lemon-lime that is deeply thirst quenching.

 Label Logic
Vinho Verde is the Portuguese term for "green wine." It comes from a variety of native grapes grown in the Minho region of northern Portugal.

Bravely Said

Minho	*MEEN-oo*
Vinho Verde	*VEEN-yo VEHR-deh*

 Poosh It!
When a Vinho Verde bottle carries no vintage year on its front label, as sometimes happens, you can confirm its youth by glancing at its "Siglo de Garantia," a government label affixed to the back of the bottle that indicates the year in which it was released.

 CULINARY SWEET SPOT

 Lightest ▲ Heaviest

 A Lovable Feast
As an aperitif or with gazpacho and other light soups; shellfish and other seafood; fish and chips; salads, especially Caesar and Caprese; dishes with fresh tomatoes; fried calamari; sushi; yogurt and sour cream; lima beans and other green vegetables

 Locally Lusty
Langoustines; cod; sardines; cuttlefish; *caldeirada* (fish stew); cabbage; sheep's milk and goat cheese

 Spend the Night Together
Slide a few bottles into a tote bag and take them to the beach.

With its lager-like texture and skid-row pricing, Vinho Verde is ideal to turn your beer-biased friends onto wine.

OTHER POURS (LIGHTER)

"I keep my fridge stocked with Fresca—it has high acidity and the flavor's not too sweet, which is how I like my wine."

—Tom Colicchio, chef and restaurateur, Craft, New York, NY

"For my favorite alternative to Champagne, I go high into the foothills of the Pyrenees in southern France to the town of Limoux. For centuries, they've made a sparkling wine called Blanquette de Limoux. Made mainly from the local Mauzac grape, this sparkler tastes only like itself. And that taste is sublimely refreshing, un-rustic, even seductive. At around ten bucks (Saint-Hilaire Blanc de Blancs is easiest to find), it's beyond a bargain."

—Peter Hellman, wine writer and former wine columnist, The New York Sun

"I love Japanese food, especially sushi and sashimi, so I have to put sake at the top of my favorite wines. Nothing is better than a little raw fish with a glass of a refreshing sake. It's the perfect pairing."

—Jean-Georges Vongerichten, chef and restaurateur, Jean-Georges, New York

"I love crisp sake with oysters, and will usually choose that over wine if the picking is good and I don't have to worry about keeping anybody else happy.

"One of the best oyster wines I've encountered was at New York's Savoy restaurant, a dry and fragrant Moscato Giallo from Italy's Alto Adige."

—Rowan Jacobsen, author, A Geography of Oysters

"Here is a real discovery, known only by real wine lovers: Château Lamothe Cuvée Velentine Blanc, a dry white wine from Bordeaux. It is bone-dry, crisp, clean, with a real sense of *terroir*, and a minerally character. Perfect for summertime drinking!"
—*Zac Posen, fashion designer*

"I love Italian whites—especially Gavi de Gavi from the Piedmont region."
—*Kevin Bacon, actor*

"I am really into white wines from Italy's Friuli region, including Le Vigne di Zamò, Scarbolo, Gravner, Bastianich, Edi Kate (who makes the only varietal Vitovska that I have ever tasted—Muscat-like, delicious!)."
—*Gillian Ballance, former wine director, PlumpJack Group, San Francisco, CA*

"I like white wines from Friuli-Venezia-Giulia and Alto Adige in Italy. There are some interesting bright whites from Ribolla Gialla; it's a really neat grape I have used in a Biancho blend and is totally delicious. There are only two acres of Ribolla Gialla in California and I buy half of them."
—*Michael Chiarello, vintner and host, Food Network's* Easy Entertaining with Michael Chiarello

"I'm from Fruili, where Picolit is a great dessert wine grape that is now being blended in with other grapes to make dry wine. It gives the wine a great glyceride feel. For the Bastianich Vespa Bianco, we blend Picolit with Chardonnay and Sauvignon Blanc to make a complex wine."
—*Lidia Bastianich, chef and and host of PBS's* Lidia's Italy

"Inspired by an on-air call from Jean-Georges Vongerichten, my Thanksgiving dinner this year included puréed sweet potatoes with goat cheese and oven-dried niçoise olives, Yukon Gold mashed potatoes with truffle butter, and sautéed green beans. For wine, I chose Dr. Karl Christoffel Mosel Riesling from Germany, and its light, semisweet character let all the flavors of my menu shine through in a wonderful way."
—*Mario Bosquez, host, "Living Today," Martha Stewart Living Radio*

"Chenin Blanc displays a beautiful balance between fruit and minerality. It makes a great companion for salads, seafood, shellfish, and charcuterie when the wine is fruity or sweet."

—Brian Duncan, owner/wine director BIN 36, Chicago, IL

"Left Foot Charley Pinot Blanc from Michigan is so compelling. I honestly can't think of another Pinot Blanc that has gotten me this excited."

—Doug Frost, master sommelier and master of wine

"White wine from the North Fork of Long Island has incredible energy. I like objective wines, those not known for their competitive streak. The wine is light, crisp, and serious. It transports the profound message of this gorgeous region and is so close to New York City."

—Alain Ducasse, chef and restaurateur, Le Jules Verne, Paris, France

"I believe in the integrity of supporting local producers, and Long Island's Channing Daughters is a favorite. The winery's vintners often make unique blends that demonstrate what New York winemakers are capable of creating. The Meditazione, a crisp white based on Friulian varietals, is nice because it pairs well with the sweet fat of pork, especially suckling pig."

—April Bloomfield, chef and co-owner, The Spotted Pig, New York, NY

"I have some Swedish aquavit, which is called 'Snapps' by the Scandinavians. It tastes of caraway seeds and dill. Aquavit is what made the Vikings the barrels of laughs that they were. It is typically served out of the freezer, really cold, with a beer to chase it." —Alex Lifeson, lead guitarist, Rush

"Sitting in a bat, or pub, in Addis Ababa, the capital of Ethopia, I had Tej—pronounced 'Tedge.' It is a honey wine that is raw, simple—it's a bit sweet like orange juice and has a similar texture. You drink it out of a small glass beaker." —Marcus Samuelsson, chef and co-owner, Aquavit, New York, NY

9 ALBARIÑO

Spanish, with Sea Legs

A WINE COLLECTOR of heroic proportions, my friend Burt has amassed a stash of wine from Burgundy so majestic that it deserves its own marble wing at the Met. But outside of the exalted vines of the Côte d'Or, and the occasional *tête de cuvée* Champagne and jeroboam of Château d'Yquem, he rarely swerves from his exclusively Burgundian beat.

You can imagine my surprise, then, when Burt and his wife, Deedee, returned from a recent trip to Spain glowing about Albariño, having been tipped off to this Spanish white in my last book, *Oldman's Guide to Outsmarting Wine*. How did these self-confessed Burghounds come to switch vinous gears? They, like many others, were enamored of Albariño's fragrant and zesty personality, an immensely likable pour that has gained favor with sommeliers and civilians alike.

Hailing from the misty, maritime Rias Baixas region of northwest Spain, Albariño reminds you of the Atlantic coast situated nearby. This wet-stones minerality runs through the wine's medium-bodied frame like a Taser, and is often joined by equally electrifying hints of citrus fruits, mint, or melon. Sometimes Albariño can show more richness and take on floral or tropical notes, bringing to mind peaches or cantaloupe.

Albariño's bracing acidity and seaside origins make it a slam dunk for seafood, providing a metaphorical lemon squeeze to anything with a shell, tentacle, or gill. Its tanginess, combined with the fact that winemakers tend to use little or no oak in its creation, make it a splendid stand-in for Sauvignon Blanc. Galicians are especially fond of using it to wash down scallops, grilled sardines, and *pulpo a la gallega*, the local favorite of boiled octopus garnished with paprika, rock salt, and olive oil.

Because it is simpatico with seafood and popular among the food obsessed, I dub Albariño the ultimate "seafoodie" wine. Survey the tables at any grand oyster depot, whether it's the Union Oyster House in Boston or Seattle's Elliott's Oyster House, and you'll know what I mean. If any doubt remains, find yourself a glass of Albariño and a plate of oysters. Sniff the wine slowly, and then inhale an empty oyster shell as if it were an oxygen mask. This is oceanfront living at its gastronomic best.

BRAVEHEARTS ON *Albariño*

"Albariño is absolutely perfect with any seafood, any time. On a recent trip to the Rias Baixas region with some fellow food and wine lovers, we paired these wines with everything from the coveted local *percebes* (barnacles) to sizzling baby eels, lobster paella to vegetable-stuffed *lampreya* (don't ask)."   —*Anthony Giglio, wine educator and author*

"I refer to Albariño as the 'lady grape of Spain' because it is aromatic, lush in the mouth, and texturally pleasing—it has everything in perfect balance."   —*Kerin Auth, co-owner, Tinto Fino, New York, NY*

"Albariño is a great seafood wine that people often forget about. One of my all-time favorites is from Lusco—it has incredible minerality and *gout de terroir.*"
—*Christopher Ycaza, wine director and general manager, Galatoire's, New Orleans, LA*

"Albariño is the closest thing Spain has to Riesling—such pure fruit and high acid. It's my favorite style of white wine from Spain. Try it from Pazo de Señorans."
—*José Andrés, chef and restaurateur, The Bazaar by Jose Andrés, Los Angeles, CA*

ALBARIÑO

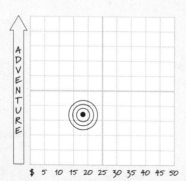

$ 5 10 15 20 25 30 35 40 45 50

 Audacious Alternative To
Sauvignon Blanc, Chardonnay

 Enthusiasts Also Like
Grüner Veltliner, low/no oak Chardonnay,
Sauvignon Blanc from New Zealand,
Moschofilero, Rueda

 Weight
Medium

 Price
Low to Medium ($12 to $25)

 Cheat Sheet
The leading white wine of Spain, Albariño is a
bright, medium-weight white with abundant
fragrance, zingy acidity, and an affinity for
sea creatures.

Label Logic
Albariño is a grape.

 Bravely Said

Albariño	Al-bah-REEN-yo
Château d'Yquem	Shah-toe dee-kem
Côte d'Or	Coat door
Pulpo a la gallega	PUL-poh ah lah ga-lee-ay-LAH
Rias Baixas	REE-yahs BA-shas

 Mark's Picks

Burgans	Boor-GANS
Do Ferreiro	Duh Fe-RAY-roh
Lagar de Cervera	LUH-gar day Sehr-VER-uh
Lusco	Loos-koh
Martin Códax	
Nora	
Orballo	Or-BAL-yoh
Pazo Serantellos	Pa-tzo Sehr-ah-TAY-yos
Serra de Estrela	SHE-ra day es-TRAY-ah

 Poosh It!
"Alvarino" is the name of the same grape in
Portugal, where it is used to make Vinho Verde
(Chapter 8).

 CULINARY SWEET SPOT

Lightest ▲ Heaviest

 A Lovable Feast
As an aperitif or with seafood of all kinds,
particularly steamed mussels, raw oysters, and
other shellfish; risotto, especially with seafood;
tangy cheeses like chèvre and feta; Caesar and
other salads; bean dishes

Locally Lusty

Scallops; grilled and boiled octopus; sardines; *bacalao* (dried salt cod); steamed mussels with *pimentón* (Spanish paprika); *percebes* (barnacles); marinated or roasted vegetables; paella

 Spend the Night Together

Though almost all of the Albariños you'll encounter are from Spain, a handful of American producers are trying their hand at the grape, including Bonny Doon (Ca' del Solo) and Bokisch. Track down one of these Albariños and compare it to the Spanish version.

10 GEWÜRZTRAMINER

The Vinous Exclamation Point

LIKE LINUS WITH his security blanket, I always seem to have wine in tow. This habit, of course, presents a challenge now that the TSA has banned carrying liquids onboard airplanes. So on a trip to Miami, I perfected the art of the "Booze Bag"—a low-grade type of roller bag found in discount stores for about $20, just sturdy enough for one rumble with baggage handlers. I was elated to find one such bag with "Bonjour" emblazoned on its strap, knowing that it had the advantage of being linguistically faithful to wine's spiritual homeland.

Stuffed with five bottles wrapped in T-shirts and Fred Perry track pants, the bag transported my wine to Miami with nary a leak, although the bag itself emerged from the claim as wobbly as a soused sailor. No matter: the experiment now a success, I placed the bag atop a public garbage can on Miami's Ocean Boulevard and respectfully bid *au revoir* to my Bonjour booze bag.

One of the bottles I toted in this rolling clothes hamper was a Gewürztraminer, in part because it was cheap enough that *I* wouldn't be shattered if *it* got shattered. But Gewürztraminer's flamboyant personality and compatibility with Latino cuisine also seemed perfectly suited to Miami.

Most Gewürztraminer hails from a place that couldn't be more psychologically or aesthetically different than South Beach: Alsace, the quaint, timber-framed region of northeastern France. From tapered, Germanic bottles springs no less than a vinous exclamation point, this golden wine erupting with a signature aroma of lychees, rose petals, and apricots, often backed by a clove-like or peppery quality true to *gewürz*'s translation from German as "spiced." Typically dry or just a shade sweet, Gewürztraminer's brash aromatics can nevertheless give the impression of sweetness, which, coupled with its Jo Malone aromatics, is why few folks are ambivalent about it. Sometimes densely textured to the point of unctuousness, this is a wine that leaves its mark.

That presence is in relative abundance in wine shops and eateries, with Alsatian Gewürztraminer going for $15 to $25 at the entry level and up to $50 or more for those of the *grand cru* rank. Trimbach and Hugel are two dependables I see often, while bottlings from Zind-Humbrecht are rarer but worth the search and added expense. Though they may not show the same level of complexity as their French counterparts, compelling efforts can be found outside of Alsace, most often from Washington State, the home of several high-quality, Booze Bag–ready versions that barely exceed $10.

Gewürztraminer's exotic intensity calls for vittles of equal exuberance. Sausage and pork chops, those mainstays of the (decidedly un–South Beachy) Alsatian diet, are classics, as is fatty fowl such as goose, duck, and dark-meat turkey, as well as oniony creations such as onion tarts. The oily texture of smoked salmon harmonizes with it, as do strong cheeses like the local lusty Muenster. Versions that have restrained alcoholic heat can run with spicy food, including the piquant flavors of Spanish fare and the ginger-and-garlic infusions of Asian and Indian cuisines.

Finally, it should be acknowledged that Gewürztraminer is the long-reigning Overlord of the Unpronounceables, having tripped up the tongue almost as long as the umlaut has inflicted its double dots on Germanic vowels and heavy-metal bands. But it *is* conquerable if you break the word into two utterable parts: Guh-VURTS and trah-mee-ner, and, of course, practice often with glass in hand.

BRAVEHEARTS ON *Gewürztraminer*

"I love Gewürztraminer that's just off-dry. That little bit of sweetness takes the high end of the spice off a hot dish. A somewhat recent discovery for me is Gewürztraminer paired with strong, blue-veined cheese like Gorgonzola. The bit of sweetness in the wine is a slam dunk with the spiciness of the cheese."

—*Ming Tsai, chef and restaurateur, Blue Ginger, Boston, MA*

"A great Indian curry with a bottle of Zind-Humbrecht is as good as life gets."

—*Al Stewart, folk-rock musician, "Year of the Cat"*

"I was in London at a curry house with musician Al Stewart. He wanted to order Gewürztraminer but I told him that I didn't want a sweet wine. He said, 'Shut up—listen, it will be just the right thing.' And it was."

—*Mick Fleetwood, drummer and namesake, Fleetwood Mac*

"I was born in the Alsace region of France, so I love the wines from my hometown. They perfectly pair with the Asian foods I like, and many of the dishes that I cook myself. These whites are very fruity and minerally, but don't have any wood tones."

—*Jean-Georges Vongerichten, chef and restaurateur, Jean-Georges, New York, NY*

"I was with Alsatian winemaker André Ostertag, and we tasted Gewürztraminer grapes off the vine at harvest. Then, later on, we tasted a fifteen-year-old bottle of Gewürz whose grapes were from the same vineyard. I was like, 'Holy %@*%, you're kidding me, *that's* the taste of the grape.' Ostertag told me that the measure of a great wine is that at some point you get to taste the grape again. Once you do, a wine's evolution is complete."

—*Paul Grieco, wine director and co-owner, Hearth, New York, NY*

"Gewürztraminer might be one of the most interesting varietals out there. It's like getting smacked in the face with a bouquet of flowers. It smells all feminine and floral but it's a powerful wine. So often, people smell it and think 'Oh, this is a sweet wine. I don't like sweet wines.' But it is not necessarily sweet. It's tricky."

—*José Andrés, chef and restaurateur, The Bazaar by Jose Andrés, Los Angeles, CA*

GEWÜRZTRAMINER

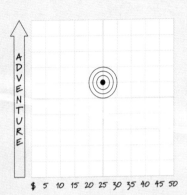

ADVENTURE

$ 5 10 15 20 25 30 35 40 45 50

 Audacious Alternative To

Chardonnay

 Enthusiasts Also Like

Viognier, low/no oak Chardonnay, Torrontés, Riesling from Austria

 Weight

Full

 Price

Medium ($10 to $50+)

Cheat Sheet

With its thrusting scents of lychees, rose water, and spice, Gewürztraminer is a collar-grabber, delivering perfume and power to sensualists who like their wines full, soft, and intense.

Label Logic

Gewürztraminer is a grape. Most of the wine comes from France's Alsace region.

 Bravely Said

Alto Adige	AHL-toe Ah-dee-zhay
Alsace	Ahl-ZASS
Gewürztraminer	Guh-VURTZ-trah-meener

 Mark's Picks

Alsace France

Albert Boxler	
Hugel	Hew-GELL
Josmeyer	JOCE-meyer
Leon Beyer	Lay-ohn Beh-yehr
Lucien Albrecht	Lew-SYEN Ahl-breckt
Marc Kreydenweiss	Krisy-deyn-vice
Marcel Deiss	Dice
Pierre Sparr	Spahr
Schlumberger	Shlum-ber-JAY
Trimbach	Treem-bakh
Zind-Humbrecht	Zint-HOOM-breckt

Beyond Alsace

Chateau Ste. Michelle (Washington State)
Cono Sur (Chile)
Covey Run (Washington State)
Hogue Cellars (Washington State)
Navarro (California)
Pacific Rim (Washington State)

 Poosh It!

Lighter and rarer manifestations of Gewürztraminer come from Italy, especially the Alto Adige region. Occasionally labeled as the aptly mellifluous "Traminer Aramatico," Italian Gewürz finds success in the hands of Alois Lageder, Cantina Tramin, Colterenzio (Kohl-teh-REHN-tsyo), and Pojer & Sandri (Po-YEHR eh SAHN-dree).

CULINARY SWEET SPOT

 Lightest   ▲   Heaviest

A Lovable Feast

Smoked fish, especially salmon; chicken and turkey; pork and smoked sausages; veal; bean dishes; richer pastas such as gnocchi; ginger- or cinnamon-inflected preparations; fruit and fruit-based sauces; spicy ethnic fare, especially Asian, Indian, and Spanish cuisine; Gorgonzola and other blue-veined cheeses; Camembert and other soft cheeses; on Thanksgiving or Mother's Day

 Locally Lusty

Choucroute garni (sausages and other salted meats in sauerkraut); foie gras; onion tarts; Muenster cheese

 Spend the Night Together

To demonstrate Gewürztraminer's lychee likeness, open a bottle and compare its fragrance with that of a can of lychees, available at many supermarkets and on the Internet. Or, for a tonier tasting, do a comparison with a bottle of the "Sugar Lychee Eau de Parfum" by Fresh (www.Fresh.com).

To see if you can detect the signature aroma of roses in Gewürztraminer, buy a rose, pluck a petal, rub it between your thumb and index finger, and compare it to the wine.

11 GRÜNER VELTLINER

Deliverer of Calm Pleasure

RECENTLY I RESOLVED to locate my inner von Trapp and get in touch with my Teutonic tendencies—in a phrase, to get my Österreich on. So a friend and I made a field trip to New York's Neue Galerie, home of Gustav Klimt's 1907 portrait *Adele Bloch-Bauer I*, the Austrian masterpiece that is one of the most celebrated portraits of the twentieth century. Locating the gold-flecked work, we meditated on its depiction of a Viennese social-ite whose serene gaze has been described by art critics as one of "calm pleasure." When the security guards weren't looking, I produced a glass vial of Grüner Veltliner I had smuggled in and we took turns knocking it back.

And then it happened: an Austrian moment, a feeling of contentment and style brought on by the interplay of art and wine. Like the Klimt, the gold-hued Grüner was pure yet luxurious, striking but subtly so—itself a deliverer of calm pleasure.

This is what Grüner Veltliner—Austria's most famous wine—is all about. No syrupy confections or oaky strangulations here. Rather than detonate in your mouth like Viognier (Chapter 15) or Gewürztraminer (Chapter 10), Grüner washes over your palate with waves of nuanced flavor—first with hints of melon or peach, then perhaps flavors of green vegetables such as snap peas or celery, and finally a characteristic afterglow of white pepper. Rarely seeing time in wood, it shows some of the citric snap of a good Sauvignon Blanc and usually comes equipped with enough heft to make it medium-bodied. After a night of indulging in its rich but stony charms, if you don't dream of gold-flecked Klimts you may very well have visions of stalactites, those mineral-rich daggers that hang in caves.

If you are to fully revel in the mystique of this wine, you need to forgo its usual sobriquets—GV and GruVee—and attempt the full mouthful: Grewn-air Felt-LEEN-air. When you do that in a good wine shop, you'll be shown bottles that typically span $15 to $40, with some best-of-breed bottles fetching double that or more. Happily, several entry-level versions below $20 are readily available, including the dependably delicious Hirsch "Veltliner #1," Loimer "Kamptal," and Huber "Hugo." For an even better deal, some producers—Hofer and Beger, to name two—bottle Grüner in fat, one-liter bottles closed with a crown cap, its high-low appearance like a Colt 45 for the wine set.

When contemplating what to serve with Grüner, the world is your oyster—literally. All manner of shellfish pair well as do a panoply of other options. It has the richness to stand up to locally lusty fare like *wiener schnitzel* and grilled sausages and the lemony zing to pierce creamy and acidic cheeses. Its peppery, green character ("Grüner" means green in German) makes it a reflexive choice for the vegetarian table—from lentil salad and quinoa to salads and grilled zucchini.

Grüner even has the goods to stand up to that Dr. Evil of food matches: asparagus—be it green or white, the latter an Austro-German delicacy known as *spargel*. This spring I plan to host an out-and-out Spargelfest, serving bottles of Grüner with a veritable lumberyard of white asparagus drizzled with hollandaise sauce—all designed to induce my next Austrian moment.

BRAVEHEARTS ON *Grüner Veltliner*

"Grüner is a very hip wine now, found on all the best wine lists, which is something that most people are not aware of. It is a dry white wine, rich and savory, with flavors of lemon and white pepper."

—*Zac Posen, fashion designer*

"I have a love affair with Grüner Veltliner. Really crisp Grüners can even pair with oysters, though I like them with sushi, edamame, and a range of Japanese cuisine. Rich, complex Grüners can go with game, and even red meat."

—Debbie Zachareas, co-owner, Ferry Plaza Wine Merchants, San Francisco, CA

"If I'm having wine by itself, I like Grüner for its moderate weight and crisp, clean flavor."

—Alfred Portale, chef, executive chef and co-owner, Gotham Bar & Grill, New York, NY

"I love how juicy, crisp, and peppery good GV can be. It's a great pinch hitter for dishes with difficult-to-pair ingredients like asparagus and dill." —Ross Outon, winner, first season of The Winemakers on PBS and beverage consultant, Austin, TX

"Grüner is wonderful to sip and wonderful to pair. It has incomparable minerality and brightness. It's trout fishing; it's back to nature."

—Helen Johannesen, wine director, Animal, Los Angeles, CA

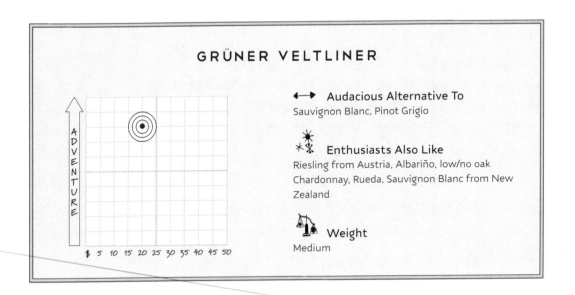

GRÜNER VELTLINER

⟷ Audacious Alternative To
Sauvignon Blanc, Pinot Grigio

✳ Enthusiasts Also Like
Riesling from Austria, Albariño, low/no oak Chardonnay, Rueda, Sauvignon Blanc from New Zealand

⚖ Weight
Medium

ADVENTURE

$ 5 10 15 20 25 30 35 40 45 50

Price

Medium $15 to $40+

 Cheat Sheet

A favorite of wine hipsters, Grüner Veltliner brings its understated grandeur to the table by way of citrus fruits and a faint peachiness, sometimes accented by nuances of green vegetables and white pepper.

 Label Logic

Grüner Veltliner is a grape.

 Bravely Said

spargel	SHPA-gel
Smaragd	Smuh-ROGGED
Spätzle	SHPETZ-luh

 Mark's Picks

Berger	
Bründlmayer	BRUN-dle-my-er
Hirsch	
Hirtzberger	
Hofer	
Huber	
Knoll	K-NOLE
Loimer	
Nigl	NEE-geh
Prager	PRAH-gehr

 Poosh It!

Who needs the Geico gecko when you have Austrian wines from the Wachau region, as those bottles sometimes carry the word "Smaragd," which is the name of a green lizard that likes to sunbathe in the local vineyards. Smaragd Grüners are from the ripest grapes and thus tend to be richer and more alcoholic.

 CULINARY SWEET SPOT

Lightest ▲ Heaviest

 A Lovable Feast

As an aperitif, or with fish, especially trout, or with shellfish such as scallops and lobster; lighter meats such as pork and veal; vegetarian creations, especially with spring vegetables such as asparagus, radishes, and watercress; lentils; peas; dishes with herbs (e.g., chervil, dill, thyme); creamy and acidic cheeses; spicy ethnic fare, including sushi and Thai food; onion flavors; Caesar salad and other piquantly dressed greens; on Thanksgiving or Mother's Day

 Locally Lusty

Wiener schnitzel (fried veal cutlet); sausages; *rindsuppe* (beef soup); goulash with *spätzle* (dumplings); *spargel* (white asparagus)

 Spend the Night Together

In springtime, create your own *spargelfest* (Leiderhosen not required).

Build a party around Grüners in one-liter, pop-top bottles.

12 LOW/NO OAK CHARDONNAY

Tiki Umbrellas Needn't Apply

MY ORIGINAL TITLE for this book was *Weaning Off Chardonnay* —a playful call to action meant to motivate readers to venture beyond wine's usual suspects. I realized, however, that even *I* don't want to abandon Chardonnay, which is the noblest of white grapes and the sole ingredient in ethereal whites like Montrachet from Burgundy. I just want to avoid the overly creamy, vanilla-tinged booze bombs whose natural partner is not food but a tiki umbrella.

If you like Chardonnay in this zaftig style—as legions still do—there is no shame in it. In the last decade, however, a growing number of enthusiasts have been pitching for Chardonnay that isn't so rich that it dominates food, opting instead for the vinous equivalent of a sinewy Weimaraner over the overgrown Tibetan mastiffs that carry the Chardonnay name.

These lean creatures are relatively easy to track. In locales such as California and Australia, many winemakers have reined in their use of new oak barrels for fermenting or aging their Chardonnay, replacing them with stainless-steel tanks or older oak barrels that don't beget the butterscotch sweetness and extra padding that new oak can impart. Instead, if they use oak at all, they do so restrainedly, more as a condiment than as a concealer of the wine's natural fruit. They also plant in cooler microclimates where the grapes can retain more acidity, and sometimes regulate vinification processes to avoid rendering the wine excessively buttery. Often labeled "unoaked," "unwooded," or even "naked," these wines are characterized less by stereotypical notes of tropical fruit and caramel and more by an appley or citrusy finesse, streamlined and lipsmackingly vibrant.

MONTRACHET: TO "T" OR NOT TO "T"?

Once and for all, we settle that great, vexing question of winedom: do you or don't you pronounce the first "t" in Montrachet, the famous *grand cru* white wine from Burgundy, France.

X "Though some people like to pronounce the 't'—like 'Mont' in Montblanc pens—I don't. Right after I opened the now closed, legendary Montrachet restaurant I asked our wine director and he confirmed: 'no t,' though a few locals in the village of Montrachet do it."

> —Drew Nieporent, restaurateur

X "I am qualified to answer because I was married at Montrachet, the New York restaurant. No, no, no to the first 't.' It is silent. Although back in the day I don't recall a single person dining in Manhattan without bragging about eating at MonTrachet."

> —Lettie Teague, wine columnist, *The Wall Street Journal*,
> and former executive wine editor, *Food & Wine* magazine

X "It is pronounced without the 't' like, Mont-réal in French."

> —Pierre de Benoist, winemaker, Domaine A. & P. Villaine, Burgundy, France

X "It is 'Mohn-ra-shay,' with the 'on' pronounced like 'pond' without the 'd.' Pronouncing it with a 't' sounds like Mount-trash-hey!"

> —Jean-Louis Carbonnier, president, Carbonnier Communications, New York, NY

FINAL TALLY: 0 FOR, 4 AGAINST THE FIRST "T"—"MOHN-RA-SHAY" IS CORRECT.

Although low oak or no oak Chardonnays can be found throughout the New World, the lion's share of it originates in New Zealand, Australia, and on the West Coast of the United States, from Washington State down to Santa Barbara, California. Happily, with these wines not requiring expensive French oak barrels, many bottles can be had for under $20.

If the New World is a gateway for experiencing Chardonnay in a leaner but approachable style, then Chablis—the region of Burgundy, France, not the deceptively named jug wine—represents Chardonnay at its most stripped down. With the area's cooler climate, famously chalky soil, and nearly complete aversion to new oak, vintners hijack the pink Cadillac that drives so many warm-climate Chardonnays and switch out its sheepskin seats for the spare elegance of cold leather. The upshot is pure Chardonnay that is lithe in frame and lemony bright, with shrimp-shell minerality and rapier thrusts of crispness.

The tariff for these angular Chardonnays is higher than that for their equivalents from the New World, with basic bottlings of Chablis averaging around $25. Bottles from *premier cru* vineyards trade in the $20 to $50 range, while the highest-quality Chablis from so-called *grand cru* vineyards fetch between $30 and $60 or more. High-end Chablis sometimes sees a brief but largely imperceptible flirtation with oak barrels, and it is one of the few white wines that can gain complexity and body as it ages.

Whether from the New World or the Old, low oak Chardonnay is like a rocket booster for food: ready to give lift. Unencumbered by oaky sweetness, it sends oysters into orbit and pierces the richness of fattier fish like salmon and swordfish. Its flinty personality harmonizes with dishes normally in the thrall of Sauvignon Blanc, including food with a "green" component like spinach, pesto, or even asparagus with its rambunctious tang. Slightly weightier New World versions have an affinity for eggy creations and the creaminess of macaroni and cheese as well as mayonnaise-based sauces.

BRAVEHEARTS ON *Low/No Oak Chardonnay*

"I like Chardonnay that is low oak. I love white Burgundy. And I also enjoy Chardonnay from New Zealand such as Cloudy Bay."

—*John Lodge, singer and bass guitarist, The Moody Blues*

"The Chardonnay style I like depends what I'm serving. For summer and the fish we catch at the lake, I like unoaked Chardonnay. EastDell, one of the vineyards I'm involved with, makes a completely unoaked Chardonnay. It's as clear as water and there's something so clean and beautiful tasting about it."

—*Dan Aykroyd, actor*

BRAVEHEARTS ON *Chablis*

"After a few years in the bottle, top-level Chablis can give you back some of the honey and butter taste. They can match so many foods, from salmon to chicken to veal, and of course all kinds of fish and goat cheese."

—*Christian Moreau, winemaker and co-owner, Domaine Christian Moreau*
Père & Fils Chablis, France

"I like Burgundy's Pouilly Fuissé, Montrachet, Chablis, but often find American Chardonnay to be too oaky."

—*Kevin Bacon, actor*

"Everyone goes through their Chardonnay period, and so did I. But California just bombed my palate. The wines there can be too big, too woody. But I dig Chablis. I prefer it with a clean piece of broiled fish and with raw seafood."

—*Sammy Hagar, vocalist, Chickenfoot, and former vocalist, Van Halen*

"These cool-weather wines have a steely purity and a limestony mineral quality that makes them unique and food friendly."

—*Jay McInerney, novelist and wine columnist,* The Wall Street Journal

"Perfect with mushrooms and shellfish. I love the flinty sensibility of this take on Chardonnay and prefer it to anything grown in California." —*Mario Batali, chef and restaurateur, Babbo, New York, NY*

"Chablis is still way underpriced for the quality you get—*premier cru* Chablis can be had for well under a hundred dollars, which is a lot less expensive than equivalent wine from other regions of Burgundy."
—*Richard Brierley, former head of North American wine sales, Christie's*

LOW/NO OAK CHARDONNAY

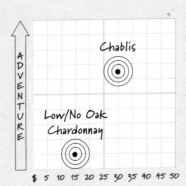

 Weight

Medium

 Price

New World: Low to Medium ($10 to $25)
Chablis: Medium to High ($20 to $60+)

 Cheat Sheet

Lighter and more food friendly than the butterballs of fame, unoaked and lightly oaked Chardonnay capture this grape at its most unadorned and provide a crisp trip through citrus and green fruits.

←→ Audacious Alternative To

Pinot Grigio, Chardonnay (oaky)

✳✳ Enthusiasts Also Like

Albariño, Grüner Veltliner, Rueda, Vermentino, Viognier, Gewürztraminer, Muscadet, American sparkling wine, grower Champagne, Prosecco

 Label Logic

Chardonnay is a grape. Chablis is a subregion of France's Burgundy region.

Bravely Said

Chablis — *Sha-blee*
Montrachet — *Mohn-rah-shay*

 Mark's Picks

New World Chardonnay
Babich (New Zealand)
Cousiño-Macul (Chile) — *Koo-SEE-nyo Ma-COOL*

Domaine Chandon
   (California)
Four Vines
   (California)
Kim Crawford
   (New Zealand)
Plantagenet (Australia)
Rex Hill (Oregon)
Saint Clair
   (New Zealand)
Snoqualmie (California) — *Snow-KWAL-mee*
Stony Hill (California)
Villa Maria
   (New Zealand)
White Truck (California)
The Wishing Tree
   (Australia)

Chablis, France
Christian Moreau — *Kree-ty-an Moh-roh*
Domaine Laroche — *Lah-rosh*
François and Jean-Marie
   Raveneau — *Rah-vuh-no*
Jean Collet — *Zhan Koh-leh*
Jean Dauvissat — *Zhan Doh-vee-sah*
J. Moreau & Fils
Louis Michel & Fils — *Loo-wee Mee-shell*
Rene & Vincent
   Dauvissat — *Do-vee-sah*
William Fèvre — *Fehv-ruh*

 Poosh It!

Among the more creative ways of signifying oak-free Chardonnay are Chehalem's "INOX" (the abbreviation of the French word for stainless steel), Morgan's "Metallico," Mer Soleil's "Silver," and Trevor Jones's "Virgin."

 CULINARY SWEET SPOT

 Lightest ▲ Heaviest

 A Lovable Feast

Lobster, crab, shrimp, and other crustaceans; oysters, clams, and mussels; all fish, especially lighter types like sole or flounder; chicken and other white meats; lemon sauces; egg dishes; pesto, spinach, and other herbal or green foods; brothy soups; vegetarian fare

 Locally Lusty

Dishes using Dijon mustard; escargot

Spend the Night Together

Although decanting—i.e., pouring wine into a glass pitcher—is typically done with red wine, either to soften its tannic bitterness or to remove sediment from an older bottle, see what happens when you let a white wine like Chardonnay sit for an hour in a decanter. How does the wine change in aromatics and taste?

13 RUEDA

Verdejo Is the Secret Sauce

LIKE SO MANY citizens of Metropolis squinting skyward wondering if it's a bird or a plane, my students are forever asking whether a wine's name refers to its grape or place. Who can blame them? The categorization of wine can be as inconsistent as the lyrics to a song by Beck or as hard to follow as signage on the New Jersey Turnpike.

A historic but revitalized region of northwestern Spain, Rueda can contribute to this uncertainty. Normally, I'd stress that Rueda is named for its region, as is typical of most European wines, as opposed to being labeled for its grape, as is done in the United States and other New World (i.e., non-European) countries. While I'd mention that it can come from various white grapes, I'd probably just leave it at that, because in most cases knowing a bunch of exotic grape names isn't going to make the wine taste any better.

But in the case of Rueda, awareness of the primary grape used in its blend, Verdejo, is integral to appreciating this wondrous wine. One reason is that wine lists in the States will sometimes list the wine not under "Rueda" but under its grape "Verdejo," so if you're scanning the list quickly—and who doesn't?—you need to be alert for either name. An ancient variety indigenous to the Rueda region and often derived from old, flavor-stoking vines, the Verdejo grape also merits recognition because it is often a key factor that sets this wine apart from other crisp whites on the shelf. In fact, producers that use at least 85% of Verdejo in the blend can add "Verdejo Superior" to the bottle's label, which they proudly do.

I'd be proud too if I were able to bring about wines that

achieve the round-but-zesty character for which the best Ruedas are admired. On the nose, you'll get a pears-and-lemon brightness coupled with some minerality and traces of peaches, flowers, or almonds. These essences echo in the wine's flavor, which is laced with a vibrancy that typically isn't as aggressive as that of Sauvignon Blanc.

Speaking of other grapes, Rueda provides the perfect escape hatch for those caught in a blind allegiance to Pinot Grigio. Just ask my friend Alison, who for years taunted me that she only had eyes for "boring old Pinot Grigio"—that is, until I sneaked some Rueda into her glass at a party; her instant, almost reflexive love of it elicited from me an exultant Dave Chappelle–style "gotcha!"

You might have a "gotcha" moment of your own when you discover that Rueda inhabits the lowest end of restaurant wine lists and averages only about $13 in wine shops. That's a microscopic price to pay for such a food-friendly pour, ideal with tapas and other Mediterranean cookery, vegetables of all kinds, and high-acid preparations like ceviche and citrusy sauces. It reigns supreme with summery foods, such as tomato, watermelon, and feta cheese—even better when the three are combined into one glorious salad. Former PlumpJack wine director Gillian Ballance calls this salad/Rueda match one of her all-time favorites.

BRAVEHEARTS ON *Rueda*

"I love whites from Rueda, especially killer old-vine Verdejos like Shaya, Agricola Castellana, and Vidal Soblechero. They are so vibrantly textured with beautiful stone fruits and citrus."
    —*Gillian Ballance, former wine director, PlumpJack Group, San Francisco, CA*

"If somebody says they drink Sauvignon Blanc, I immediately recommend Rueda. It is clean, with good acidity, like the lemon on the side of a shrimp cocktail. Ruedas with a high percentage of the Verdejo grape tend to be very aromatic, sometimes with tropical notes like mango and passion fruit."

—*Kerin Auth, co-owner, Tinto Fino, New York, NY*

"Rueda is crisp, fresh, and fruity, with flavors of grapefruit, lemon, and gooseberry. It is not quite as intense as Sauvignon Blanc from New Zealand, but it has a chalky, mineral backbone that makes it stand apart."

—*Mollie Battenhouse, sommelier and wine director, Maslow 6, New York, NY*

RUEDA

ADVENTURE

$ 5 10 15 20 25 30 35 40 45 50

← → **Audacious Alternative To**
Sauvignon Blanc, Pinot Grigio

☀ **Enthusiasts Also Like**
Sauvignon Blanc from New Zealand, Moschofilero, Grüner Veltliner, Vermentino, Albariño, low/no oak Chardonnay, Riesling from Australia

⚖ **Weight**
Medium

💲 **Price**
Low ($8 to $20)

☑ **Cheat Sheet**
Powered by the native grape Verdejo, Rueda is the *madre* of all wine bargains, a value-priced palate pleaser with vibrancy, ample aromatics, and a richness usually unencumbered by oak.

💡 **Label Logic**
Rueda is a region. Its primary grape is Verdejo, which is often blended with other grapes such as Viura and Sauvignon Blanc. "Verdejo Superior" designates that a bottle comprises at least 85% Verdejo.

🗨 **Bravely Said**

Bogovantes	*Boh-go-VANT-ays*
Porrón	*Por-OWN*
Rueda	*Roo-AYE-dah*
Verdejo	*Vehr-DAY-yoh*

Mark's Picks

"Basa"
   (Telmo Rodriguez)

Blanco Nieva	*BLAN-coh Knee-AY-vah*
Pie Franco	*Pie-ay FRAN-koh*
Con Class	*Cone Klass*
(Cuevas de	*KWAY-VAS day*
Castilla)	*Cass-TEE-ya*
Marques de Riscal	*Mar-CASE day Rees-KAHL*
Martinsancho	*Mar-teen-SAHN-cho*
Montebaco	*Mon-teh-BAH-ko*
Naia	*Nah-yah*
Pedro Escudero	*PEY-dro Es-koo-DEH-roh*
Shaya	*SHY-ah*

Poosh It!

Before the region's revitalization in the 1980s, Rueda was known only for wines of the polar opposite character: dark, oxidized, and anything but refreshing.

  CULINARY SWEET SPOT

Lightest ▲ Heaviest

A Lovable Feast

As an aperitif; seafood of all types; feta and other tangy cheeses; summer salads; ceviche; fresh tomatoes and tomato-based sauces; citrus sauces; garlic, pesto, and other Mediterranean flavors; vegetarian fare

Locally Lusty

Bogavantes (lobster) and *cigalas* (langoustines) *a la plancha* (salted and grilled on a metal plate); tapas of all types; gazpacho

Spend the Night Together

Try imbibing Rueda via a *porrón*, a glass pitcher traditionally used with the Spanish sparkler cava. Like a bong for wine, its tapered spout allows a group of people to drink from it without having to make lip contact. Using a non-bubbly like Rueda has the advantage of avoiding the hard-to-swallow foam that comes with drizzling cava into your mouth. KegWorks.com and other Internet retailers carry *porróns*.

14 VERMENTINO

Right for Sprite-ing

AT THE RISK of being blacklisted from the world's cineplexes, I hereby render a confession. I have developed a habit of smuggling wine into movie theaters, especially at flicks that require a bit of self-anesthetization, namely those exceeding two hours, imposing subtitles, or featuring the freneticism of Renée Zellweger. While I am of course not actually advising you to do this, my method is as follows. I purchase a 20-ounce bottle of Sprite (or another soda with tinted plastic), empty it out, and carefully pour in the wine—most of which fits inside.

I call this process "Sprite-ing" the wine—and, as you can imagine, it is also well suited to taxicabs, sporting events, and time spent with teetotaling in-laws. I find myself doing this often with Vermentino, a wine that is not only affordable and unsuspiciously translucent, but has a lemon-lime character that matches the saltiness of movie popcorn and the sourness of Jujubes.

Though grown in France and in the Italian regions of Liguria and Tuscany, Vermentino is most often associated with the Italian island of Sardinia. The windswept hills and granite soil of this Mediterranean isle produce a wine that is typically medium weight, though it is sometimes plumper, with sassy notes of citrus and a clean, appetite-amping finish, with rarely a trace of oak. You would be correct if this reminds you of Pinot Grigio, but Vermentino typically has something extra to offer, with more pronounced floral aromatics and occasionally accents of herbs or almonds. It can show a faint bitterness on the finish, which only serves to make the wine more interesting and palate cleansing.

While Vermentino works wonders on its own as an aperitif, a wine of this vibrancy cries out for the company of seafood, whether it's a simple grilled sea bass or Sardinian specialties such as roasted sardines or clams with pasta. Its acidity harmonizes with Mediterranean flavors, from capers and olives to tomato sauces and the most garlicky of pestos. It also has an affinity for creations of the green persuasion, such as salads, artichokes, green beans, and broccoli rabe.

Vermentino may have four syllables, but they pass through the lips so easily that the name sounds like the invention of a couture house or Ferrari factory. When you ask for it in a wine shop, you'll find that its price is as gentle as its pronunciation, usually residing in that sweet spot of $10 to $20. It doesn't get better with age, so look for the youngest bottle you can find. And although it is not yet a prime-time player, it is starting to gain a following. New York restaurateur Joe Campanale recently told me that he overheard one of the diners in his dell'anima restaurant triumphantly announce to her friends: "No Pinot Grigio for us tonight—*we're* going with Vermentino."

BRAVEHEARTS ON *Vermentino*

"With its racy acidity and occasional herbaciousness, Vermentino is the wine I recommend for a dyed-in-the-wool Sauvignon Blanc drinker or someone who wants to make the transition from martinis or gin and tonics to wine."

—*Lou Amdur, owner, Lou's Wine Bar, Los Angeles, CA*

"I've been drinking a lot of Vermentino this summer—it's very popular by the glass at restaurants. I drink it at the beach, at barbecues, or as an aperitif on hot days." —*Alfred Portale, chef, executive chef and co-owner, Gotham Bar & Grill, New York, NY*

"I hate it when restaurants don't have affordably priced wine. Wine shouldn't be elitist like that. Sometimes you just want to relax with a good Vermentino."

—*Gavin Rossdale, solo artist and former vocalist and guitarist, Bush*

"Vermentino—I love it because it is food friendly. It makes you want a second glass." —*Lidia Bastianich, chef and host of PBS's* Lidia's Italy

"I enjoy Vermentino because of its balance and subtlety. The virtue of a wine like this is that it naturally complements myriad classic seafood dishes from places like Liguria and the Mediterranean coast. Its ripe fruit makes for an intense and complex pairing."
  —*April Bloomfield, chef and co-owner, The Spotted Pig, New York, NY*

"There is something special about Vermentino from the northern Sardinia province of Gallura. It reveals a highly aromatic wine of jasmine, Asian pears, Key lime and nectarines balanced with the seering backbone of acidity that makes it an incredibly fun wine to match with many dishes from asparagus to seafood stew to a salad of olives with Pecorino sardo, arugula, and walnuts."
  —*Shelley Lindgren, wine director and co-owner, A16, San Francisco, CA*

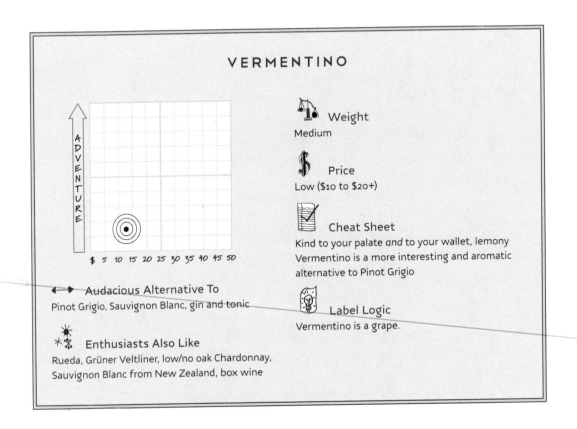

VERMENTINO

ADVENTURE

$ 5 10 15 20 25 30 35 40 45 50

Weight
Medium

Price
Low ($10 to $20+)

Cheat Sheet
Kind to your palate *and* to your wallet, lemony Vermentino is a more interesting and aromatic alternative to Pinot Grigio

Audacious Alternative To
Pinot Grigio, Sauvignon Blanc, gin and tonic

Label Logic
Vermentino is a grape.

Enthusiasts Also Like
Rueda, Grüner Veltliner, low/no oak Chardonnay, Sauvignon Blanc from New Zealand, box wine

Bravely Said

Aragosta	*Ah-rah-GO-stah*
Gallura	*Guh-LUR-uh*
Liguria	*Lee-GOOR-ee-ah*
Vermentino	*Vehr-men-TEEN-oh*

 Mark's Picks

Antinori (Tuscany)	
Argiolas (Sardinia)	*Ahr-JOH-las*
Cabras "Cielo Bleu" (Sardinia)	
Campo al Mare (Tuscany)	
Fattoria di Magliano (Tuscany)	*Faht-to-REE-ah dee Mah-lee-AH-no*
Fratelli Pala "Crabilis" (Sardinia)	
Santadi (Sardinia)	
Sella e Mosca (Sardinia)	

 Poosh It!

"Fresca Flask" is the pet name I use for a wine-filled soda bottle.

 CULINARY SWEET SPOT

Lightest ▲ Heaviest

 A Lovable Feast

As an aperitif; seafood of all kinds; calamari *fritti* and other fried dishes; risotto; capers, olives, eggplant, and other Mediterranean accents; tomatoes and tomato sauces; pesto sauces; salads; green veggies such as broccoli rabe and green beans; spicy fare

 Locally Lusty

Roasted sardines; *sa merca* (roast fish with ziba, a local herb); clams with pasta; *aragosta alla castellanese* (lobster sautéed with tomatoes, onion, garlic, and lemon); gnocchi with tomato sauce; pecorino cheese; artichokes

 Spend the Night Together

Contrast a tasting of Pinot Grigios with Vermentinos. Which type provides more enjoyment?

Since we've already established that Vermentino is the kind of casual wine that fits unconventional maneuvers, here's another. Instead of cutting off the foil capsule on a bottle's neck, try this shortcut: grasp the entire capsule with one hand, and while twisting it a bit like a motorcycle throttle, slide it forcefully off the end of the bottle. Although it doesn't work with every bottle, more often than not it peels away so easily that you feel like a magician doing the tablecloth trick.

CAMPANALE'S BICYCLETTE

As a former sommelier at New York's Babbo restaurant and currently the beverage director and co-owner of the Italian hot-spots dell'anima and L'Artusi, Joe Campanale really knows his *vino Italiano*. That is why I was especially impressed when he elected to make me and a friend an unpretentious Italian drink called a Bicyclette, apparently named for its ability to make enthusiasts zig-zag home on their bicycles. Also a favorite of London celebrity chef Fergus Henderson, its crisp, bittersweet character is perfect for priming the appetite.

INGREDIENTS

Campari
White Wine (dry and simple)
Ice

Pour a few ounces of Campari into a wineglass. Fill with ice, and then add wine to your taste. (It is typically made with equal parts Campari and white wine.) Finish with a lemon twist.

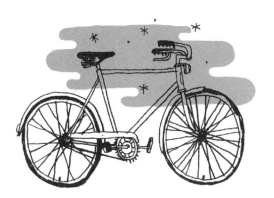

15 VIOGNIER

Hits the V-Spot

A NEAT LITTLE way to gauge a wine's aromatic intensity is to pour a yourself a small taste, drink it, and then sniff the empty glass. If the aroma emanating from the glass is pronounced, you know you're dealing with a major scent-maker.

The perfect wine to try this with is Viognier, a white that can have knee-wobblingly intense notes of peaches, mangoes, apricots, or other tropical fruits, joined by a rich, round texture and a finish that stretches out like a desert highway. It can be so bold and distinctive, so evocative of peaches and cream, that I liken it to Torrontés, the floral Argentine white, but with supplemental swagger. To invoke two phrases I've learned from HBO: it's "yoked," as vainglorious Johnny Drama of *Entourage* once said of his biceps, and it "brings the ruckus," as daffy slickster Leon Black of *Curb Your Enthusiasm* once described his sexual powers. For those with a yen for the softness and weight of Chardonnay but with less or no oak, Viognier can really hit your V-Spot.

This is not to say that Viognier is always so lushly perfumed and densely textured. In its homeland of the northern Rhône, where it goes by the name of its subregion, Condrieu, it can show restraint, with wiry acidity on the tongue and minerality on the palate. France's climate plays a role in rendering such a style, as does whether a winemaker chooses to use new oak barrels—or any oak at all. Either way, Condrieu is a special-occasion manifestation of the grape, priced as it is at $50 to $100 or more, a victim of scarce, expensive vineyard land; E. Guigal, M. Chapoutier, and Georges Vernay are blue chips. For a better deal, look to France's Languedoc-Roussillon region, where producers such as Jean-Luc Colombo, Laurent Miquel, and R. Gassier get it done, albeit with less complexity, for under $20.

Under the New World's relatively robust sunbeams, you're likely to experience Viognier in all of its voluptuousness, but even here it can sometimes have a lean, citrusy bent, especially when it originates in a cooler subregion and vintners forgo the use of oak. In California, Alban, Cold Heaven, Calera, and Fess Parker are perennial performers in the $20 to $25 range. Respectable versions from Australia and Chile clock in at half that price, including Angove's, Oxford Landing, and Yalumba's "Y Series" from the former and Cono Sur and Viu Manent from the latter.

There was a period in the 1990s when experts predicted that Viognier would become as popular as Chardonnay, which, of course, never came to be. Consumers were likely daunted by its challenging name, which is indeed drowning in vowels. Even so, Viognier is far from obscure and regularly appears in many stores and restaurants.

Foods that mirror Viognier's plump and tropical profile are its trustiest companions. It craves the company of richer-tasting seafood such as crab, lobster, scallops, and tuna, even more so when it comes dressed in a creamy sauce. Fruit-based preparations are another natural choice, be it salmon in an orange-miso glaze or pork loin stuffed with apples. Viognier will also pluck all the right sitar strings with the spice and fruit of Indian cuisine.

BRAVEHEARTS ON *Viognier*

"Lush and peachy, Viognier is feminine and Rubenesque—overindulgence in a glass. Viognier is more compelling than similarly priced Chardonnays and goes much better with cheese than any red wine."
—*Colin Averas, sommelier, DGBG Kitchen and Bar, New York, NY*

"Many wines this fragrant have a lighter body, like Riesling. But Viognier has the unusual, almost schizophrenic combination of a heady aroma *and* a full body. Both Viognier and Gewürztraminer have a potent aroma and full body. But to me, Viognier is more about fresh fruit and flowers, whereas Gewürztraminer is more spicy and smoky.

"Famed Rhône vintner Marcel Guigal once told me that the vines will die if you just look at them cross-eyed."
—Josh Jensen, winemaker and owner, Calera Wine Company, Hollister, CA, on the Viognier grape's notorious fragility

"The flavor profile for Viognier goes from fresh fruit flavors of peach, pear, apricot, to wet stone, honey, grapefruit, citrus peel, vanilla (not from the oak barrels), as well as additional hard spices of cardamom and anise. If you like the mouthfeel of Chardonnay but want to try something different, then Viognier may be of interest.

"Viognier really shines with fish and everything from Mexican chilies to Thai food to sushi. It seems to be made for cuisine that customarily has beer or Champagne paired with it—that is, ethnic cuisines with some fiery spice. The other key pairing is anything with a soft goat cheese and or walnut oil."
—Morgan Clendenen, winemaker and co-owner, Cold Heaven, Santa Rita Hills, CA (a Viognier-only winery)

"For the richness of the food here in New Orleans, I'm a big fan of well-made Condrieus and other Viogniers. The thing you have to watch is that the wine isn't so rich that it becomes flabby—i.e., lacking in acidity."   —Christopher Ycaza, wine director and general manager, Galatoire's, New Orleans, LA

"The ideal food pairing with it is an obscene amount of steamed Dungeness crab, homemade aioli, and a few other dipping sauces."
—Andrew Adam, winemaker, Conway Family Vineyards, Rancho Arroyo, CA

VIOGNIER

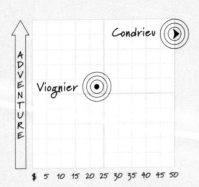

Condrieu

Viognier

ADVENTURE

$ 5 10 15 20 25 30 35 40 45 50

 Audacious Alternative To

Chardonnay

 Enthusiasts Also Like

Gewürztraminer, Torrontés, Riesling from Austria, low/no oak Chardonnay

 Weight

Full

 Price

Viognier: Medium ($10 to $30)
Condrieu: High ($50+)

 Cheat Sheet

At its best, Viognier primes passions and closes deals with its exotic aromas and crème brulée texture.

Label Logic

Viognier is a grape.

 Bravely Said

Condrieu	Coh'n-DREE-uh
Languedoc-Roussillon	Lan-guh-dok
	Roo-see-yohn
Viognier	VEE-oh-nyay

Mark's Picks

New World
Alban (U.S.)
Angove's (Australia)
Calera (U.S.)
Casa Silva (Chile)
Cline (U.S.)
Cold Heaven (U.S.)
Cono Sur (Chile)
Fess Parker (U.S.)
Oxford Landing (Australia)
Pride Mountain (U.S.)
Robert Hall (U.S.)
Viu Manent (Chile)
Yalumba (Australia)
Zaca Mesa (U.S.)

France

M. Chapoutier (Condrieu)	Shah-pooh-tyay
Domaine de Gournier (Languedoc-Roussillon)	Goohr-nyay
E. Guigal (Condrieu)	Gee-gahl
Georges Vernay (Condrieu)	
J & F Lurton (Languedoc-Roussillon)	
Jean-Luc Colombo (Languedoc-Roussillon)	Coe-lon-bow
Laurent Miquel (Languedoc-Roussillon)	
Paul Jaboulet (Condrieu)	Jah-boo-lay
R. Gassier (Languedoc-Roussillon)	GAS-ee-yay
Wild Pig (Languedoc-Roussillon)	

Poosh It!

Virginia, once the home of our great Oenophile-in-Chief, Thomas Jefferson, is emerging as an interesting source of Viognier. Because Virginia is less sunny than California, these "double V's" (Virginia Viogniers) tend to be less alcoholic and more delicate than their Golden State counterparts. Try Chrysalis, Horton, or Veritas.

CULINARY SWEET SPOT

Lightest ▲ Heaviest

A Lovable Feast

Crab, lobster, scallops, and other richer seafood; chicken, duck, turkey, and guinea hen; pork and ham; fruit-infused sauces and glazes; cream and butter sauces; butternut squash and sweet potatoes; coconut-milk curries, sesame shrimp, satays, and other Thai flavors; Chinese and Indian fare; nuts and nut-based oils; most kinds of cheese; on Thanksgiving or Valentine's Day

Locally Lusty

Condrieu: seafood terrines; deep-fried fish

Spend the Night Together

Ace wine marketer Jean-Louis Carbonnier told me that he likes to "*aviner le verre*" or "get the glass drunk" with a bit of wine before he pours himself a full glass. Viewed by some as a ritual of wine geekery and by others (including wine staff of New York's Babbo restaurant) as an important technique, it is also known as "priming the glass" or a "wine wash," performed to remove any extraneous odors from the glass. Try it with Viognier and see if it makes a difference.

LOCALLY LUSTY GASTRONOMY

"I always take such great pleasure exploring wines and foods in the places they're from. In Italy, I remember white truffle–covered pastas in Piedmont with earthy Barbarescos. In Vicenza, Italy, the local *bigoli* (square spaghetti) are dressed with the drippings from roasted duck and paired with Amarone or Ripasso reds. In eastern Sicily this summer, my wife, Antonia, and I salt-roasted just-caught *spigola* (sea bass) and paired it with dry, local whites made from Carricante and Catarratto grapes."

—Anthony Giglio, wine educator and author

"It's not by chance you have the wine and you have the food, both from a particular region. It's a symbiosis. The wine and the food of a region evolve together."

—Ariane Daguin, owner and co-founder, D'Artagnan, Newark, NJ

"I love tasting local dishes and local wines when I travel. A few favorites are drinking Tokaji Aszu in a great little restaurant in Budapest, Castello di Ama Chianti in a small restaurant in San Gimignano, and a Goerges Vernay Condrieu in an outdoor café in Avignon."

—Laurie Hook, chief winemaker, Beringer Vineyards, Napa, CA

"I will never forget sipping Chianti among the vineyards at the Fonterutoli estate in Tuscany while hunters searched for wild boar in the surrounding forests, or drinking Fiano [a dry full-flavored white from Italy's Campania region] after tasting the heartiest bean soup at Marenna restaurant in the town of Sorbo Serpico."

—Donatella Arpaia, food/entertaining authority and restaurateur, Mia Dona, New York, NY

"I was in Croatia this summer and drank local wines, sitting by the ocean, eating freshly-caught seafood. Drinking and eating locally absolutely makes sense."

—Todd English, chef and restaurateur, Olives, Charlestown, MA

PINK

ROSÉ: ADVENTURE & PRICE AT A GLANCE

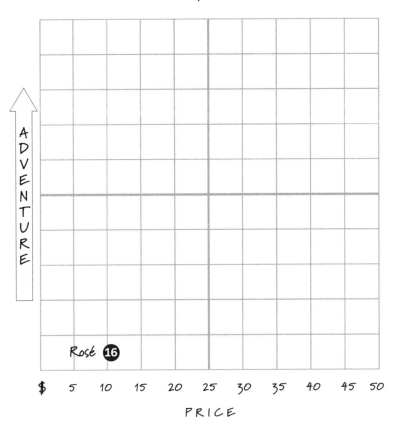

ADVENTURE

Rosé **16**

$ 5 10 15 20 25 30 35 40 45 50

PRICE

16 ROSÉ

Sunset in Your Glass

WHEN I WAS planning my "Rosé Renaissance" seminar for the Aspen Food & Wine Classic, my mission was to turn vice into virtue. Despite rosé's currently fashionable status, there are still many who, at first sight, dismiss it as the stuff of clown cars, cotton candy, or Rush Limbaugh's ties. It is misjudged as the vinous equivalent of Mariah Carey's hemline or Donald Trump's hairline. It is guilty not by association, but by pigmentation. So rather than offer apologies, I decided to celebrate rosé's color spectrum by providing each Aspen attendee his or her own "Rosé Ruler," a homemade card featuring a row of Pantone-like color samples, from "light pink" to "watermelon" to "russet" to "ruby."

While the idea that anyone would want to go around analyzing pink wine with a designer's precision is, of course, meant to be cheeky, the point I was making was that rosé is a wine that entertains long before it even passes your lips. Its comely colors have in fact been likened to a sunset in a glass. With better bottles, its bouquet will live up to its look, refreshing you with juicy red fruits like raspberries, cranberries, or watermelon, joined sometimes by floral essences, citrus fruits, or perhaps a whiff of minerals. And then there is the taste: not the sucrose serum of a bad white Zinfandel, but a dry, clean thirst-slaker with the body of a light red and the crispness of a white.

Though rosé is sometimes made by blending red and white wines together, the dominant method of production is known as *saignée* (from the French *saigner*, "to bleed"), whereby the juice of red-wine grapes is bled off before the skins can make it fully red. After fermentation, what results is typically a medium-bodied affair, one which deftly straddles the foods we associate with white and red wine. Dry rosé is so versatile that I'm reluctant to impose *any* parameters on your food choices, though I'll proffer one rule of thumb. To achieve rosé nirvana, follow my "Rosé Rule of P": serve it with anything pink—lobster, shrimp, ham, pork—or anything Provençal—such as bouillabaisse, salade Niçoise, or grilled sardines.

Speaking of Provence, that paradisiacal region of sun-kissed slopes and lavender meadows remains the locus of rosé's spiritual soul, especially when it is from the ancient soils of Bandol. But the pink stuff prospers throughout France, from Tavel in the nearby Rhône Valley to Anjou in the Loire. Knowing how many gratifying Spanish *rosados* and Italian *resatos* there are you might say that most of Mediterranean Europe sees things through a rosé-colored lens. The New World has developed its own passion for the pink, typically in the form of more fruit-forward and creamy concoctions such as SoloRosa from Napa and Paso Robles's Tablas Creek.

Wherever it originates, it is almost always moderately priced, with most bottles ringing up between $8 and $20, with the exception of showpiece rosés such as France's celebrated Domaine Tempier and Domaines Ott; the latter is so à la mode that the cognoscenti have given it their own nickname—"the D.O."—though with its $40 price tag, you might want to give its ubiquitous bowling-pin-shaped bottle an "N.O." Finally, dry rosé's greatest advantage is in its power to refresh: short of retreating to a triple-spray outdoor shower or clipping one of those portable fans to the base of your wineglass, there is no better restorative in the swelter of a summer eve.

BRAVEHEARTS ON *Rosé*

"When I visit my sister in the southwest of France, we take an empty jug to the local supermarket and the pink stuff spills out like cool water. It is my version of madeleines only tons more fun.

"I'm told by one of my oldest friends that I have the wine palate of an old French lady with too much lipstick and a tattered Hermès scarf. I assume he means my taste in wines has more to do with Proustian references than a desire for surprise. But if you catch me in the summertime, I'll be in my old housedress drinking nothing but rosés. I'll take any Tavel you've got, also Domaines Ott or the very pale Petale de Rosé. I go through cases of the stuff as if it were pink Kool-Aid . . . but way better with grilled sausages, guac and chips, hard Italian cheese, and Thai noodles. —*Jodie Foster, actress*

"Rosé is my summer gulping wine—I love the spice and fresh fruit flavors. I mostly drink it in the summer on all occasions—on its own, with grilled foods, with cheese, sausages, etc."
—*Daniel Johnnes, wine director, Daniel Boulud's Dinex Group, New York, NY*

"One of my favorite wine experiences was with a couple of friends on a Sunday afternoon, sitting in a park overlooking Sydney Harbour with a loaf of white bread, a bag of fresh prawns, and a bottle of rosé."
—*Kevin Judd, winemaker and co-founder, Cloudy Bay Vineyards, New Zealand*

"I find rosés typically very easy drinking, floral in the nose, yet with excellent body. An excellent one is Nine Vines Rosé from Angove's in Australia." —*Zac Posen, fashion designer*

"I drink an inordinate amount of rosé in the summer—not just rosé from France, but from all over the world."
—*Drew Nieporent, restaurateur, Tribeca Grill and Nobu, New York, NY*

"I have recently discovered Chinon rosé from the Loire Valley. It is perfect for summer and the only one that has so beautifully reminded me of my late mother's favorite of the 1960s, Rosé d'Anjou. It is fresh, not too sweet, and for me filled with nostalgia!"
—*Lynn Redgrave, the late actress*

"Château Margillière Rosé 'Cuvée Hautes Terres' mirrors the colors and aromas of the south of France. This gourmand rosé is refreshing and adapts perfectly to our summertime rituals, particularly if it is consumed at the heart of its source in Provence."
—*Alain Ducasse, chef and restaurateur, Le Jules Verne, Paris, France*

"I'd like to do a high-end rosé called 'Pink Bear,' which would feature my body as a dancing Pink Bear. I've got the Pink Bear body."

—*Dan Aykroyd, actor, joking about how he'd like to expand his eponymous portfolio of wine*

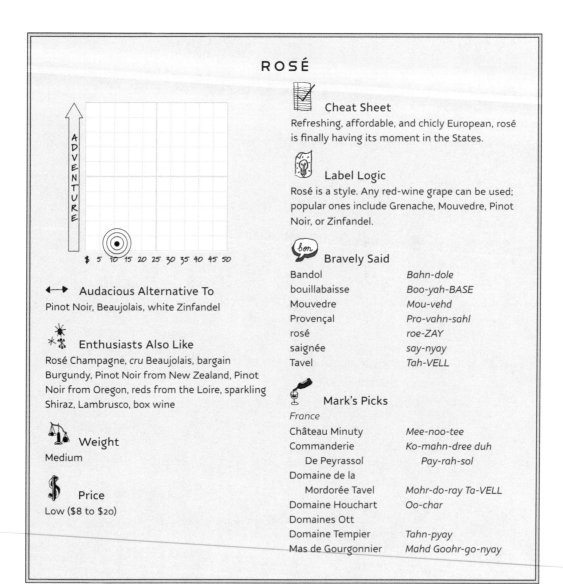

ROSÉ

Cheat Sheet

Refreshing, affordable, and chicly European, rosé is finally having its moment in the States.

Label Logic

Rosé is a style. Any red-wine grape can be used; popular ones include Grenache, Mouvedre, Pinot Noir, or Zinfandel.

Bravely Said

Bandol	Bahn-dole
bouillabaisse	Boo-yah-BASE
Mouvedre	Mou-vehd
Provençal	Pro-vahn-sahl
rosé	roe-ZAY
saignée	say-nyay
Tavel	Tah-VELL

Mark's Picks

France

Château Minuty	Mee-noo-tee
Commanderie	Ko-mahn-dree duh
De Peyrassol	Pay-rah-sol
Domaine de la	
Mordorée Tavel	Mohr-do-ray Ta-VELL
Domaine Houchart	Oo-char
Domaines Ott	
Domaine Tempier	Tahn-pyay
Mas de Gourgonnier	Mahd Goohr-go-nyay

Audacious Alternative To

Pinot Noir, Beaujolais, white Zinfandel

Enthusiasts Also Like

Rosé Champagne, *cru* Beaujolais, bargain Burgundy, Pinot Noir from New Zealand, Pinot Noir from Oregon, reds from the Loire, sparkling Shiraz, Lambrusco, box wine

Weight

Medium

Price

Low ($8 to $20)

Mark's Picks (continued)

Italy (rosato)

Alois Lageder	*Ah-Low-is Lah-GAY-duhr*
Cantalupo "Il Mimo"	*Eel Mee-moh*
Castello di Ama	

Spain (rosado)

Bodegas Muga	*Moo-gah*
CVNE	*Coo-NAY*
Marqués de Cáceres	*Mar-KESS deh KAH-seh-res*
Tapeña	*Tah-pay-nyah*

United States

A-to-Z Wineworks
Bonny Doon Vin Gris
Deep Sea "Sea Flower"
Etude Rosé of Pinot Noir
Kuleto
SoloRosa
Soter
Tablas Creek
Wölffer   *Wowl-fer*

Other

Angove's Nine Vines (Australia)
Crios de Susana Balbo Rosé of Malbec (Argentina)
Jindalee (Australia)
Turkey Flat Grenache (Australia)

 Poosh It!

A quirky, singular pick is Spain's Bodegas R. López de Heredia Viña Tondonia (Ton-DOE-nee-ah) rosado, which is typically copper-orange in color, pricey for a pink drink at about $30, and released from the winery a good ten years after the vintage. Complex, singular, and the darling of insiders, it manifests some of the tangy, slightly oxidized, hazelnut-almond personality you'd expect from dry sherry.

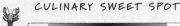 CULINARY SWEET SPOT

Lightest   ▲   Heaviest

 A Lovable Feast

As an aperitif or with almost anything; spicy ethnic food like Indian and Chinese; smoked meats and other barbecue fare; chicken stir-fry; turkey burgers; nachos; potato salad; vegetarian dishes; salads; red peppers, anchovies, and other tapas-oriented fare; shrimp, lobster, pork, lamb, bacon, and other "pink" foods; sushi; teriyaki dishes; paella; on Valentine's Day, Independence Day, or Mother's Day; with brunch

 Locally Lusty

Provençal standards such as *pissaladière* (pee-salad-YAIR, onion tart); dishes with aioli (garlic mayonnaise); fried oysters; salade Niçoise; ratatouille; *petits farcis* (little stuffed vegetables); tapenade

 Spend the Night Together

Create your own Rosé Record, recording every shade you see over a period of time. Not only will doing this get you drinking more rosé, but you'll be amazed at the variation in pigmentation.

TASTING WHILE TRAVELING

"I told NBA superstar Grant Hill, 'We're going on a wine tour of Napa next week, so you better be in shape.' He told me, 'Don't worry, Coach, my wife Tamia and I were in France drinking wine last week, so we're in shape.'"

—Mike "Coach K" Krzyzewski, head coach, Duke University men's basketball team and U.S. national team

"The Orient Express has a killer wine list—everything you want, they have. Basically, if you see a wine region out of the window of the train, you can order it from the train's cart."

—Courtney Taylor-Taylor, lead singer and guitarist, The Dandy Warhols

"Being a Canadian, your experience with libations begins with beer. When I was twenty-one and had just started on *Beverly Hills, 90210*, I had a girl-friend who was a wine lover and we started taking trips to Napa . . . Many of the winemakers had daughters who were teenagers who happened to think that Jason Priestley was the coolest guy in town. That would lead to my being taken into the winery's caves and doing barrel tastings. So I got fast-tracked into wine appreciation in a way that most young people don't get to be."

—Jason Priestley, actor

"At least once on every tour a select few band members and crew members find a nice restaurant and splurge on an epic meal . . . It's such a great way to leave the strange world of rock and roll touring behind. It's a tradition that we have all promised to keep alive our entire lives. I'm already looking forward to those days long in the future where we all are old and falling apart, laughing at our shared memories."

—Nick Harmer, bass guitarist, Death Cab for Cutie

"A few years ago, my wife and I were spending a fabulous few days in Champagne at Château de Corcelles, a magical seventeenth-century château outside of Reims. One very special evening we ate by ourselves in the garden, surrounded by ancient sculptures and perfectly disheveled hedgerows. We drank a bottle of 1990 Henriot Cuvée Des Enchanteleurs, it tasted of smoke and apples, and the bubbles were perfectly ticklish on the tongue, cutting wonderfully against a rich lobe of foie gras and cherry compote. The Champagne was so delicious that we stuck with it for the evening, and it held its own nicely against a crispy squab."

—Jeff Corwin, host and executive producer, Animal Planet's "The Jeff Corwin Experience"

"The idea of a picnic with a bottle of wine and baguette is an essential part of the mystique of wine. Wine doesn't have to be elitist. Europeans get it right—they view wine as a useful and reasonably priced mood enhancer."

—Gavin Rossdale, lead singer, Bush and solo artist

"When I travel, I go into a local grocery store and literally spend hours there looking around. I gather up stuff—wineglasses, mini-stoves, bamboo steamers—and send it all home."

—Guy Fieri, chef and television host

"I went to South Africa to film a movie and visited the Franschhoek Valley, a short journey from Cape Town. Being with girlfriends in a foreign country amongst the beautiful scenery of Franschhoek made it one of my most special wine tasting experiences. When I travel, I bring back wines and share them along with the stories of my journey. It brings people I love around the table, and we share in the adventures together." —*Hilary Swank, actress*

"Whilst traveling I tend to try local New World wines, which have certainly improved dramatically over the last two decades. It's always good to discover a rising star, but in Europe, I swiftly revert to the elite race of the Super Tuscans. When I first set eyes on a bottle of Sassicaia, I knew instantly that it was going to be something very special. It has one of the most beautifully designed labels of any wine, and the producers' remarkable attention to detail is even more evident in every drop of this grand elixir. The Super Tuscans don't adhere to all the traditional winemaking rules, it is their style and individuality that I find hugely appealing. Ornellaia, Solaia, and Tignanello each bring a different bouquet of flowers to the evening, so I'm always happy to receive any of them as guests at short notice."

—*Nick Rhodes, keyboardist, Duran Duran*

REDS

REDS: ADVENTURE & PRICE AT A GLANCE

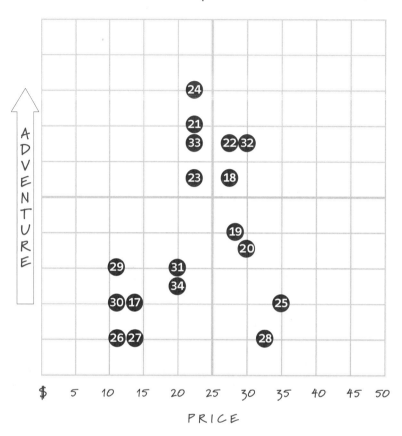

17. *Cru* Beaujolais	**26.** Côtes du Rhône
18. Bargain Burgundy	**27.** Malbec
19. Pinot Noir from New Zealand	**28.** (Good) Merlot
20. Pinot Noir from Oregon	**29.** Montepulciano d'Abruzzo
21. Reds from the Loire	**30.** Nero d'Avola
22. Aglianico	**31.** Petite Sirah
23. Bargain Bordeaux	**32.** Priorat
24. Cahors	**33.** Reds from Portugal
25. Classic Cabernet	**34.** Reds from Washington State

17 *CRU* BEAUJOLAIS

The Serious Side of the Gulpstream

WHEN I SEE *cru* Beaujolais on a wine list, I snipe it off with the reflexes of an over-caffeinated biathlete. At a time when so many bottles in restaurants aren't worth their altitudinous markups, it is often one of the few bottles to achieve the vinous hat trick of affordability, versatility, and universal likability.

Beaujolais, you ask? Isn't that the late-autumn happy juice derided by critics as little more than a confection created with all the craft of Keebler elves?

That's Beaujolais nouveau, the simple quaff from grapes that are picked, fermented, and bottled all in a matter of weeks, then rushed to market with fanfare as France's first wine of the new vintage. With pinkie-extenders writing it off as little more than a one-note, Bubblelicious-in-a-glass and Americans no longer quite as excited about its annual ritual, Beaujolais nouveau of late has indeed lost some of its, well, "bojo." Despite its diminished popularity, I nevertheless welcome Beaujolais nouveau as I do a good swig of spiked cranberry juice: clean and crisp, it is a refreshing rite of autumn. And why would anyone want to frown upon a wine that still inspires jubilation around the world?

Cru Beaujolais, however, is a different story. It offers a richer, more interesting take on Beaujolais, one that is available year-round and is considered the best of the Gamay-based wine for which France's Beaujolais region is known. Such so-called "serious Beaujolais" is light-to-medium bodied and highly fragrant, dialing up bright red fruits such as raspberries and cranberries, flowers like violets, and sometimes a touch of topsoil. Its vibrant acidity and absence of bitter tannins makes it taste even better when given a good chill. Being a light red, it is also famously versatile with a range of foods, deftly accenting all but the heaviest of dishes. Bistro staples, piscine flesh like salmon and mahi-mahi, and dishes high in acid are especially transcendent, and it never met a picnic basket, baguette, or summertime grassy knoll that it didn't like.

On average $12 to $20 at retail, *cru* Beaujolais delivers significant felicity for your francs. Note, though, that these bottles don't trumpet themselves as "*cru* Beaujolais," so consumers instead have to look for one of the ten villages, or *crus*, from which they spring (see the full on list on page 126). For those who familiarize themselves with some of these villages, the emphasis of their village name over "Beaujolais" is actually an advantage, as it sidesteps the happy-juice stigma of Beaujolais nouveau and thus makes for an affordable-but-chic present for a discerning friend. Especially giftable are the wines of Daniel Bouland, which combine artisanal quality with a handsome, all-script label.

Though exceptions abound, each *cru* has a slightly different personality, with Moulin-à-Vent and Morgon often denser and more complex, while Brouilly, Juliénas, and Chiroubles are typically a bit more delicate. No matter where it's from, *cru* Beaujolais aims to please. Once on Valentine's Day at Chicago's Blackbird restaurant, I ordered a St.-Amour from an artisan producer and it hit the bull's-eye with its chilled flavors of cassis and blueberries, tangy acidity, and obvious powers of linguistic seduction.

BRAVEHEARTS ON Cru *Beaujolais*

"I like Fleurie—it tastes best in a Parisian bistro."

—*Al Stewart, folk-rock musician, "Year of the Cat"*

"One of my great wine memories is years ago drinking Fleurie from big black mugs I'd call 'tankers' at bistro Chez L'Ami Louis in Paris.

"I love *cru* Beaujolais. At my restaurant Corton, we crafted a wine list to include high-quality, inexpensive wines like Moulin-à-Vent and Chiroubles."

—*Drew Nieporent, restaurateur, Tribeca Grill and Nobu, New York, NY*

"I love the simplicity and stimulating flavors of a good Beaujolais. The '*crus*' have more body and intensity but are still unpretentious, delicious drinking."

—*Daniel Johnnes, wine director, Daniel Boulud's Dinex Group, New York, NY*

"On my own time and my own dime I prefer light-bodied reds like single-village Beaujolais to heavier red wines. They are true refreshments, delivering flavor without weighing me down."

—*Marnie Old, author,* Wine Secrets, *and wine educator*

"I drink more *cru* Beaujolais more often than any other red wine type. From a good producer, it is almost always ranges between 'good' and 'amazing.'"

—*Lou Amdur, owner, Lou's Wine Bar, Los Angeles, CA*

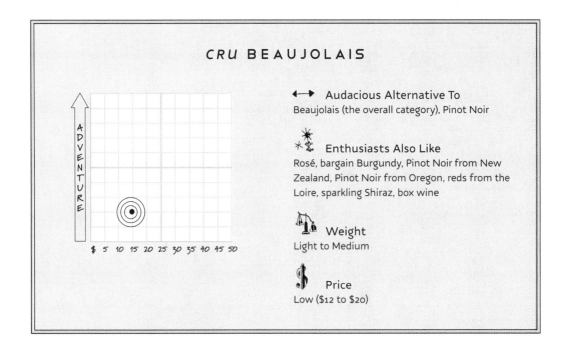

CRU BEAUJOLAIS

←→ **Audacious Alternative To**
Beaujolais (the overall category), Pinot Noir

Enthusiasts Also Like
Rosé, bargain Burgundy, Pinot Noir from New Zealand, Pinot Noir from Oregon, reds from the Loire, sparkling Shiraz, box wine

Weight
Light to Medium

Price
Low ($12 to $20)

Cheat Sheet

A gutsier, more serious alternative to the Beaujolais nouveau style most drinkers know, *cru* Beaujolais delivers a refreshing, exuberant, and sometimes surprisingly complex red without picking your pocket.

Label Logic

Beaujolais is a subregion in the Burgundy region of France. Gamay is the grape. *Cru* Beaujolais refers to one of ten "villages" in the best part of the Beaujolais region. The ten Beaujolais *crus*, or "villages," are:

Brouilly	Broo-yee
Chénas	Shay-na
Chiroubles	Shee-roobl
Côte du Brouilly	Koht dyoo Broo-yee
Fleurie	Flehr-ee
Juliénas	Jool-yeh-nahs
Moulin-à-Vent	Moo-lahn-ah-vahn
Morgon	More-gawn
Régnié	Ray-nyay
St.-Amour	Sahn Tah-moor

Bravely Said

Beaujolais	Boh-joh-lay

Mark's Picks

Clos de la Roilette	Rwah-let
Daniel Bouland	
Georges Duboeuf	Duh-BUFF
Jean Folliard	Fohl-yar
Jean-Paul Brun	
Joseph Drouhin	Drew-AHN
Louis Jadot	Jah-DOE
Marcel Lapierre	
Michel Tête	Mee-shell TEHT
Pierre-Marie Chermette	Shary-met
Potel-Aviron	Poh-tel Ah-vi-rhon

Poosh It!

You can avoid having to remember the name of artisanal producers of Beaujolais (and other wines) by learning the names of elite importers who specialize in that category and are thus themselves a good marker of quality. Appearing on the bottle's back label, some of the best importers of small-batch *cru* Beaujolais are: Louis/Dressner, Kermit Lynch, Weygant-Metzler, and Robert Chadderdon.

 CULINARY SWEET SPOT

Lightest ▲ Heaviest

A Lovable Feast

Vastly versatile, including richer fish such as swordfish and salmon; grilled sausage; salami, prosciutto, and other charcuterie; fried foods; acidic foods such as tomato sauces, goat cheese; teriyaki dishes; Thanksgiving

Locally Lusty

Bistro fare such as roast chicken, *pot-au-feu*, pâtés, pork and duck rillettes; ratatouille

Spend the Night Together

Because Beaujolais nouveau makes many people associate all Beaujolais with late autumn, try switching gears and hosting a *summertime* celebration with chilled bottles of *cru* Beaujolais.

Contrast *crus* known for richer Beaujolais (e.g., Moulin-à-Vent) and those associated with more delicacy (e.g., Brouilly).

18 BARGAIN BURGUNDY

Seek "Shake Shack" and "Mayberry's Best"

WEDDINGS. SUSHI. EYE SURGERY.

Certain purchases are incompatible with the term "bargain," lest we transgress natural law, antagonize the gods, or bring on a gastrointestinal Waterloo. Many drinkers would add red Burgundy to this list, not for medical or karmic reasons but because a moderately ambitious bottle of this famous Pinot Noir from eastern France can fetch $80 or more. Add to this the fact that the wine is fiendishly inconsistent in quality and its region is as complicated as the federal tax code, and you wonder why someone jonesing for Pinot would even bother with Burgundy.

The answer is that when it is really good, it can stop time. After my friend Evan shared a bottle of the fabled 1978 La Tache with me, I emailed him that the wine was "a run at vinous perfection: a 'sinus clearing' [Evan's term], utterly unforgettable nose of Asian spices and forest floor, and a hauntingly silky, minutes-long finish more mood-lifting than anything with a childproof lid." Admittedly, *that* bottle was a rarity whose monetary value approximated that of a low-mileage MINI, but it provides insight into how sometimes just one transcendent Burgundy is enough to inspire the kind of obsessive love that eventually makes mincemeat of 401(k)s and marital bonds.

So can the thrifty drinker experience a sliver of the magic that is good Burgundy without resorting to a life of ransom notes? The answer is yes, though this bargain Burgundy, however enjoyable, will be far less concentrated and complex than the finer bottles. Without saddling you with the region's geographic or hierarchical intricacies or attempting to cover every strategy, here are two simple ways (and a few names therein) to smoke out bargain Burgundies—which, in relative terms, means Burgundy around $40 or less:

1. *Seek "Shake Shack"*: as with Danny Meyer's beloved New York burger stands, look for a humble offering from a top producer. At Shake Shack, the burgers are made to Meyer's exacting specifications—even incorporating a sirloin-brisket mix that used to be ground at Meyer's acclaimed Eleven Madison Park across the street from the original Shack. Adjusting for Burgundy, then, you should look for wine from the generic, entry-level "Bourgogne Rouge" category, which means that the grapes come from anywhere throughout Burgundy rather than from a specific village or vineyard. But do so from a top producer, whose resources and ambition can imbue even the most humble of offerings with a bit of the allure for which their upscale bottles have gained fame. Generally the least expensive type of red Burgundy, with prices ranging from about $18 to $40 at retail, the best vintners for Bourgogne Rouge include Nicolas Potel, Joseph Drouhin, and Faiveley.

2. *Seek "Mayberry's Best"*: another approach is to pursue top producers from a modest, less familiar locale—"Mayberry," we'll call it. Though the best restaurant in Mayberry probably won't have access to top resources enjoyed by an elite, big-city restaurant, its cuisine can still provide abundant pleasure at a fraction of the price charged by a Michelin three-star. So for Burgundy, look for the best producers in less exalted Burgundy villages, such as the appellations of Mercurey, Savigny-lès-Beaune, and Chorey-lès-Beaune. When I consulted him, Burgundy guru Allen Meadows also recommended trying Chassagne-Montrachet, an elite source of white Burgundy, but overlooked for its reds. Though generally slightly more expensive than Bourgogne Rouge, these can often be found for $25 to $50.

Being from a cool, mercurial climate, red Burgundy generally tends to be lighter, crisper, and earthier than the fruit-forward Pinot Noirs from warmer climates like California. Bargain Burgundies can be svelter still, displaying the region's telltale signs of cherry earth but backed by a firm spine of acidity so that they can sometimes taste a bit hollow and sharp for those used to New World Pinot. But if you already appreciate the subtlety of red Burgundy, or are open to its understated appeal, these wines can satisfy at a price that won't crack your monocle.

The probabilities for pleasure are even greater when there is a capable merchant or sommelier to act as your divining rod. A visit to Michael Mina's XIV in Los Angeles—where the wine director became excited that anyone even knew to ask for this neglected category and then pointed me to a delightful, under-priced Bourgogne Rouge—convinced me that there is no other wine type where a wine pro can better prove his mettle. Show me a rewarding Malbec and I'll nod approvingly; point me to a great bargain Burgundy and I'm washing your car.

Bargain Burgundies cry out for a good chill as much as they demand the company of food, and are ready to embrace everything from fleshier fish, roast chicken, pork, and veal to native Burgundian favorites such as beef bourguignon, coq au vin, escargot in garlic butter, and Époisses cheese. But most bargain Burgundy is ultimately simple stuff, and it is relieving to hear the the advice of veteran consultant and auctioneer Dennis Foley, who, despite having been to more fancy wine dinners than most, told me that there is no better pairing with moderately priced Burgundy than pepperoni pizza.

BRAVEHEARTS ON *Bargain Burgundy*

"Though it is of course possible to drink for even less at the generic Burgundy level (called "Bourgogne"), stick to the very top producers. In particular, two domains that seem to never miss with their examples are Domaine Michel Lafarge and Domaine Mugneret-Gibourg."

—*Allen Meadows, publisher and owner, Burghound.com*

"Good producers will make wine from less famous villages. For example, Mercurey from Faiveley is wonderful."

—David Chan, violinist and concertmaster, Metropolitan Opera, New York, NY

"When it comes to wines, I personally prefer those from the beautiful Burgundy region in France. These wines are elegant and have a delicate balance of flavors, never heavy or overly fruit-forward. They are very versatile and pair well with almost any cuisine."

—Laurent Tourondel, chef and restaurateur

"No description necessary, it's that good."

—Wine list at Vine Street Café (Shelter Island, NY), describing a Savigny-lès-Beaune

BRAVEHEARTS ON *Upmarket Burgundy*

"Drinking Romanée-Conti from the barrel, I had a moment when time completely stopped. I was experiencing things that I didn't know were possible in wine. It was an image of perfection that people strive for—and here it was achieved."

—David Chan, violinist and concertmaster; Metropolitan Opera, New York, NY

"Crazy as it sounds, even my hit song 'Mas Tequila' was written after a few glasses of wine. I think I was drinking the acclaimed '85 Domaine de la Romanée-Conti Richebourg."

—Sammy Hagar, vocalist, Chickenfoot, and former vocalist, Van Halen

BARGAIN BURGUNDY

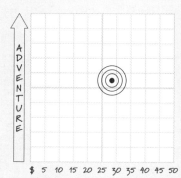

$ 5 10 15 20 25 30 35 40 45 50

 Audacious Alternative To
Pinot Noir (the overall category)

 Enthusiasts Also Like
Cru Beaujolais, Pinot Noir from Oregon, Pinot Noir from New Zealand, reds from the Loire, rosé

 Weight
Light

 Price
Medium to High ($20 to $50+)

Cheat Sheet
The search for bargain Burgundy need not be quixotic if you focus on quality producers, particularly those who make generic Bourgogne Rouge and bottlings from less heralded villages.

 Label Logic
Burgundy is a region. The wine known as red Burgundy is 100% Pinot Noir.

 Bravely Said

Bourgogne	*Boor-goh-nyuh*
Chassagne-Montrachet	*Shah-SAHNNE Mohn-rah-SHAY*
Chorey-lès-Beaune	*Sho-ray-lay-Bone*
Époisses	*Ay-pwoss*
Mercurey	*Mair-coo-ray*
Savigny-lès-Beaune	*Sah-vee-nyee lay Bone*

 Mark's Picks
Bourgogne Rouge

Bouchard	*Boo-SHAR*
Champy "Signature"	*Shahm-pee*
Faiveley	*FAVE-ah-lee*
Louis Jadot	*Jah-DOE*
Michel Lafarge	*Lah-farzhe*
Mugneret-Gibourg	*Mew-yuh-reh Jhee-boor*
Joseph Drouhin	*Drew-ahn*
Laboure-Roié	*Lah-bow-ray WAh*
Leroy	*Luh-RWALL*
Nicolas Potel	*Poe-tell*
Olivier Leflaive "Cuvée Margot"	

Mark's Picks *(continued)*

Less Celebrated Villages

A & P de Villaine   *deh VEE-lehn*
   (Mercurey)

Bernard Morey   *Bear-NAHR More-AY*
   (Chassagne-
   Montrachet Rouge)

Bouchard   *Boo-SHAR*
   (Savigny-lès-Beaune)

Bruno Clair
   (Savigny-lès-Beaune)

Champy
   (Chorey-lès-Beaune)

Faiveley (Mercurey)   *FAVE ah-lee*

Château de Chamirey
   (Mercurey)

Jean-Pierre Charton
   (Mercurey)

Joseph Drouhin   *Drew-ahn*
   (Chorey-lès-Beaune)

Leroy
   (Savigny-lès-Beaune)

Louis Jadot
   (Savigny-lès-Beaune)

Louis Latour
   (Chassagne-
   Montrachet Rouge)

Maurice Ecard   *Ay-CAHR*
   (Savigny-lès-Beaune)

Philippe Colin   *Koe-LAHN*
   (Chassagne-
   Montrachet Rouge)

Simon Bize   *See-mon Beez*
   (Savigny-lès-Beaune)

Tollot-Beaut
   (Chorey-lès-Beaune)

 Poosh It!

A favorite of Napoleon, the gastronome Brillat-Savarin, and Burghounds across the globe, the nutty, runny cheese Époisses de Bourgogne is so malodorous that French authorities are rumored to have once banned it from public transport.

 CULINARY SWEET SPOT

Lightest   ▲   Heaviest

 A Lovable Feast

Salmon, swordfish, and other substantial fish; roast chicken, duck, and other fowl; pork; veal; pizza, especially with pepperoni and other meats; vegetarian fare; Thanksgiving, Valentine's Day, or Mother's Day

 Locally Lusty

Beef bourguignon; coq au vin; escargot in garlic butter; Époisses de Bourgogne

 Spend the Night Together

Do a comparative tasting of bargain Burgundy and Pinot Noir from California. The differences are sometimes dramatic. Which tastes richer? Which has an earthier edge?

19 PINOT NOIR FROM NEW ZEALAND

Silken and Shockable

"GIVE IT A SHOCK."

These four words have revolutionized the way I drink lighter red wine like Pinot Noir. It is my shorthand for asking for the wine slightly chilled, a way to disarm the servers who secretly scoff at this request being nothing more than tableside bombast.

What they don't realize is that imposing ten minutes of ice-bucket time on a lighter red has the miraculous ability to focus its flavors and diminish its alcoholic heat.

Few wines are more "shockable" than Pinot Noir from New Zealand. The Kiwis' take on this coveted, challenging grape is one of lightness and purity over the relatively rich fruit of California Pinot or the overt earthiness often characterizing red Burgundy (Chapter 18). Though richer versions exist, New Zealand Pinot shines brightest when it shows restraint and elegance, supplying a dose of red-berry magic that is as refreshing, tangy, and straightforward as a fistful of chilled raspberries. Better bottles will also have the silky, smooth texture that makes the wine so craveable.

You can't fault New Zealand Pinot Noir if it doesn't thrill with the prismatic nuances that typify the finest red Burgundy, as the latter has had a head start of a good seven hundred years. In fact, New Zealand has been doing noteworthy Pinot for only about the last twenty years, still finding its way with relatively young vines and new winemaking talent, with the greatest strides made in the regions of Martinborough and Central Otago. The world's southernmost wine-growing zone, mountainous, picturesque Central Otago is a sensation among the Pinot passionate, who recognize the potential in the region's intense sunlight, day-to-night temperature swings, and other favorable conditions. Winemakers are advancing the quality of Pinot there, as well as the vineyard acreage devoted to it, with the gravity-defying force of the bungee jumping for which the locals are famous.

Produced by mostly upstart, boutique wineries, Pinot Noir from New Zealand comes to the States in relatively scant, though rising, supply—which, when combined with its aforementioned dependability, means that putting out an APB on particular producers isn't needed. Even so, know that the wineries Felton Road, Craggy Range, and Te Muna Road consistently fire the fancy of insiders. Pricing ranges between $15 and $35, with exceptional cases above that.

Pinot Noir's chill-worthiness is joined by a wondrous compatibility with food, so much so that I nickname it *Pivot* Noir, as it glides so easily among the foods we associate with white wine and those which pair with reds. New Zealand's renditions are no exception, as they are willing bedfellows with all but the lightest of sea creatures and the heaviest of beasts. Local gastronomes are partial to serving it with dishes infused with wild thyme, which became commonplace in Otago after Chinese gold miners brought it to the region in the 1800s. Pinot is also a tradition with the abundance of wild hare that populates the local hills. And the end of "Duck Day," which marks the start of Otago's waterfowl-hunting season, just wouldn't be the same without pairing your catch with a bright and delicate glass of local Pinot.

BRAVEHEARTS ON *Pinot Noir from New Zealand*

"Pinot's home is in Burgundy. It goes to California and Oregon to do business, but to New Zealand to have fun. New Zealand is colder climatically than any other Pinot growing area, but it has more ultraviolet light than any other Pinot growing area. There's some evidence that New Zealand Pinots ripen on U/V rather than heat, which might account for their freshness and vibrancy.

"The best duck dish I have ever seen with our Pinot was done by a Brisbane chef: he skinned a duck, then made a confit of the meat, which he shredded and mixed with a reduced stock from the bones. The shredded meat was then rolled in the skin, like a sausage, and roasted until the skin was crispy."

—*Nigel Greening, owner, Felton Road Wines, Central Otago, New Zealand*

"I love the silky, elegant texture, depth of flavor, and range of aromatics and flavors that Pinot Noir can provide. Grilled steak, an heirloom tomato salad, and a lovely bottle of Pinot are a great combination."

—*Laurie Hook, chief winemaker, Beringer Vineyards, Napa, CA*

"Pinot works great with mushrooms, truffles, hard cheeses like Edam, and red meat birds like duck and squab."

—*Todd English, chef and restaurateur, Olives, Charlestown, MA*

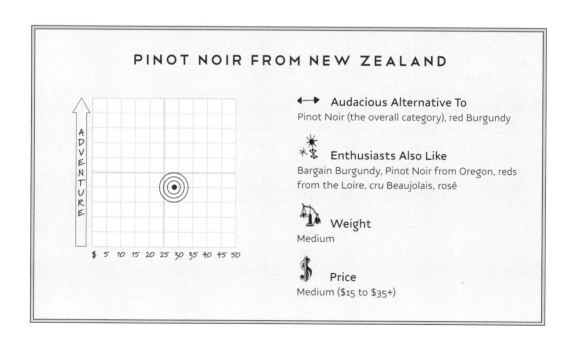

PINOT NOIR FROM NEW ZEALAND

↔ Audacious Alternative To
Pinot Noir (the overall category), red Burgundy

✳❧ Enthusiasts Also Like
Bargain Burgundy, Pinot Noir from Oregon, reds from the Loire, *cru* Beaujolais, rosé

⚖ Weight
Medium

$ Price
Medium ($15 to $35+)

ADVENTURE

$ 5 10 15 20 25 30 35 40 45 50

Cheat Sheet

Often light on its feet and crisply appointed, Pinot Noir from New Zealand is a feisty upstart of a wine, able to consistently satisfy.

 ### Label Logic

Pinot Noir is a grape.

 ### Bravely Said

Central Otago   *OH-ta-go*

 ### Mark's Picks

Anthem
Ata Rangi   *Ah-tah Rain-gee*
Craggy Range
The Crossings
Felton Road
Mt. Difficulty
Rippon
Roaring Meg
Sherwood Estate

 ### Poosh It!

As Felton Lane's Nigel Greening confirmed for me, it is a pivotal time for New Zealand Pinot Noir, as the vines of some of its longer established vineyards are becoming just old enough (twenty to thirty years) to produce wines of significant complexity.

CULINARY SWEET SPOT

Lightest   Heaviest

 ### A Lovable Feast

Vastly versatile, including roast chicken; richer fish; lamb; bacon; salads and salad dressing; beets; tomatoes and tomato sauce; mushrooms, potatoes, beets, and other earthy delights from the Greenmarket; truffle and truffle oil; most kinds of cheese; Thanksgiving, Valentine's Day, or Mother's Day

 ### Locally Lusty

Thyme-infused dishes (e.g., new potatoes roasted with thyme); hare and rabbit (e.g., spiced rabbit rillettes); wild duck; "pork and puha" (Māori specialty of pork and watercress boiled with potatoes)

Spend the Night Together

To see how much temperature affects a wine's taste, try chilling one bottle for ten minutes (in a bucket with ice and water) and compare its taste to a second bottle of the same kind that hasn't been chilled. If you wish, try making a third bottle very cold (over twenty minutes in an ice bucket) and notice the difference between it and the less chilled bottles?

CHILLING WINE, EVEN SOME REDS

"I'll sometimes throw an ice cube in wine, especially in the summer. I'm not afraid to do it. Follow your taste."

—*Joe Montana, football legend*

"I put most reds in the fridge for ten to fifteen minutes, especially in the summer. Who wants a glass of hot red? If it's too cool, it can always warm up in the glass."

—*Kerin Auth, co-owner, Tinto Fino, New York, NY*

"If you secretly add ice cubes to your whites because you like them cold, you can show your face! My trick is to fill an ice cube tray with a few white wine types like Sauvignon Blanc and Chardonnay, then pop out the cubes and keep them in a bag in the freezer. When you want to chill down a glass without watering it down, add a wine cube."

—*Leslie Sbrocco, wine consultant and author*

"When I was in college in Rome twenty years ago, the wine we were served in the cafeteria—and just about everywhere else—was *fresco*, which translates as 'fresh' but really means 'cool.' The temperature of the red wine reminded me of the cold jug wines my grandfathers poured on the Sundays of my childhood."

—*Anthony Giglio, wine educator and author*

"I went on holiday in Mexico and the restaurant served a bottle of Jordan Cabernet quite cool. It was so elegant that way. Since that time, I find myself chilling reds a good way."

—*Gavin Rossdale, lead singer, solo artist and former vocalist, Bush*

"When I ask a waiter to bring an ice bath in a restaurant for red wine, they look at me like I'm crazy . . . I chill the wine just enough to take the heat off and move the alcohol into the background."

—*Monte Pitt, owner, Patton Valley Vineyards, Willamette Valley, OR*

"You really have to make sure the ice and water reaches all of the way to the top of the ice bucket or the bottle won't fully chill. If they're not doing this in a restaurant, you have to say 'No, no, no—more ice, more ice!' You have to be a bit of a pain in the ass."

—*Chazz Palminteri, actor and writer,* A Bronx Tale

20 PINOT NOIR FROM OREGON

Fine-Boned and Ego Free

IF THERE EVER was a divine sign validating the inclusion of Oregon Pinot Noir here, it appeared one soggy night in June. After organizing reams of notes I had made on this wine in preparation for writing about it, I made a midnight mission to the small bar at New York's Blue Ribbon Brasserie, where next to me a bespectacled banker type dressed down in fleece was paying his check. As he was doing so, the wine-savvy bartender called out to him, "I hope we get an allocation of your wine this year."

Not a little surprised that someone connected to wine was so randomly in my midst, I couldn't resist asking him what he did.

"I co-own Patton Valley Vineyards in Oregon—we specialize in Pinot," he said. With that, I shook my head incredulously and showed him my gigantic binder with "Oregon Pinot" scrawled on the cover. I then proceeded to quiz him about the Oregon wine scene with the zeal of a cub reporter, while the bartender looked on, amazed at the serendipity of this encounter.

In truth, I didn't *need* a signal from above to confirm this wine's greatness. Benefiting from the state's cool climate and high-quality soil, good examples of Oregon Pinot have a fine-boned delicacy that extends from their shimmery ruby trans-lucence to their cherry-cranberry perfume and silky texture. I like to think of it as a hypothetical love child of California Pinot and red Burgundy (Chapter 18), as it displays certain attributes of each of these major Pinot types. Like Californian Pinot, it is generally fruit-forward and approachable, favoring bright berry flavor over Burgundian earthiness. But it displays not the fruit, oak, and alcohol that often marks Pinot from sun-swaddled

California, but a slender frame and succulent acidity—which is unsurprising given Oregon and Burgundy's similar geographic latitudes. It may also show some sweet spice from the moderate use of oak and also veer toward the exotic with subtle notes of violets, black tea, or forest floor. Like Natalie Portman, it is that rare specimen that combines purity with sensuality, freshness with foxiness.

Oregon winemakers are a profile in fortitude, coping as they do with the state's incessant rainfall and the notorious fickleness of the Pinot grape. With only a few decades of experience on the world's wine stage, they remain mostly a cooperative and modest bunch, more L.L.Bean-earnest than the Prada-posh you sometimes see in Napa. The heartland of all of this is Oregon's Willamette Valley, a corridor of verdant hills located just south of Portland. Willamette Valley is headquarters for many of Oregon's finest Pinot players, including Erath, Domaine Serene, Elk Cove, and St. Innocent. In shops, the good stuff typically begins at $25, and sometimes double that for vineyard-designated bottlings, but wineries like A-to-Z Wineworks and Siduri have figured out how to do pleasurable Pinot that barely tops a twenty-spot.

Being a light, crisp red, Pinot Noir pairs beautifully with all but the weightiest of creations, but the undeniable cat's-meow partner for Oregon Pinot is salmon, a pairing which is as quintessentially Oregonian as a Pendleton blanket or the labyrinthine Powell's Books. Whichever way you serve it, know that it is light enough to serve cool, a subject expanded upon in Chapter 19, Pinot Noir from New Zealand.

BRAVEHEARTS ON *Pinot Noir from Oregon*

"They've got magic up there in Oregon. I love Beaux Frères—it's very concentrated. I also love Domaine Serene."

—*Sammy Hagar, vocalists, Chickenfoot, and former vocalist, Van Halen*

"Oregon Pinot and especially Domaine Serene have an easy-drinking quality. I normally open this wine when I am cooking something a little less spicy. Its cherry flavors and hints of cinnamon go well with most red meats."   —*Floyd Cardoz, executive chef, Tabla, New York, NY*

"I really love the more fruit-forward style of Pinot—versus Burgundy barnyard—that they make in the Willamette Valley."

—*Jason Priestley, actor*

"Pinot Noir that is elegant and nuanced engages me the most. One of my favorite pairings for Pinot Noir is halibut with a truffled cream sauce, but I also enjoy it with sushi and sashimi."

—*Brian Duncan, owner and wine director, BIN 36, Chicago, IL*

"When I was interviewing in Portland, Oregon, after finishing neurosurgery training, I had dinner with the head of the practice and he ordered an Eyrie Pinot Noir. It was so incredibly good that when I was back in Michigan, my wife and I hunted for it everywhere. We finally came upon it at a Whole Foods store and served it at my wife's birthday party."

—*Dr. Sanjay Gupta, chief medical correspondent, CNN, and neurosurgeon*

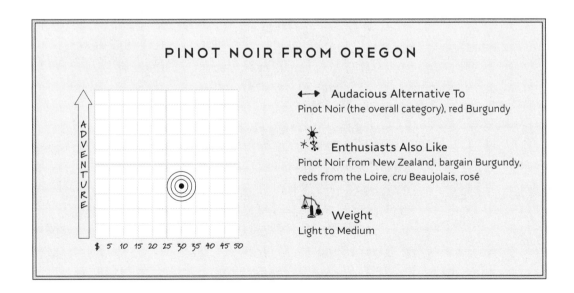

PINOT NOIR FROM OREGON

ADVENTURE

$ 5 10 15 20 25 30 35 40 45 50

←→ **Audacious Alternative To**
Pinot Noir (the overall category), red Burgundy

Enthusiasts Also Like
Pinot Noir from New Zealand, bargain Burgundy, reds from the Loire, *cru* Beaujolais, rosé

Weight
Light to Medium

Price
Medium ($15 to $50+)

 Cheat Sheet
Often lighter than California Pinot but more approachable than red Burgundy, Pinot Noir from Oregon, at its best, tastes as pure as a pine needle and bright as the sun glinting off an alpine creek.

 Label Logic
Pinot Noir is a grape.

 Bravely Said

Oregon	OHR-i-gun (not OH-ri-gone)
Pinot Noir	Pee-noh N'wahr
Sous bois	Sue bwa
Willamette	Will-AM-it

 Mark's Picks

Adelsheim	Ah-dells-hime
Amity	
Ann Amie	
A-to-Z Wineworks	
Beaux Frères	Bow Frayr
Benton-Lane	
Domaine Drouhin	Drew-ahn
Domaine Serene	
Erath	EE-rath
Firesteed	
Patton Valley	
Ponzi	
St. Innocent	
Siduri	Sih-door-ee
Soter	

 Poosh It!
The term "forest floor" (or, in French, *sous bois*) is a common descriptor for Pinot-based wines, meant to describe an earthiness evocative of mushrooms or dried leaves.

CULINARY SWEET SPOT

Lightest ▲ Heaviest

 A Lovable Feast
Vastly versatile, including roasted duck, chicken, and other fowl; pork loin and other porcine preparations, including bacon; veal; lamb; mushrooms and mushroom sauce; tuna (including tuna tartare), swordfish, and other rich fish; sushi and sashimi; truffles; goat cheese and other tangy cheeses; Brie and other soft cheeses; Thanksgiving, Valentine's Day, and Mother's Day

 Locally Lusty
Salmon, especially baked over alder wood

 Spend the Night Together
Try skewering a few salmon fillets and baking them over alder-wood coals, in the manner of a native Northwestern salmon bake, which is how they do it on the last night of Oregon's International Pinot Celebration held in July. More on this festival, a veritable Woodstock for the Pinot passionate, can be found at www.IPNC.org.

Use Oregon Pinot as the centerpiece of a red-wine-and-fish dinner to once and for all debunk the only-white-wine-with-fish rule.

21 REDS FROM THE LOIRE

Looks Like Red, Acts Like White

WHEN I DECIDED to bring Chinon, a red from France's Loire Valley, to Thanksgiving dinner at my relatives' house, I realized that I needed to do something to neutralize what could be perceived as a highly unpatriotic act. So I borrowed a friend's '67 Chevy Chevelle SS, a brilliant-blue vintage muscle car loaded with an overpowered 396 "Big Block" V8 engine. With this beast setting off car alarms as we roared out to my relatives', I contemplated the unlikely, if alliteratively satisfying, combination of the Chinon and the Chevelle; it was a cross-cultural match with cinematic flair: French wine, American thunder.

My family was pleased with both my transportation *and* the wine, even if the former made the latter arrive a bit shaken and stirred. The Chinon nevertheless embodied what I love about Loire Valley reds—namely, how their light-to-medium weight and zesty red-berry flavors are splendidly versatile with food, including the spectrum of flavors on Turkey Day. Fashioned from the Cabernet Franc grape, Chinon's subtle "green" flavor—often evocative of green olives, green pepper, or even pine needles—gives it a uniquely punchy personality that can be invigorating during sleep-inducing repasts like Thanksgiving.

It's not always love at first sip with these wines. With the Loire's northerly, challenging climate, its reds are less about ripe fruit and more about acidity, minerals, and the kind of savoriness favored by those who ask for their martinis extra dirty. It isn't just Chinon that evinces this kind of personality, but also Bourgeil, another Cabernet Franc–based wine from a neighboring district. Bourgeil is similar in taste to Chinon, but not as easy to find on American shelves. Even rarer still is a third Loire red—red Sancerre or, "Sancerre Rouge," which is lighter still and entirely

from Pinot Noir, a fact that will stump even the savviest somme-
liers, as Sancerre is normally known for its piercing Sauvignon
Blanc—powered whites. But before dismissing red Sancerre as a
Trivial Pursuit curiosity, know that it was the audience favorite
of the six deliciously svelte reds I taught in my "Looks Like Red,
Acts Like White" seminars at the Aspen Food & Wine Classic.

I included the Sancerre Rouge in those seminars because
it, like other Loire Reds, is typically light and tangy enough to
operate like a zesty white—stoking the appetite, cleansing the
palate, and thus functioning as the prototypical "food wine."
It's no surprise, then, that Loire reds are as much an earmark of
Parisian bistros as are faded mirrors, dark-leather banquettes,
and snappish servers. Bistro fare such as roast chicken, coq au
vin, steak frites, salads, chèvre, are all gustatory triumphs, as
are herbal sauces and leafy vegetables, which harmonize with the
wine's "green" notes.

It is vital to choose Loire reds with care. From the wrong
hands or in years where the grapes didn't get sufficiently ripe,
they can be cruelly herbaceous and acidic, better suited to jump-
starting Chevelles than to stimulating gastric juices. Your extra
efforts will be rewarded, however, when you get a good one and
revel in its raspberry-inflected fruit and modest price tag.

BRAVEHEARTS ON *Reds from the Loire*

"Chinon and other Loire reds are a groovy choice for those beginning
to emerge from drinking overoaked reds."

—*Lou Amdur, owner, Lou's Wine Bar, Los Angeles, CA*

"Loire reds are not big and overextracted. They are civilized country
wines—a great value, eminently drinkable, and great with food."

—*Colin Averas, sommelier, DGBG Kitchen and Bar, New York, NY*

"Loire reds may be a bit edgy by themselves, but with food—holy
$@%@! Reds from the Loire don't get their due. The value for the

price is terrific. Loads of dusty dry earth with plums, cherries, and strawberries. Sometimes they're so good that you go into a fourth dimension—that is, all senses become engaged."

—*Paul Grieco, wine director and co-owner, Hearth, New York, NY*

"It can get tedious trying to pair similar tastes in wine and food. I'd rather pair opposites, like an acidic wine with buttery food. That's more interesting to me. It's why I also like fish with lighter reds. And, anyway, pairing opposites is how we usually drink in restaurants—so you have four people ordering different things but one bottle of wine."

—*Tom Colicchio, chef and restaurateur, Craft, New York, NY*

LOIRE REDS

$ 5 10 15 20 25 30 35 40 45 50

ADVENTURE

$ Price
Low to Medium ($15 to $30)

Cheat Sheet
A world away from the oaky fruit bombs that line store shelves, Loire reds are light, snappy slingshots of raspberry flavor and earth, sometimes edgy with hints of olives and herbs, but dependably affordable and food friendly.

Audacious Alternative To
Pinot Noir, Merlot

Label Logic
Chinon and Bourgeil are regions: Cabernet Franc is their grape. Sancerre is also a region; its reds derive from the Pinot Noir grape.

Enthusiasts Also Like
Bargain Burgundy, *cru* Beaujolais, Pinot Noir from New Zealand, Pinot Noir from Oregon, rosé

Bravely Said

Chinon	*She-non*
Chevelle	*She-vell*
Bourgeil	*Boor-GOY*
Sancerre Rouge	*San-sair Roozh*

Weight
Light to Medium

Mark's Picks

Bernard Baudry	*Bow-dree*
Charles Jouget	*Jhu-geh*
Château de la Grille	*Greey*
Domaine de la Perrière	
Gerald Spelty	
Jean-Maurice Raffault	*Raff-oh*

 Poosh It!

The notation "Vieilles Vignes" (Vee-yay Veen) on some bottles of Chinon and other wines translates to "Old Vines." Though it carries no legal definition, it usually means wine that comes from vines generally older than thirty years. Such vines yield fewer grapes and are thus usually more concentrated, often leading to more flavorful wine.

CULINARY SWEET SPOT

Lightest ▲ Heaviest

 A Lovable Feast

Grilled salmon; roast chicken (especially if herb-rubbed); duck; coq au vin; steak frites; vegetables, especially sharper ones like eggplant and zucchini; thyme, saffron, rosemary, and other herbs and herbal sauces; tomato-based dishes; cheese, especially zesty types

 Locally Lusty

Crottin de Chavignol (rounds of goat cheese); rillettes (a type of pork paté); dishes with lentils

 Spend the Night Together

Host a decadent gathering in honor of Rabelais, the sixteenth-century French writer, native son of the town of Chinon, and, as this book's opening quote shows, a staunch adherent of "drinking bravely." His salty satires often mention feasts fueled by the copious consumption of Chinon.

Right before you finish making a sauce, try adding a spoonful of the Chinon (or other light red) that you are going to drink. The wine in your glass will pick up on the added zip to the sauce.

OTHER POURS (RICHER)

"I find myself riding the line between aggressive new styles and classic old world wines. For every exciting new Languedoc—rich red from the South of France—I hear about, I reach for a mature Châteauneuf-du-Pape and the world is right again. There isn't a right or wrong; there is only a 'what am I in the mood for today?' and that's a wonderful thing."

—David Welsh, lead guitarist, The Fray

"I have a soft spot for the rich, red Sagrantino-based bottlings of Umbria where I keep my second home, but I also love the exuberant blast of Dolcetto, the nobility of Barolo, and the volcanic complexity of the wines from the slopes of Mount Etna. On rare occasions when I'm not behind the Mozzarella Bar at Osteria Mozza, I have been known to uncork a bottle of rare and elusive wine from my friend Manfred Krankl's Sine Qua Non winery."

—Nancy Silverton, baker and co-owner, Osteria Mozza, Los Angeles, CA

"I tend to drink a lot of Zinfandel. I think of it as the Golden Retriever of red wines; it loves everything at the table and can handle a lot of tastes. I like to pour it out of the magnum if I'm with a group."

—Michael Chiarello, vintner and host, Food Network's Easy Entertaining with Michael Chiarello

"I like the Syzygy—pronounced 'Szz-eh-jee'—'Saros 134' from Walla Walla, Washington. Winemaker Zach Brettler has made a wine of such beautiful intensity it's hard to put the glass down. It's an unusual blend of Tempranillo, Malbec, and Cabernet. This effect is just exceptional."

—Kyle MacLachlan, actor

"My favorite reds are elegant and balanced wines—a good Pinot Noir, a Sangiovese, wines from the Languedoc region or the Rhône Valley. They are so versatile and could easily be paired with fish or meat, and I love that they smell like berries."

—*Jean-Georges Vongerichten, chef and restaurateur, Jean-Georges, New York, NY*

"While Shiraz is the undisputed king of Australian reds, I have always been drawn to the more subtle power of Grenache from Down Under, perhaps because it reminds me of Pinot Noir in its purity and overall deliciousness. Try Burge Family, Clarendon Hills, Château Reynella, d'Arenberg, Magpie Estate, Pirramirra, Rusden, Turkey Flat, Tintara, Two Hands, and Yalumba."

—*Anthony Giglio, wine educator and author*

"I've loved just about every wine from the d'Arenberg winery in the McLaren Vale region of Australia. Their Shirazes called 'The Laughing Magpie' and 'The Dead Arm' as well as their white blend, 'The Stump Jump,' all knock my socks off."

—*Nick Harmer, bass guitarist, Death Cab for Cutie*

"Petra—a rich "Super Tuscan" from Italy—is an exceptional red whose vines are planted on some of the noblest *terroir* in Tuscany, and are for me the essence of the region."—*Alain Ducasse, chef and restaurateur, Le Jules Verne, Paris, France*

"From Italy, I love these two Super Tuscans: Donna Olimpia 'Millepassi,' a blend of Cabernet Sauvignon, Merlot, and Petit Verdot, and Antinori's 'Guado al Tasso,' a blend of Cabernet Sauvignon, Merlot, and Syrah.

"I love Boekenhoutskloof Winery's 'The Chocolate Block' from South Africa, a blend of Syrah, Grenache, and other grapes." —*Hilary Swank, actress*

"Allegrini Palazzo della Torre, a full-bodied red from the Veneto in Italy, I call the 'sweet dreamer.' Every time I drink it I have sweet dreams—guaranteed.

"Valduero Reserva, a full-bodied red from Spain's Ribera del Duero region, is a class act with three great gear changes from palate to swallow to hangin' around.

"Cuvée Christine from Pax Wine Cellars, a lush Syrah-based red from California's Sonoma County, is pure sexy power, one of my 'go-to' bottles."

—*Matthew McConaughey, actor*

"A red that is close to my heart comes from the region of Nemea. This region produces a wine that consists 100% of the grape Agirgitiko. For all intents and purposes, we could call this the Cabernet Sauvignon of Greece."

—*Michael Psilakis, chef and co-owner, Anthos, New York, NY*

"I like to drink Domaine de la Grange des Peres, a rich red from the Languedoc-Roussillon region, Domaine Hauvette, a rich red from Provence, Château La Conseillante, a red from Bordeaux's Pomerol region, and Château Lynch-Bages, the red Bordeaux."

—*Dave Stewart, musician and co-founder, The Eurythmics*

"I'll never forget one meal I had in the Loire Valley. We were served roasted foie gras with a 1976 Späburgunder—Pinot Noir—Trockenbeerenauslese, a sweet, dessert wine style. It was like the nectar of the gods with the sea-salted and fatty foie gras."

—*John Besh, chef and restaurateur, Restaurant August, New Orleans, LA*

"I really dig sangría. The key is to let the fruit sit overnight with the wine in the fridge, so that the fruit gives up some of its juice to the wine. Although any wine will do, my ideal choice is a French wine from a grape called Valdiguié, which is a fruity, almost sangria-like red wine."

—*Lou Amdur, owner, Lou's Wine Bar, Los Angeles, CA*

"When I smell glögg, warm wine with spice and honey, I know it's Christmas. Some would say that you shouldn't adulterate wine with sugar and spices, but we Scandinavians are less traditional."

—*Marcus Samuelsson, chef and co-owner, Aquavit, New York, NY*

22 AGLIANICO

Square Jaw and a Mean Streak

JOIN ME, FAIR READER, on a journey into recesses of a lair seen by few—George Clooney's personal study at his Italian country house. Feast your eyes on the wood-paneled walls, tufted club chairs, and stuffed stag's head looming over the room. Behold the glittering Venetian daggers on display, and the tar stains on his silvery Suomy motorcycle helmet. Breathe in the scent of rich leather, espresso bean, and Cohiba smoke. And on his phone: Heidi Fleiss on speed dial.

Okay, so I haven't really seen Clooney's study, but when I drink Aglianico, this is the kind of manly setting I conjure—omitting, *of course*, the hotline to Heidi.

Like the celebrated actor, Aglianico is all about old-school masculinity—a big, rich, son-of-a-bitch that doesn't really care whether you like its powerful display of sour cherry and black currants and scents of tobacco, tar, leather, or bitter chocolate. In its youth, Aglianico can be a rebel without a cause, up in your face with tannins that transform your jaw space into a portable sandbox. But with time, some of that unchecked virility mellows into leading-man elegance, so much so that this Southern Italian pick is often dubbed the "Barolo of the South."

This is no small accomplishment for a wine hailing from the bottom half of the boot. If the famous *New Yorker* cover exaggerating the centrality of Manhattan were applied to Italy's most prestigious wines, it would show Northern Italy large, with indisputable greats like Barolo, Barbaresco, and Brunello highlighted; Southern Italy, in contrast, would be relegated to the cover's depiction of New Jersey, a barren sliver of land with little to show for itself. That is, with the exception of Aglianico, an ancient grape, which has experienced a renaissance in the past decade thanks to improved grape growing, the use of French oak barrels and modern vinification equipment, and other enhancements that injections of capital can bring.

Although Aglianico is grown throughout Southern Italy, most bottles that make it here are from the Taurasi area of the Campania region and, heading east, the aggressive-sounding Vulture area of Basilicata. Taurasi does Aglianico at its most formidable and prestigious. In the wine store, make sure you look for the place name "Taurasi" on the label, as it is usually emphasized rather than the grape Aglianico. Although Basilicata's Aglianico del Vulture can be slightly less intense, it too is a chest-thumper, as is appropriate for a wine named for an extinct volcano whose slopes are thought to sometimes add a distinctly earthy edge to it.

Aglianico is starting to make its presence known. The most famous producer from the region of Campania is Mastroberardino, which believed in the potential of Aglianico well before many of its current competitors even got their boots on. In Basilicata, Paternoster is king of the volcano, with a variety of well-knit options, including its famous "Don Anselmo" cuvée. That selection and a slew of others, such as Feudi di San Gregorio's swaggeringly-titled "Serpico," are priced for collectors in the $50 to $80 range, which is actually a good deal if you consider that you're getting the quality of Barolo at about half the price. Happily, options below $25 are increasingly available, including Terredora and Feudi di San Gregorio's "Rubrato."

When deciding what to eat with Aglianico, you need only recall what Paulie and his crew in *Goodfellas* lovingly devoured in their privileged prison cell. Start with salami, "prosciutt," and hunks of cheese, preferably smuggled to the table in brown paper bags. The pasta course should feature a re-creation of Vinnie's meat-studded tomato sauce, better if it has razor-sliced garlic, Paulie style. For the main, opt for something like steak, completely rare if you dare. So you get the picture: Aglianico pairs best with the upper limits of fat and protein—perfect for Atkins adherents, but not as good for herbivores.

BRAVEHEARTS ON *Aglianico*

"Aglianico is great with the picante regional food of Basilicata—vegetables like fava beans, chicory, and wild greens, dishes topped with peperoncini and fenesi, a pepper that is dried and then fried. Locals also drink it with breads using durum wheat and whole-grain pastas, as well as *luganiga*, a thin sausage that is the best in Italy."

—Lidia Bastianich, chef and and host of PBS's Lidia's Italy

"Aglianico happens to be a topic I have spent hundreds of hours researching. It means 'Hellenic,' the Latin word for Greek, from where it was heralded over three thousand years ago.

"I find Aglianico to have a pleasant spice quality like cloves, black pepper, and allspice and incredible structure with firm tannins and vibrant acidity. It's great with braised pork shoulder with chestnuts, *maccaronara*—thick spaghetti-like pasta—with a tomato-based Neapolitan ragu, and house-made sausages. Some favorites are Paternoster and Elena Fucci from Basilicata and Antonio Caggiano from Taurasi."

—Shelley Lindgren, wine director and co-owner, A16, San Francisco, CA

"Like ripe rich berries dusted in earth, with a subtle, sexy barnyard character. At Animal, it is the perfect wine for my die-hard California-palate-driven clientele. It complements our richer sauces, our poutine with Cheddar and oxtail gravy, and our rib-eye with escargot butter."

—Helen Johannesen, wine director, Animal, Los Angeles, CA

"Aglianico is a big, bad southern Italian packed with acid and tannin—and the potential to strip the enamel right off your teeth! But if the grapes were picked at maturity, the tannins can become fairly supple. It makes me want tomatoes and sardines."

—Ross Outon, winner, first season of The Winemakers on PBS and beverage consultant, Austin, TX

"My heritage is a mix of Neapolitan and Barese, so naturally I am drawn to the wines of Campania and Apulia. Among the reds of Campania, Taurasi is my favorite, but Feudi di San Gregorio also produces a single-vineyard named Piano Di Montevergine; it is exceptional, since is made from Aglianico grapes that provide elegance and power in the same glass. I sometimes think of it as the perfect offspring created by a Bordeaux and a Burgundy."

—*Donatella Arpaia, food/entertaining authority and restaurateur, Mia Dona, New York, NY*

AGLIANICO

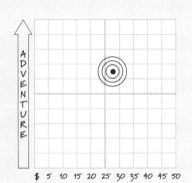

 Audacious Alternative To
Cabernet Sauvignon, Zinfandel

 Enthusiasts Also Like
Petite Sirah, Cahors, reds from Portugal, classic Cabernet

 Weight
Full

 Price
Medium ($12 to $50+)

 Cheat Sheet
Southern Italy's most prestigious red, Aglianico plays for keeps with a high-testosterone surge of black currants and sour cherry, with hints of earthiness and leather, often buttressed by muscular tannins that soften over time.

 Label Logic
Aglianico is a grape. It is primarily produced in the Taurasi area of Campania and the Vulture area of Basilicata, both in Southern Italy.

 Bravely Said

Aglianico	*Ah-LYAH-nee-ko*
Barbaresco	*Bahr-BAH-res-ko*
Barolo	*Bah-ROW-low*
Brunello	*Brew-NEHL-low*
Campania	*Kahm-PAH-nee-ah*
Taurasi	*Tah-oo-RAH-zee*
Vulture	*VOOL-too-reh*

 Mark's Picks

Alois	
Antonio Caggiano	
Elena Fucci	*Foo-chee*
Feudi di San Gregorio	*FEH-oo-dee Sahn Greh-GOH-ryo*
Mastroberardino	*Mass-tro-bear-ahr-DEE-no*
Paternoster	
Terredora	*Tear-ah-DOOR-ah*

Poosh It!
Aglianico's history as a wine for big shots dates back to ancient Rome, where it was used to make Falernian wine, considered the best juice of that era. According to the writings of Pliny the Elder, Julius Caesar drank it in 60 B.C. to celebrate his conquests of Spain.

CULINARY SWEET SPOT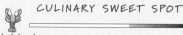

Lightest ▲ Heaviest

 A Lovable Feast

Steak, lamb chops, and other red meat; *salumi* such as prosciutto; wild game; red-sauced (e.g., puttanesca) and or meat-sauced pastas; pizza; for Father's Day

 Locally Lusty

Luganiga (sausage); *cutturidde* (lamb stew); cheeses such as provolone, pecorino, and buffalo mozzarella; osso buco; braised pork shoulder; polenta; dishes using peperoncini and other peppers

Spend the Night Together

The rustic, southern Italian origins of Aglianico and the hearty foods served with it bring to mind "fare la scarpetta," the Italian expression for using a piece of bread to mop up the last bits of a delectable sauce. "Scarpetta" translates to "little shoe," which is the shape the bread takes when you are scooping up the sauce. In your Aglianico-amped feasts, be sure to try your own shoe scooping, and with practice you can call yourself an accomplished *scarpettaro*.

23 BARGAIN BORDEAUX

Pedigree Lost, Value Found

WHEN I EVALUATE a barrage of wines at one sitting as I did while judging the Bordeaux Wine Bureau's "Today's Bordeaux" competition, friends imagine such an event to be an orgiastic feast of Hefnerian proportions: if one glass gives pleasure, one hundred must yield sensory nirvana. The truth is, however, that you're so focused on giving each wine a fair shake that the experience is hardly hedonistic. And if the intense concentration required of you doesn't sap the romance, the fact that you and your fellow judges are hocking a good one after every taste surely does.

Inelegant expectorating aside, the Bordeaux tasting proved to me that a whole world of respectable wine exists beyond the *grands vins* for which France's Bordeaux region is known. This "other Bordeaux" in fact comprises most of the region's production, and yet what we hear about are the trophy bottles priced for those in the employ of Goldman Sachs. Peel back this gilded curtain, however, and you'll see that technological innovation, which has raised the game of so many of the world's viticultural regions, has also greatly benefitted some of Bordeaux's humble estates.

But how to find them? Although bargain bottles can be sourced throughout the vast Bordeaux region of Southwest France, I find that it is easiest to start with a few dependable designations. The most obvious choice is wine labeled simply "Bordeaux" or "Bordeaux Superiéur" which signifies a basic bottling that uses Bordeaux grapes but doesn't fall under a more specific appellation or growing zone. In the hands of a good producer such as Reignac or Château Le Conseiller—you can have a solidly pleasurable wine.

Or, consider an unsung estate from the subregion of Médoc or Haut-Médoc. Although the Médoc is home to many of Bordeaux's most prestigious châteaus, it also contains a bevy of humble estates making perfectly enjoyable wine. Among these are Château Belle-Vue, Château Senejac, and Château Greysac, the last of which gets my vote for one of the most dependable and plentiful bargain Bordeaux on the market.

Finally, look to one of Bordeaux's up-and-coming "satellite" appellations, such as Fronsac, Lalande-de-Pomerol, or the Côtes de Castillon. The last has been a particularly fruitful source of values for me, with estates like Château Cap de Faugères, Château Côte Montpezat, and Château Brisson among the most consistent overachievers.

Because there is such a broad array of bargain Bordeaux, you should follow the lead of The Dandy Warhols' frontman and Bordeaux fanatic Courtney Taylor-Taylor and seek the recommendation of a trusted merchant—more so here than with most wine types. Courtney told me that he routinely asks his local seller to round up the best values from Bordeaux, and hosts a pizza party with friends to identify the crowd pleasers. He then buys multiple cases of those wines, "cleaning them out" of it.

Produced from grapes of modest quality, bargain Bordeaux won't rearrange your molecules the way a *premier cru* like Château Haut-Brion can. These are uncomplicated, everyday wines, faithful to the European conception of wine as an accent for food, not as an object of worship. To be sure, disappointing bottles can be thin-tasting or downright bitter. But a good one can have a surprisingly satisfying core of blackberries and currants, backed by pretty notes of licorice, sweet tobacco, or wet earth that evince a sense of place. With Bordeaux's relatively cool, maritime climate, its weight will typically be medium-to-full, sometimes with tannic grip, but not of the type that makes the wine particularly age-worthy.

Gift givers and party hosts will appreciate the fact that even when it's inexpensive, Bordeaux's stately, timeless labels lend an aristocratic cachet to any occasion; you can rest assured that tradition-bound Bordeaux wines have not warmed to the critters, lip prints, bare feet, and other tawdry imagery adopted elsewhere.

The labels may not be casual, but the food you enjoy with it should be. Stews, hamburgers, meatloaf, spaghetti Bolognese, pizza, and any other cheap feeds are ideal.

BRAVEHEARTS ON *Bargain Bordeaux*

"I believe in the concept of 'breaking bread' with wine—of the conviviality that wine brings. When I was a young man in London and had no money, friends and I would have big dinners with lasagna and cheap cuts of meat and cheap but good Bordeaux. I'd go to a local wine shop and ask for good 'third pressings' of inexpensive Bordeaux."

—*Gavin Rossdale, solo artist and former vocalist and guitarist, Bush*

"When the bands the Strokes, Jet, the Vines were coming to our house for dinner, we needed a lot of wine. So I bought two cases of Bordeaux priced at eight to twenty dollars a bottle. I have Bordeaux dating back to '53, but I also have Bordeaux that I got for ten dollars a bottle that is indistinguishable from an '89 Château Clerc-Milon. Côtes de Castillon, such as Clos des Lunelles, is a %#$@ing monster of a value.

"Red Bordeaux has a deep earthiness—the smell and taste of ancient minerals of the earth, and there's romance about it, with references to 'a glass of claret' throughout English literature."

—*Courtney Taylor-Taylor, lead singer and guitarist, The Dandy Warhols*

BRAVEHEARTS ON *Upmarket Bordeaux*

"The musician Al Stewart ("Year of the Cat") turned me on to the Bloodline of the Holy Vine. He told me, 'Burgundy is for sex, but Bordeaux is for intellect.'"   —*Tori Amos, singer-songwriter*

"Burgundy is for lovers in a hurry—for when you want to make love that night. Fine Burgundy has such a special, different taste that the effect is immediate. Fine Bordeaux is for a long-term affair."

—*Julio Iglesias, music legend*

"Château Margaux is my celebration selection. I normally pick up a bottle of this when I'm celebrating a successful business meeting, or when I'm out to dinner chopping it up with business colleagues and close friends."

—*Busta Rhymes, hip-hop artist*

"I lived in France. I have untold memories of drinking wine there. So, I love my traditional red Bordeaux. Who doesn't? And yes, I'm partial to Saint-Estèphe, St.-Julian, and Pomerol, especially Château Pétrus."

—*Jodie Foster, actress*

BARGAIN BORDEAUX

ADVENTURE

$ 5 10 15 20 25 30 35 40 45 50

 Weight
Medium to Full

 Price
Low to Medium ($15 to $30)

 Cheat Sheet
Beyond the marquee wines of Bordeaux lies a plethora of overachieving choices for the cost-conscious.

 Label Logic
Red Bordeaux wines are always a blend of up to five grape types: Cabernet Sauvignon, Merlot, Cabernet Franc, Malbec, and Petite Verdot; they are usually dominated by Cabernet or Merlot.

◄—► **Audacious Alternative To**
Merlot, Cabernet Sauvignon

✳✾ **Enthusiasts Also Like**
Reds from Washington, Côtes du Rhône, classic Cabernet, (good) Merlot, big wine

Bravely Said

Bordeaux	*Bohr-DOE*
Côtes de Castillon	*Kahs-tee-yohn*
Fronsac	*Frohn-sahk*
Haut-Brion	*Oh Bree-ohn*
Médoc	*May-DOK*
Petite Verdot	*Puh-teet Vehr-doe*
Supérieur	*Soo-pay-ree-uhr*

Mark's Picks

Bordeaux or Bordeaux Supérieur

Bel-Air "Grande Cuvée"	*Coo-vay*
Conseiller	*Kohn-say-ay*
Domaine de Courteillac	*Cur-tay-ak*
Dourthe No. 1	*Dooth*
La Cour d'Argent	*La Koor Dar-zhen*
Le Pin Beausoleil	*Luh Pahn Bow-so-lay*
Reignac	*Ray-nyak*

Médoc and Haut-Médoc

Belle-Vue	*Bell-view*
Caronne Ste. Gemme	*Kah-rone Sahn Jhaym*
Charmail	*Shar-my*
d'Agassac	*dah-gah-sack*
Greysac	*Greh-zahk*
Larose-Trintaudon	*Lah-ROSE Trent-oh-DOAN*
Senejac	*Say-nay-zhahk*

Côtes de Castillion

Brisson	*Brie-sohn*
Cap de Faugères	*Fo-gehr*
Clos des Lunelles	*Cloh day Lew-nehl*
Côte Montpezat	*Kot Mohn-puh-zah*
La Vieille Cure	*Lah-viyeh*
L'Estang	*LAY-stahgn*

Poosh It!

Bordeaux is also known for Lillet ($15), a blend of white wine and citrus liqueurs that makes for a crisp, refreshing aperitif and versatile base for mixed drinks.

 CULINARY SWEET SPOT

Lightest ▲ Heaviest

A Lovable Feast

Stews; hamburgers; meatloaf; pasta Bolognese; pizza; smoked tofu; mushrooms and other earthy veggies; Parmigiano-Reggiano, aged Gouda, and other hard and semihard cheeses

Locally Lusty

Lamb; Bordelaise sauce (brown sauce with shallots and red wine)

Spend the Night Together

To celebrate the wine "steals" you uncover, rent the sixth season of HBO's *The Sopranos* and watch the episode entitled "The Ride." In it, Tony and his nephew Christopher come upon some bikers robbing a liquor store and proceed to steal what they were stealing—several crates of fine Bordeaux.

24 CAHORS

Medieval on Your Tongue

WHEN MY FRIEND Laurent described to me how he drinks red wine from his native Cahors, a wine region in France's Southwest, I immediately thought of professional hockey.

"The key with Cahors," he explained, "is to open the bottle the night before and drink it twelve to twenty-four hours later, with either lunch or dinner the next day." Without doing this, he warned, this fiercely tannic wine will be like "zee head butt," with a "rough, opaque, and monodimensional" taste.

Ah, I thought, this is like a vinous version of hockey's penalty box: the imposition of a time-out to tame the overly aggressive. While I was no stranger to decanting a young, astringent wine to soften its tannic assault, I had never before relegated a bottle to such a lengthy hiatus. To test this method, I opened a bottle of Cahors at eight o'clock one night, and found the wine to be distractingly dry and deficient in fruit, as is the case with many young bottles of Cahors. But after twenty hours exposed to the air in a spacious glass pitcher, the wine, while still quite dry, had mellowed to the point where its plummy flavor and tinges of smoke and leather were the perfect foil to a juicy hamburger.

Not only does Cahors get medieval on your tongue in texture, it also gets medieval historically, since it achieved global fame in the Middle Ages as a syrupy concentrate dubbed the "black wine." Drinkers are often surprised to learn that it originates from the Malbec grape, which, of course, is also responsible for the sizzlingly popular Malbec from Argentina (Chapter 27). But the two wines are about as similar as Los Angeles is to New York, with Argentine Malbec as lush and welcoming as a palm-lined beachfront in Malibu, while Cahors is as brooding and mercurial as a New York winter.

But that winter doesn't have to be one of discontent—if you decant Cahors for a sufficient time and secure the right nourishment. Take it from Laurent when he advises not to even think about having it without food, which for him, encompasses regional favorites such as foie gras, rounds of fried sausage, duck confit, and hard and sheep's milk cheeses. Hearty, fatty, rustic cuisine is thus the order of the day—and also includes such locally coveted fare as cassoulet, wild game, and roasted walnuts.

Of course, not every bottle of Cahors begins life with a truncheon of tannin. To appeal to global tastes, some winemakers are making Cahors that is lighter and more approachable, and these tend to be in the $12 to $20 range, including Château du Cèdre's "Héritage," Georges Vigouroux's "Pigmentum," and Château Lagrézette's "Zette Rouge." These producers and others also have rarer, more upmarket bottlings at $30 or more, which are more likely to be in the classically ornery style that benefits from years of bottle aging or adherence to Laurent's Law of Decanting.

BRAVEHEARTS ON *Cahors*

"This is not a wine for little girls. It is not for delicate foods but ones that are rich and distinctive in taste. The Cahors region is agricultural and so the food is seriously nourishing to give the farmers strength—cassoulet, daube of beef, venison, wild boar . . ."

—*Ariane Daguin, owner and co-founder, D'Artagnan, Newark, NJ*

"Though the profile of Cahors can run the gamut, one I had brought onto Corton's list was from a fantastic small winery—Clos Siguier—and from a vintage that had had quite a bit of sun. It was supple, dark, jammy, tasting of overripe plum and blackberry—the characteristics I have found California red wine drinkers cherish. They'd pay only $40 at Corton for a luxurious, velvety wine, and the next day, they'd be calling me to find out the nearest place they could purchase a case of it."   —*Elizabeth Harcourt, sommelier, Corton, New York, NY*

"I asked at a winery why their red wine tasted better at the winery than at home. They told me that they open it up the first thing in the morning and let it breathe throughout the day. Now when company is coming over, my wife and I will sometimes do the same thing. The wine has less sting and you can taste it on all parts of your tongue, not just the front."

—*Dr. Sanjay Gupta, chief medical correspondent, CNN, and neurosurgeon*

CAHORS

ADVENTURE

$ 5 10 15 20 25 30 35 40 45 50

⟷ Audacious Alternative To
Cabernet Sauvignon, Syrah

✳ Enthusiasts Also Like
Aglianico, Petite Sirah, reds from Portugal, Malbec

⚖ Weight
Full

$ Price
Low to Medium ($12 to $40+)

✓ Cheat Sheet
An intriguing style, Cahors is an old-school, batteries-not-included kind of wine, often requiring some combination of aging, decanting, and rich food for the drinker to fully appreciate its rustic charm.

💡 Label Logic
Cahors is a region in France's Southwest. The wine is primarily made from the Malbec grape.

Bravely Said

Cahors	*Cah-or*
Laguiole	*La-yoll*
Rocamadour	*Row-cah-mah-door*

Mark's Picks

Château de Haute-Serre	*Oht-Sayr*
Château Famaey	*Fah-mah-ay*
Château Haut-Monplaisir	*Oh Mohn-play-Zire*
Château Lagrézette	*Lah-gray-Zeht*
Clos de Triguedina	*Trih-gway-DEE-nah*
Clos la Coutale	*Koo-tal*
Georges Vigouroux	*Vee-goo-roo*
Zette	*Zeht*

Poosh It!

When tasters refer to a wine like Cahors as "tight," they mean that the wine lacks expressiveness and needs more time to "open up," either through decanting or cellaring. Being "tight" isn't necessarily a negative; in fact, many quality reds start life with tightly-wound tannins.

 CULINARY SWEET SPOT

Lightest ▲ Heaviest

 A Lovable Feast

Beef and lamb dishes, especially if charred or smoked; dishes featuring pork, duck, squab, and rabbit; wild game; bresola, and other *salumi*; garlicky dishes; Parmigiano-Reggiano, Manchego, and other hard cheeses; Roquefort and other blue-veined cheeses

 Locally Lusty

Foie gras; cassoulet; duck confit; fried sausage; cheeses such as *cantal* (hard cow's milk), *laguiole* (semihard cow's milk), and *rocamadour* (goat cheese); walnut and walnut oil; black truffles; wild mushrooms

 Spend the Night Together

You can order a decadent array of Cahors-friendly meat products—foie gras, game birds, sausages, and the like—from your local butcher or Web sites like www.Dartagnan.com, www.Lobels.com, and www.hudsonvalleyfoiegras.com.

25 CLASSIC CABERNET

Old Guard, New Verve

WOULD YOU SIP a great wine through a stick of licorice? You would if you were Nicki Pruss, winemaker at Napa's storied Stag's Leap Wine Cellars, one of the winners of the legendary 1976 Paris Tasting that put California on the vinous map. When we met recently, she told me that she'll occasionally slurp the winery's $100 Fay Vineyard Cabernet through a slice of Red Vines licorice. After draining her glass this way, Pruss will gobble down the licorice, which by then has become fully "Fay-infused." "The flavor combination is perfect," she explains.

Leave it to Californians to make serious wine without taking themselves too seriously. At a time when an increasing number of grapes and regions beckon to the drinker, it's easy to overlook the pleasures of "classic" Cabernet—i.e., Cabernet Sauvignon from long-established California wineries—which, for many American wine enthusiasts, myself included, is the first stop on our journeys in fine wine. Like an alt rocker who rediscovers the majesty and swagger of Zeppelin, it is rewarding to rediscover these old-guard producers, as many have access to prime vineyard land and are innovating with as much passion as any winemaker out there.

Fine versions of classic Cabernet are typically plush and powerful, a bicep-flexing display of flamboyantly ripe black currants and plums, joined by layers of oaky sweetness and often a minerally or smoky dimension. They are also sometimes markedly tannic, a quality that allows some of the best examples to improve in the bottle for fifteen years or longer. Though the majority of classic Cabs are made in this tooth-staining, ultra-rich style, these days some estates deliver the goods with a bit more restraint and subtlety.

Because man cannot live on wine and licorice alone, you would do well to serve Cabernet with anything that brings revenue to your local cardiologist. Red meat, of course, ranks high on the list, with glory points for fattier cuts, as greasy, protein-rich foods tend to tone down a wine's tannic pucker. Another artery-clogging tannin-tamer is cheese, especially stink bombs like Roquefort and Stilton, which can soften an edgy Cabernet. A rich, plummy wine like Cabernet also has a special affinity for black pepper and the meaty embrace of mushrooms, black olives, and roasted nuts.

Though a staple of wine shops and steakhouses, classic Cabernet is not a particularly good value when contrasted with less exalted wine types, as it often comes from grapes grown in the immoderately-priced vineyards of Napa Valley. But the classics' lack of trendiness and generally larger production runs often translates to better prices than bottles of similar quality from boutique producers. Premium classic Cabernet starts at about $30 and can fetch well over $100 a bottle, while entry-level bottles hover in the $20 to $30 range.

BRAVEHEARTS ON *Classic Cabernet*

"A friend gave me case of '94 Caymus (Special Selection) and it is one of the best wines I ever tasted. I loved it so much that I named my king shepherd Caymus!" —*Chazz Palminteri, actor and writer,* A Bronx Tale

"Christmas Eve, prime rib, Yorkshire pudding, roasted potatoes, and several bottles of older Napa Valley Cabernet Sauvignon—delicious. Shafer, Caymus, and Spottswoode are always great."

—*Laurie Hook, chief winemaker, Beringer Vineyards, Napa, CA*

"Sterling Napa Cabernet Sauvignon I drink occasionally when I'm with a couple of friends at home relaxing or on the road after a show."

—*Busta Rhymes, hip-hop star*

"Francis Ford Coppola invited me to Napa to participate in a screen test for the movie *Dracula*. He invited me to come to the library at his winery. I thought we were going to see books, but instead there were all of these fantastic California Cabs. I ended up completely drunk."

—*Antonio Banderas, actor*

"One of my favorite experiences was drinking Far Niente Cabernet with my favorite English couple in a BYOB restaurant in Los Angeles called Sawtelle Kitchen."

—*Cesar Millan, National Geographic Channel's "Dog Whisperer"*

"Dollar for dollar, classic California Cabernets like Beringer offer better value for your money than more trendy California Cabernets."

—*Joe Montana, football legend*

"I once had a meeting with a record executive who added Cherry Coke to his Opus One. It was cute, but not a trick that I wanted to use."

—*Gavin Rossdale, solo artist and former vocalist and guitarist, Bush*

"Napa makes such great wine because the winemakers there have such high standards. If the wine isn't great, they're not going to put their name on it. Among those I like are Far Niente, Shafer, Del Dotto, and Stag's Leap."

—*Mike "Coach K" Krzyzewski, head coach, Duke University men's basketball team and U.S. national neam*

"I actually got to work the crush at Joseph Phelps in Napa. I'd get picked up in the morning at 6:15 and got to do a bit of everything— punch downs, pump overs, washing out barrels, and accompanying former winemaker Craig Williams when he was testing grapes for the harvest." —*Alex Lifeson, lead guitarist, Rush*

"On colder days, rainy days, or just days that are a little darker than most I'll crave a big red wine and that usually means I'm reaching for one from the Napa Valley. Stag's Leap, Silver Oak, Shafer are huge favorite producers in that region. All three wineries' Cabernets are incredible and seem to complement most of what I cook or what I am feeling emotionally.

"During college, when I first started drinking wine and could only afford cheap stuff, I had no idea that wine could be so amazing. I just assumed for years that all reds basically tasted the same and all whites were Chardonnay. That was until I was given a bottle of Silver Oak Cabernet Sauvignon. I can still remember how amazing that bottle tasted. And suddenly, I was forced to rethink my entire wine paradigm." —*Nick Harmer, bass guitarist, Death Cab for Cutie*

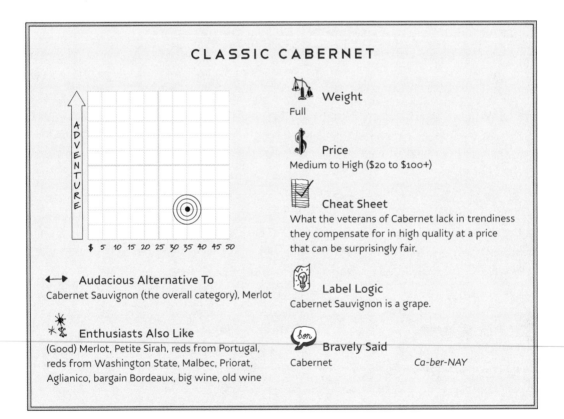

CLASSIC CABERNET

ADVENTURE

$ 5 10 15 20 25 30 35 40 45 50

Weight
Full

Price
Medium to High ($20 to $100+)

Cheat Sheet
What the veterans of Cabernet lack in trendiness they compensate for in high quality at a price that can be surprisingly fair.

Label Logic
Cabernet Sauvignon is a grape.

Audacious Alternative To
Cabernet Sauvignon (the overall category), Merlot

Enthusiasts Also Like
(Good) Merlot, Petite Sirah, reds from Portugal, reds from Washington State, Malbec, Priorat, Aglianico, bargain Bordeaux, big wine, old wine

Bravely Said
Cabernet   Ca-ber-NAY

Mark's Picks

Under $30

Beaulieu Vineyard "Rutherford"	*Beau-lew*
Beringer "Knights Valley"	
Gallo Family	
J. Lohr "Seven Oaks"	
Louis Martini	
St. Supéry	

$30 and Up

Beringer (Private Reserve)	
Cakebread	
Caymus "Special Selection"	*Kay-mus*
Chappellet "Napa Valley Signature"	
Frog's Leap	
Hess Collection	
Joseph Phelps	
Newton	
Shafer	
Silver Oak	
Stag's Leap Wine Cellars	
Trefethen	*Truh-FEH-thun*

 Poosh It!

Finer examples of Cabernet are sometimes said to evince hints of mint or eucalyptus.

 CULINARY SWEET SPOT

Lightest ▲ Heaviest

 A Lovable Feast

Heavier meat such as sirloin steak, filet mignon, lamb chops, especially when grilled or smoked; venison or other game meats; firm cheeses (e.g., Dry Jack, Manchego, Parmigiano-Reggiano, Cheddar); blue-veined cheeses (e.g., Roquefort); mushrooms and root vegetables; dishes with black olives; walnuts, pecans, and other nuts, especially toasted; hamburgers, ribs, and other rich barbecue fare; dark chocolate; on Independence Day or birthdays

Spend the Night Together

Follow Nicki Pruss's iconoclastic lead and finish off a classic Cab with some Red Vines licorice. Find it at www.RedVines.com or www.CandyCabinet.com.

26 CÔTES DU RHÔNE

Meaty, Spicy, Big, and Savory

WANT TO ACCOMPLISH the dual objective of making a red wine taste better while leaving your waiter flabbergasted?

Do what wine guru Lettie Teague did when we had lunch at New York's acclaimed Eleven Madison Park. After the wine was poured, she confidently scooped up a piece of ice and plopped it into her glass. When the waiter shot her a look as if she had hop-scotched on a papal tomb, she explained that she acquired this technique from the late, legendary wine writer Alexis Bespaloff.

"It's his four-second rule," she explained, "You float a bit of ice in the wine for four seconds to tone down the taste of alcohol and make it more refreshing."

The wine Lettie cooled was a Côtes du Rhône, which is the kind of simple, unpretentious pour that was well suited to such an unconventional maneuver. Though there's nothing new or trendy about it, Côtes du Rhône remains unappreciated in some circles and thus deserves attention for its long-standing role as a frugal conduit to the spicy berry goodness of France's southern Rhône Valley.

Most Côtes du Rhône wines originate in the expansive flat-lands of this sunny region. Some express themselves as medium-bodied, juicy, and evocative of raspberries or strawberries. Others tend toward a darker, denser, somewhat tannic style. Such variation is influenced by the combination of grapes, which is usually dominated by supple Grenache but may also have signific-ant infusions of other grapes, especially peppery Syrah. Modern techniques have allowed winemakers to make the wine in a more polished, oak-driven style, though the most interesting rendi-tions retain some classic Rhône rusticity, with notions of licorice, cracked pepper, earthy funk, or even a bacony meatiness.

If we're going to mention bacon, we need to talk about Côtes du Rhône's food affinities, which center on robust country food such as cassoulet, charcuterie, and onion soup. There's no need to gorge grandly: grilled mushrooms, garlicky roast chicken, pizza, and hamburgers bring the love, the last even more so if topped with bacon and cheese. Richer Mexican food is well advised, as is Middle Eastern fare like lamb stew. One of the most seductive pairings to pass my lips was a Côtes du Rhône with *kibbe*, the torpedo-shaped croquettes made of bulgur and lamb.

Not long ago, I swiped the wine list from New Orleans's Herbsaint Restaurant to remind myself that Côtes du Rhône comprised two of the least expensive wines on this well-edited document, a common occurrence in good eateries. The situation is just as heartening in wine shops, where bottles of Côtes du Rhône usually duck $20 and don't raise eyebrows at $10 or less. Marquee names include E. Guigal, Paul Jaboulet Aîné's "Parallèle 45," and Delas. Decent versions of Côtes du Rhône are also increasingly finding their way into box wine (Chapter 45), which—like our four-second ice rule—won't disgrace this unpretentious *vin de soleil*.

BRAVEHEARTS ON *Côtes du Rhône*

"Outside of my husband's wine—Destino Wines in Napa—I tend to prefer something from the Côtes du Rhône. In general, I'd say that delicious to me means dry, full, and elegant."   —*Bebe Neuwirth, actress*

"Côtes du Rhône are meaty, satisfying reds at moderate price-points. I like Domaine de l'Oratoire, Domaine de la Renjarde, and many others."
—*Peter Granoff, master sommelier and co-owner, Ferry Plaza Wine Merchants, San Francisco, CA*

"Côtes du Rhône wines can have the magic of a complex wine but still be very affordable. They can be smooth and fruity or big and tannic."
—*Jenny Lefcourt, co-owner, Jenny & François Selections and importer of "From the Tank" box wines, New York, NY*

FUNNELING FOR A CHILL

I can't say that I was surprised when I discovered how my friend William chills his favorite Pinot Noirs from Oregon and other light reds. Being a tinkering type whose company creates elegantly simple home entertainment systems, he has devised a similarly easy approach to instilling wine with a light chill: he fills a baking funnel with ice and pours the wine through. When he has company over, he swaps the plastic funnel for a beautiful pewter version that is designed to aerate wine by filtering the fluid through five small holes in the funnel's base. Not only does it hold a good scoop of ice, but the funnel will catch everyone's eye as it streams the wine in all directions against the inside of a glass or decanter. An elegant, unusual gift for a wine sophisticate, it is called the "Fluted Wine Funnel," and is available at Royal Selangor (RoyalSelangor.com) for about $70.

"I love Rhône wines—they can be great steak wines and particularly good with barbecue."

—Alfred Portale, chef and co-owner, Gotham Bar and Grill, New York, NY

"I love wines made from black Grenache grapes, with an intense nose of wild red fruit marmalade. They have a nice structure that is strong in the mouth with round velvet tannins. I think of the Châteauneuf-du-Pape reds, also from the southern Rhône. Château Rayas is my favorite."

—Joël Robuchon, chef and restaurateur, L'Atelier de Joël Robuchon, New York, NY

"I like to hang around people who like barnyardy aromas."

—Todd English, chef and restaurateur, Olives, Charlestown, MA

CÔTES DU RHÔNE

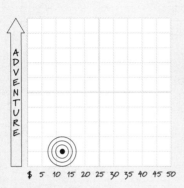

 Audacious Alternative To
Zinfandel, Cabernet Sauvignon

 Enthusiasts Also Like
Montepulciano d'Abruzzo, reds from Washington State, (good) Merlot, Malbec, Nero d'Avola, bargain Bordeaux, box wine

 Weight
Medium to Full

 Price
Low ($8 to $20+)

 Cheat Sheet
Often sold for a song, Côtes du Rhône deserves discovery for its spicy, strapping personality that sometimes carries some of the characteristic earthiness seen in the reds of southern Rhône.

Label Logic
Côtes du Rhône is a general place name that refers mostly to wine from grapes grown in the southern Rhône Valley. Several types of grapes are permitted, with Grenache dominant and Syrah and Mouvèdre also common.

 Bravely Said

Côtes-du-Rhône	*Coat-doo-Rone*
Grenache	*Gruh-NASH*
Mouvèdre	*Move-vehd*
Vacqueyras	*Vah-keh-rahss*

 Mark's Picks

M. Chapoutier	*Shah-poo-tyay*
Château de Beaucastel	*Bow-kahs-TEHL*
Delas	*Duh-lah*
Domaine de la Renjarde	*Ruhn-jharde*
Domaine de l'Oratoire	*lo-rah-twahr*
Domaine d'Estezargues	*deh-stay-ZAR-gwoy*
"From the Tank" (3L)	
Domaine le Garrigon	
E. Guigal	*Ghee-GAL*
Jaboulet	*Jah-BOO-leh*
Jean-Luc Colombo	
"Les Abeilles"	
Perrin & Fils	*Peh-rahn ay Fees*
VRAC	

 Poosh It!
Though it sounds like a goddess from Norse mythology, Vacqueyras is an oft-overlooked southern Rhône appellation that is considered a step up from Côtes du Rhône, offering a bit more complexity and a characteristically dark, tarry personality. It typically rings up between $20 and $35.

A Lovable Feast

Casual, robust fare, including chili, ribs, stews, hamburgers, and bacon; roast chicken; garlicky dishes; pepper and pepper sauces; richer Mexican food; Middle-Eastern fare such as *kibbe* and marinated lamb kabobs; Gruyère, Emmenthaler, and other dry cheeses

 Locally Lusty

Cassoulet, charcuterie, onion soup; French regional cheese such as Saint-Nectaire (semisoft cow's milk)

 Spend the Night Together

To fully appreciate the spicy, earthy dimension marking many Côtes du Rhône, find yourself a sample of each of these: black pepper, damp earth, burnt leaves, and charcoal. Now open a few different bottles of Côtes du Rhône and see if you can identify any aroma matches.

27 MALBEC

Bulletproof Lusciousness

I KNEW SOMETHING was different when I spied the bulletproof glass in the Volkswagen Cabriolet.

It was Sunday night in São Paulo, Brazil, and we were blowing red lights on our way to one of the city's best *churrascarias*. It wasn't starvation that inspired this cannonball run, but São Paulo's infamously mean streets, which explains why the driver—not an escaping operative but a local twenty-something gym trainer—would fortify her girlie car like a Humvee in Kabul.

The meal was worth braving bullets for, however, not so much for the table's orgy of skewered animal flesh but for the wine we had with it, a Malbec from neighboring Argentina. A mouth-filling red, this Malbec was like a chocolate-covered plum encased in a velvety box—and was one of those category-defining wine memories forever etched into my brain's hippocampus.

Argentine Malbec is likely to be one of the most familiar of the Brave New Pours, as few wine types have come so far so fast into the good graces of the wine-passionate; I even included it in my first book, and I'm such a fan that I needed to include it here. Whereas in its original homeland of France it is used in small quantities blended into red Bordeaux and survives as a stand-alone in the black wine of Cahors (Chapter 24), it has found its soul mate in the high desert climes and soils of Argentina. Though single-varietal Malbec was barely a blip on American radar screens fifteen years ago, infusions of money and winemaking talent into Argentina—and especially into the marquee region of Mendoza—have launched this grape so successfully that it is now the envy of other up-and-coming wine locales around the world.

Malbec couldn't have gone prime time if the wine weren't as

amiable and generous as a South American after two stiff caipi-rinhas and a soccer win. Mouth-coating and velvety, it is a lesson in vinous voluptuousness, all ripe plums and blackberries, with traces of dark chocolate or mocha, and noticeable but typically soft tannins. The best ones often show a minerality reminiscent of graphite or asphalt or sometimes a whiff of leather.

Attesting to Malbec's profile is that producers are starting to deem it established enough to export their highest-end ver-sions—showpieces which run $50 or even double that. At the same time, however, Malbec remains very much a value, its retail sweet spot operating in the $10 to $20 range, thanks in part to Argentina's relatively inexpensive vineyard land and labor as well as favorable exchange rates.

As the aforementioned *churrascaria* mission suggests, Malbec is a natural for meat eaters, as it should be, with Argentina so cel-ebrated for its fire-grilled beef. And I have yet to see a lasagna or cheeseburger that didn't take to it like a Brazilian to a soccer chant. It will also have vegetarians in its thrall, especially with dishes dominated by meatier ingredients such as mushrooms, beans, and black olives.

BRAVEHEARTS ON *Malbec*

"I'm Proustian by nature. I tend to have emotional connections with wines, like a handicapper who bets on a horse because he likes the name. For that reason, I love the best Riojas, Malbecs, and Brunellos di Montalcino, since they evoke memorable moments in Andalucia, Mendoza, and Tuscany, respectively. But I'm not a fool: the good ones from those regions are so good!"   —John Lithgow, actor

"Malbec is an unbelievable bang-for-your-buck Cab substitute with the near-perfect grape growing *terroir* of Argentina behind it. With the snow-covered Andes and sixty-year-old vineyards as our backdrop, I recently feasted with Argentine winemakers on beef empanadas, all kinds of sausages, and huge slabs of succulent local beef—with Malbec as the perfect partner. Salads are an afterthought in Argentina."

—*Heather Willens, importer and owner HW Wines, Buenos Aires, Argentina*

"With a big, spicy red like Malbec, I'd make my Gaucho Steak with Chimichurri Sauce or Bloody Mary Flank Steak."

—*Guy Fieri, chef and television host*

"I like the full body of Argentine Malbec but I drink Tignanello, a Super Tuscan blend of Sangiovese, Cabernet Sauvignon, and Cabernet Franc when I want something mad sophisticated." —*John Leguizamo, actor*

"I love the jamminess and the fruitiness of Malbec. It works exceptionally well with the spice-crusted steak I do at Tabla. I also open this wine for people who are not big wine drinkers, as it is easy to like." —*Floyd Cardoz, executive chef, Tabla, New York, NY*

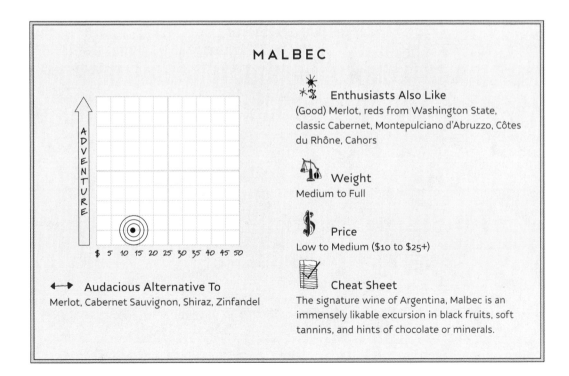

MALBEC

Enthusiasts Also Like
(Good) Merlot, reds from Washington State, classic Cabernet, Montepulciano d'Abruzzo, Côtes du Rhône, Cahors

Weight
Medium to Full

Price
Low to Medium ($10 to $25+)

ADVENTURE

$ 5 10 15 20 25 30 35 40 45 50

Audacious Alternative To
Merlot, Cabernet Sauvignon, Shiraz, Zinfandel

Cheat Sheet
The signature wine of Argentina, Malbec is an immensely likable excursion in black fruits, soft tannins, and hints of chocolate or minerals.

Label Logic

Malbec is a grape.

 Bravely Said

Churrascaria	*Choo-rah-scah-ree-ah*
Malbec	*Mahl-bec*
Mendoza	*Men-DOH-sah*

 Mark's Picks

Alamos	*AH-lah-mos*
Altos Las Hormigas	*AHL-tos Las Hor-MEE-gahs*
Catena Zapata	*Kah-TAY-nah Sah-PAH-tah*
Familia Zuccardi	*Fah-MEEL-ee-ya Zoo-KAHR-dee*
La Posta del Viñatero	*Lah POS-tah del Veen-ah-TEHR-oh*
Luigi Bosca	*Loo-EE-gee BOS-cah*
Maipe	*Mah-AY-peh*
Norton	
Septima	*Sep-teem-ah*
Sur de los Andes	
Susana Balbo (Dominio del Plata)	*Bawl-boh*
Terrazas de los Andes	*Tear-RAH-sahs day los AN-days*
Trivento	*Trih-VEN-toh*
Viña Cobos	*VEEN-yah Koh-bos*

 Poosh It!

Feline fanciers have an extra reason to meow for Malbec: the prevalence of cat-inspired cuvees, including "El Felino," a Malbec from Viña Cobos, whose label features an angular, folk-art rendition of a jungle cat, and Budini, which depicts the long-legged pampas cat that likes to roam the Andean foothills of Argentina.

CULINARY SWEET SPOT

Lightest — Heaviest

 A Lovable Feast

Steak, lamb, sausage, and other meats, especially barbecued or grilled; hamburgers; stews; pizza, especially with meat or mushrooms; pasta with meat sauces; richer vegetarian preparations; Manchego and other firm cheeses.

 Locally Lusty

Empanadas, especially stuffed with spicy beef; *cordero patagónico* (rack of lamb); *bife de chorizo* with *papas rusticas* (spicy sausage with potatoes); chimichurri (spicy green) sauce

🌙 **Spend the Night Together**

Aside from grilled *gaucho* steaks, nothing goes better with Malbec than watching a game of soccer, the South American passion that borders on obsession, christened "the beautiful game" by Brazilian footballer Pelé.

28 (GOOD) MERLOT

Dial "M" for Minefield

DOES THE DREADED "M" word really deserve its scarlet letter? Sure, you could almost hear Merlot casks across the world exploding when Miles gave his infamous "I am not drinking any %#$@ing Merlot" rant in *Sideways*. The truth is that before his red Saab ever hit Freeway 101, Merlot was already choking on its own vines, a victim of its rock-star popularity in the '90s, rampant overproduction, and subsequent cratering in quality.

The result was a market flooded with Merlot that is reminiscent of a shirtless Schwarzenegger in the present day: fleshy and soft—an unfortunate snapshot of what should never be. Cheap Merlot can be so devoid of flavor that it should be dubbed "Snore-low," a shallow, weedy basin of blandness where there should be deep, ripe fruit. Expensive Merlot can be the opposite: overripe, sun-baked fruit plagued by more wood than a foreclosed Miami condo.

But while the post-*Sideways* world abandoned Merlot for Pinot pastures, an interesting thing happened: the state of Merlot started to improve. As Merlot-maven Jeff Bundschu told me, significant plots of "commodity Merlot" grapes in California have been pulled out and replanted with more popular varietals. The Merlot grapes that remain are on average of high quality. Moreover, true believers in Merlot have learned to keep crop yields low and to plant the grape in the cooler, hillier areas that the vine favors.

Even with these enhancements, the Merlot market is still somewhat of a minefield. When it's good, it will be a medium-to-full-bodied mélange of plums and black cherries, often with slightly less heft and acidity than Cabernets of similar rank. The archetypal Merlot has velvety smooth tannins, though examples from cool climates or blends with Cabernet can display more structure. Some combination of plums, cocoa, coffee, smoke, or cedar are typically present in Merlot at its most complex and voluptuous.

With careful selection so vital, Merlot is the kind of wine where a knowledgeable merchant or sommelier can really shine. They would likely steer you first to Washington State, whose climate and winemaker ambition powers the country's most consistently exciting Merlots (Chapter 34). Many Washington Merlots require at least a $30 commitment, but Château Ste. Michelle and Snoqualmie consistently get the job done for less than $20. In California, Napa blue-chips like Duckhorn, Pride, and Beringer are virtuosos of the grape, though the toll is typically $40 or more to sample their craft.

Looking to more exotic locations, Long Island Merlot proves that two wrongs *can* make a right. Its earthy, balanced Merlots suggest that the North Fork may finally have a signature grape in the making.

Elsewhere in the New World, Chile is emerging as a Merlot avenger, with Casa Lapostolle, Cono Sur, and Montes Alpha all doing the grape proud for about $25 a bottle. Pomérol and Saint Emilion, comprising the so-called "right bank" of France's Bordeaux region, have long been the world's template for complex, Merlot-dominant blends, though much of it is priced vertiginously. A new fascination of mine has been Merlot from Italy, which is grown throughout the country and at a range of prices. A waiter at Los Angeles's Osteria Mozza turned me on to the medium-bodied, minerally embrace of a Tuscan Merlot, which was *bellissimo* with the restaurant's sausage-studded orecchiette.

Speaking of nourishment, you'll never fail when matching Merlot with the hearty, meaty, and cheesy. Upmarket versions are natural partners for rack of lamb, steak, goose pâté, and game meats, while moderately-priced bottles have an affinity for hamburgers, sausages, and hearty pasta dishes. Although chocolate might be overpowering for some palates, I find that it harmonizes with richer, cocoa-inflected renditions of Merlot.

BRAVEHEARTS ON *(Good) Merlot*

"My secret is this: I drink two glasses of wine during the last five songs of a Fleetwood Mac set. I enjoy being a little naughty—it's my little treat at the end of the show. It's the *only* place I ever have wine without food. It's always Sterling or Frog's Leap Merlot or my own blend.

"I'm a Merlot freak. I love reds but I don't like heavy, dense, syrupy wines. Merlot is mellow—it doesn't hit you over the head."

—*Mick Fleetwood, drummer and namesake, Fleetwood Mac*

"I like Merlot from the Maipo Valley, Chile—particularly the Santa Ema Reserve, which has notes of chocolate, and a bit of coffee. It's very reasonably priced and is a good companion to heavier meals."

—*Bruce Greenwood, actor,* Star Trek (2009)

"Merlot, when done right, can be a very seductive wine with much of the complexity and earthiness of a Cabernet in combination with the fruit and approachability of a Pinot Noir. There is an absolute reason why it was king of the reds for so many years. Lighter and more red-fruit than most Cabernets. Meatier and more substantial than most Pinots. It is much less hot and more subtle than Zins."

—*Jeff Bundschu, president, Gundlach Bundschu*

"It was two A.M. and we had pizza and a bottle of Duckhorn Merlot."

—*Mike "Coach K" Krzyzewski, on how he accepted an offer to coach the U.S. national basketball team in the 2012 Olympics*

"Petra's 'Quercegobbe,' a rich Merlot from Tuscany, is an easy all-around red; it's never out of style—you can't go wrong with it."

—*Matthew McConaughey, actor*

"Once, in Paris, my wife Natasha and I cooked a fun dinner for our hosts, who graciously surprised our mouths with a bottle of 1947 Pétrus from their cellar. At the Marché des Enfants Rouges, the oldest food market in Paris, we secured some white asparagus, a pint of wild morels, rabbit, fingerling potatoes, and those stupendously tart little wild strawberries. It was an evening that I often reflect upon, especially when I am sweltering in a remote jungle, tragically wine-less, noshing on questionable field rations, while plucking leeches from my ankles."

—*Jeff Corwin, host and executive producer,* Animal Planet's "The Jeff Corwin Experience," *on Bordeaux's famed Château Pétrus, which is virtually 100% Merlot*

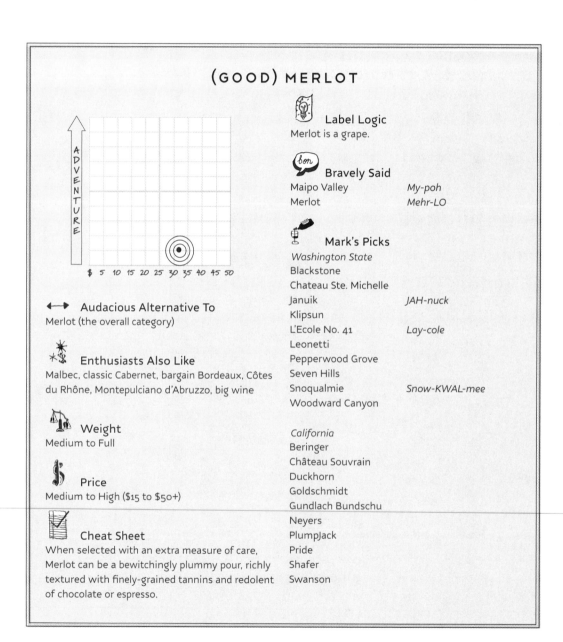

(GOOD) MERLOT

Label Logic

Merlot is a grape.

Bravely Said

Maipo Valley	*My-poh*
Merlot	*Mehr-LO*

Mark's Picks

Washington State
Blackstone
Chateau Ste. Michelle

Januik	*JAH-nuck*
Klipsun	
L'Ecole No. 41	*Lay-cole*

Leonetti
Pepperwood Grove
Seven Hills

Snoqualmie	*Snow-KWAL-mee*

Woodward Canyon

California
Beringer
Château Souvrain
Duckhorn
Goldschmidt
Gundlach Bundschu
Neyers
PlumpJack
Pride
Shafer
Swanson

Audacious Alternative To

Merlot (the overall category)

Enthusiasts Also Like

Malbec, classic Cabernet, bargain Bordeaux, Côtes du Rhône, Montepulciano d'Abruzzo, big wine

Weight

Medium to Full

Price

Medium to High ($15 to $50+)

Cheat Sheet

When selected with an extra measure of care, Merlot can be a bewitchingly plummy pour, richly textured with finely-grained tannins and redolent of chocolate or espresso.

ADVENTURE

$ 5 10 15 20 25 30 35 40 45 50

Mark's Picks *(continued)*

Long Island, NY
Bedell
Lenz
Shinn Estate
Wölffer   *Wowl-fer*

Chile
Casa Lapostolle
Concha y Toro
Cono Sur
Montes
Santa Ema

France
Château Beauregard   *Bow-rah-gahr*
   (Pomerol)
Château du Cauze   *dew Cose*
   (Saint Emilion)
Château Mazeyres   *Mah-zeyhr*
   (Pomerol)
Christian Moueix   *Moe-ex*
   (Saint Emilion)
Château Monbousquet   *Mohn-boos-keh*
   (Saint Emilion)

Italy
Cusumano   *Koo-soo-MAH-no*
Falesco   *Fah-LES-koh*
Mezzacorona   *METS-sah-koe-ROH-nah*
Planeta   *Plah-NET-ah*
Sorbaiano   *Sore-bah-YAH-no*
Stella

 Poosh It!
The subtle irony of the movie *Sideways* is that though Paul Giamatti's character memorably blasts Merlot, the end of the movie reveals his dream wine to be Cheval Blanc, a Bordeaux which actually contains a substantial amount of Merlot in its blend.

 CULINARY SWEET SPOT

Lightest   Heaviest

 A Lovable Feast
Red meat such as beef tenderloin and lamb; goose pâté and rich terrines; sausages, hot dogs, and other grilled fare; rich pasta dishes; hearty casseroles; hard and blue-veined cheeses; cranberry and other ripe berry sauces; chocolate; Thanksgiving, Independence Day, and Mother's Day

Spend the Night Together
At your next dinner party, don't tell your guests that you're serving Merlot until after they praise it—which they will, if you choose the good stuff.

29 MONTEPULCIANO D'ABRUZZO

Full Monty, Half Priced

I'M CONVINCED THAT deep in the bowels of a dusty wine cellar, in the sinister flicker of candlelight, there exists an annual meeting of a "Secret Society to Confuse Wine Drinkers." Under the shadow of the group's secret crest—consisting of a question mark trapped in a wine bottle—and dressed in hooded robes, the members have dreamed up curiosities such as making the "extra dry" designation on Champagne mean sweeter than "dry"; Petite Sirah be neither petite nor Syrah; "Fumé Blanc" and "Sauvignon Blanc" mean the same thing; and wine labeled as "private reserve" and "special selection" not necessarily be distinguished wines at all.

Another of the Society's creations has to be "Montepulciano," which is not only a challenge to force through your lips (Mawn-teh-pool-CHA-noh), but can refer to either "Vino Nobile di Montepulciano," named for Montepulciano, a town in Tuscany, or the completely different wine "Montepulciano d'Abruzzo," named for the Montepulciano grape. It is the kind of ambiguity that George Carlin could have surely riffed on.

We're focusing on Montepulciano d'Abruzzo, as it is the source of remarkable value. Although the grape is grown throughout central Italy, the primary region for it is in the hills of Abruzzi, which is midway down the boot on Italy's east coast. Once synonymous with mass-produced, industrial dreck, this area has seen an upsurge in quality thanks to technological advancements.

Imbibers can now look to Montepulciano d'Abruzzo as a source of uncomplicated, easy-drinking pleasure. Offering generous notes of tart cherries or blackberries, joined by injections of earth, licorice, or black olives, it is a "full monty" of flavor and, you might say, the Platonic ideal of a simple-but-satisfying Italian red, one that Billy Joel would sing about if "Montepulciano" had a partner-in-rhyme. But you don't need to be a piano man to appreciate the wine's robust flavors and soft, sometimes velvety mouthfeel.

Though there are luxury versions, most bottles of Montepulciano d'Abruzzo fall in the $8 to $15 range, with more than a few bobbing under $10—which is one of the finest examples of vinous humanitarianism I know of. When folks are racking their brains for a low-risk, low-fuss pour to complement Sunday night pizza or pasta, this is what they want.

In fact, I'll venture to say that Montepulciano has never met a red sauce it didn't like. One of my most memorable experiences with it was at A16, the San Francisco hot spot specializing in Neapolitan-style pizza and cuisine from the region of Campania. To wash down the restaurant's charred, fennel-sausage pizza with glasses of Montepulciano is to experience life exactly the way it should be.

BRAVEHEARTS ON *Montepulciano d'Abruzzo*

"Montepulciano d'Abruzzo is one of the best reds for a non-Italian lover to become a believer. The best, underrated producer is Rimbaldi, great with lasagna or baked ziti."

—*Inez Ribustello, sommelier and co-owner, On the Square, Tarboro, NC*

"Hearty and earthy, Montepulciano d'Abruzzo is just about the best food wine around. Pair the lighter, fruitier styles with simple tomato-sauced pastas or pizza margherita. Deeper, richer styles, often aged in oak barrels, will pair best with braised, rich meats, such as lamb shanks, short ribs, or beef cheeks."

—*Mollie Battenhouse, sommelier and wine director, Maslow 6, New York, NY*

"It's come a long way, and is still getting better. Chewy, big, bold—people love it. Definitely not for fish, but great with lamb, chorizo, and other meaty meats. A nice December treat."

—*Helen Johannesen, wine director, Animal, Los Angeles, CA*

"My Italian boyfriend is who got me hooked on wine. There wasn't one specific wine that he introduced me to but the Italians appreciate cuisine paired with wine and he helped integrate that into my life. I was mostly a beer drinker with everything I ate before I met him."

—*Hilary Swank, actress*

"When made from high-quality grapes, Montepulciano d'Abruzzo is a straightforward gulp with a nicely spicy flavor that goes with the typical countryside cooking. At old-fashioned wine bars, they have a grill with skewers of lamb rolled in herbs you eat seconds off the grill while drinking a good glass of Montepulciano.

"For expensive, small-production Montepulciano, track down Emidio Pepe and Valentini. These wineries shroud their winemaking in mystery and their low crop yields and the age of the vines make for wines of incredible intensity and flavor."

—*Dean Gold, owner/chef, Dino, Washington, DC*

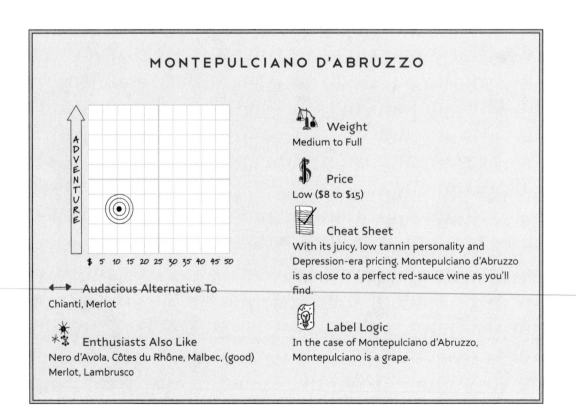

MONTEPULCIANO D'ABRUZZO

ADVENTURE

$ 5 10 15 20 25 30 35 40 45 50

Audacious Alternative To
Chianti, Merlot

Enthusiasts Also Like
Nero d'Avola, Côtes du Rhône, Malbec, (good) Merlot, Lambrusco

Weight
Medium to Full

Price
Low ($8 to $15)

Cheat Sheet
With its juicy, low tannin personality and Depression-era pricing. Montepulciano d'Abruzzo is as close to a perfect red-sauce wine as you'll find.

Label Logic
In the case of Montepulciano d'Abruzzo, Montepulciano is a grape.

Bravely Said

Chianti	*K'yahn-tee*
Montepulciano d'Abruzzo	*Mawn-teh-pool-CHA-noh Dah-BROOT-soh*
Vino Nobile	*Vee-no NO-bee-lah*

 Mark's Picks

Catina Frentana	*Kan-TEEN-ah Fren-TAH-nah*
Dino Illuminati	
Ercole Velenosi "Quattro Mani"	*ER-Koe-leh Veh-leh-NO-zee*
Il Conte	
Marchesi Dè' Cordano	*Mar-KEH-see day Cor-DAH-noh*
Nicodemi	
Poliziano	
Rimbaldi	
Stella	
Valle Reale	*VAL-leh Ray-AH-leh*

 Poosh It!

With a name fit for an Italian magician, Dino Illuminati is one of Abruzzo's most important vintners of the Montepulciano grape, both in affordable ("Riparosso" or "Illico") and mega-rich, upmarket ("Pieluni") bottlings.

 CULINARY SWEET SPOT

 Lightest ▲ Heaviest

 A Lovable Feast

Pizza, especially topped with meat, mushrooms, or other earthy tastes; old-school, Italian classics such as lasagna, tortellini, manicotti, eggplant parmigiana, ravioli; tomato, meat, and mushroom sauces; grilled chicken, steaks, and lamb; veal chops; hamburgers; rich stews; olives and olive tapenade.

 Locally Lusty

Roast lamb, especially *arrosticini* (skewered pieces of mutton, often accompanied by olive oil–drenched bread)

Spend the Night Together

Call your favorite pizzeria to ask if you can BYOB there. If you get the green light, buy some Montepulciano d'Abruzzo and have yourself a Montepulciano-and-pizza feast.

BRINGING IT

"Hide it down by your side and don't tell anybody."

> —Drew Bledsoe, football great, on sneaking wine into restaurants that don't allow BYOB, based on his experience at a Montana eatery

"BYOB is the centerpoint of my religion.

  "I decant my Bordeaux at home and funnel it back into the opened bottle. It avoids the chance that the sommelier will shake the bottle in my face and create a red cloud. I always give a taste to the sommelier and sometimes to the waiter, too. It just creates a good feeling."

> —Al Stewart, folk-rock musician "Year of the Cat"

"We heartily encourage BYOB. You let guests bring their own wine, and they're coming back. I've lost sommeliers over this subject. We'll sell more wine in the long run, and we're making people happy."

> —John Besh, chef and restaurateur, Restaurant August, New Orleans, LA

"When we had the band Duran Duran over to dinner, we learned that those guys love wine so much that they had a special flight-case built just to have good wine with them on tour, mostly Bordeaux from the '80s, worth about twenty thousand dollars. When I asked keyboardist Nick Rhodes about why he went to these lengths, he explained, 'Have you ever played Boise? It's times like that, at least there's this.'"

> —Courtney Taylor-Taylor, lead singer and guitarist, The Dandy Warhols

30 NERO D'AVOLA

The Maternal Cheek Pinch

SOME TIME AGO, my friend Ricardo—a Milan-reared George Hamilton doppelganger minus thirty years and a few shades of burnt sienna—explained to me a critical difference between American mothers and those in Italy:

"When you get home from school, mothers here ask about your homework. In Italy, the first thing they want to know is what the school served you for lunch."

This overriding passion for food and family makes me think of Nero d'Avola, a maternal cheek pinch of rich black fruit, soft tannins, and floral perfume so likable that if you're not careful, it may end up doing your laundry and fixing you a steaming bowl of pasta fagioli.

The best known and most-planted red grape of Sicily, Nero d'Avola is a shining example of how far this island known for its fiery volcano and equally fiery mobsters has come in wine production. While fifteen years ago Sicily was virtually one big clearinghouse for undistinguished bulk wine, today ambitious young winemakers are rediscovering the region's potential and using technology to revive ancient varietals, the most exciting of which is Nero d'Avola. If you like Syrah or Malbec, then Nero is an alluring alternative, sporting a medium-to-full body, aromas of crushed blackberries, and tannins that typically tread gently on your palate. Some versions show shades of tar, chocolate, violets, or a savory herbaceousness reminiscent of tarragon or rosemary.

This drinkability is priced to move. It is entirely possible to find a good Nero at your local wine store for $12 and many bottles never vault the $20 mark. While the finest versions from producers such as Feudo Maccari and Morgante go for twice as much, these tend to be exceptions to the rule. In a phrase, Nero rarely requires much *dinero*.

Get your highlighter out because this point cannot be over-emphasized: like the aforementioned Montepulciano d'Abruzzo (Chapter 29), Nero d'Avola is a consummate pizza wine. Its juicy, gutsy personality has made it for me the perfect partner with pies from across the country, from the smoky prosciutto pie at Phoenix's Pizzeria Bianco to the coal-blistered beauties of Totonno's in Brooklyn. But a pizza oven isn't necessary to coax out Nero's culinary capabilities—almost any hearty fare is a contender, from lasagna to winter stews to grilled lamb chops. If you want to go native, try Nero with *arancini*, the deep-fried rice croquettes that are a staple of the Sicilian table.

BRAVEHEARTS ON *Nero d'Avola*

"My grandfather was from Sicily—and in Italy wine is just part of the meal—they 'get it' over there and don't have the taboos that we have here."   —*Joe Montana, football legend*

"Nero d'Avola is a warm-hearted, full-bodied wine with home-cooked meals such as noodles with rich tomato and meat-based pasta sauces and braised meats. Most of them are affordable and put a smile on your face from the moment you open them."

   —*Debbie Zachareas, co-owner, Ferry Plaza Wine Merchants, San Francisco, CA*

"Nero has a piercingly spicy volcanic scent that makes me think of fire and brimstone and tastes like pomegranate meets homemade beef jerky. I love it with lamb burgers, grilled octopus, and any pasta made with black olives."   —*Marnie Old, author,* Wine Secrets, *and wine educator*

"Nero d'Avola is an ancient grape, and its best wines taste like chocolate-covered cherries, providing a wonderful depth of fruit that I often pair with margherita pizza, fresh ricotta with olive oil, spaghetti nero with sardines, rack of lamb, and pork chops.

"One of the mistakes often associated with Nero d'Avola also happens with Chianti—once a person tries one they believe the rest will taste the same. Nero d'Avola has a range of flavors and quality. It is one of my favorite varietals in Italy and extremely important to Italian history and culture. Try Tenuta La Lumia 'Don Totò,' Planeta 'Santa Cecilia,' and Gulfi."

—*Shelley Lindgren, wine director and co-owner, A16, San Francisco, CA*

"Nero d'Avola is ideal with a simple dish, like pasta with chicken tossed with basil, mint, garlic, and olive oil. So pure."

—*John Besh, chef and restaurateur, Restaurant August, New Orleans, LA*

"Nero d'Avola is all about dark plums and dark chocolate. I like Tasca d'Almerita and Cusumano, the latter of which is a killer red for less than twelve dollars, and is so great with braised short ribs."

—*Inez Ribustello, sommelier and co-owner, On the Square, Tarboro, NC*

"I think Nero d'Avola is the grape variety that has shown the most improvement of any type in Italy. . . . If you've been disappointed by Nero in the past, try another, especially one that is a notch above the typical seven-dollar Nero you often see."

—*Lou Amdur, owner, Lou's Wine Bar, Los Angeles, CA*

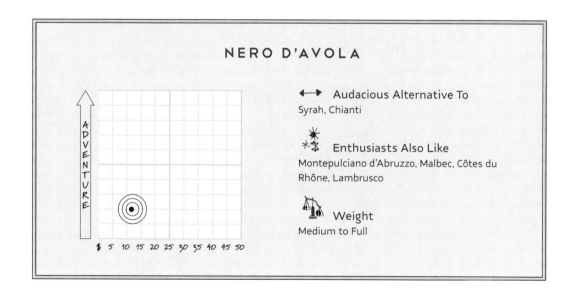

NERO D'AVOLA

↔ Audacious Alternative To
Syrah, Chianti

✴ Enthusiasts Also Like
Montepulciano d'Abruzzo, Malbec, Côtes du Rhône, Lambrusco

⚖ Weight
Medium to Full

ADVENTURE

$ 5 10 15 20 25 30 35 40 45 50

Price

Low ($10 to $25+)

 Cheat Sheet

Those who savor Syrah have much to like in revitalized Nero d'Avola, a rich red reminiscent of black fruit, chocolate, and tar.

 Label Logic

Nero d'Avola is grape.

 Bravely Said

Nero d'Avola   *Neh-roe da-voh-lah*

 Mark's Picks

Ajello	*Eve-YAY-low*
Colosi	*Co-LOW-see*
Cusumano	*Koo-soo-MAH-no*
Feudo Arancio	*FEH-oo-do Ah-RAN-cho*
Feudo Maccari "Sala"	*Mah-CAHR-ee Sigh-ya*
Gulfi	*GOOL-fee*
Morgante	*More-GAHN-tay*
Planeta	*Plah-NET-ah*
Rapitala	*Rah-pee tah-LAH*
Villa Pozzi	*Veel-lah POE-tzee*

 Poosh It!

"Nero d'Avola" translates as "the black grape from Avola."

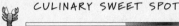 **CULINARY SWEET SPOT**

 Lightest ▲ Heaviest

 A Lovable Feast

Pizza, especially with black olives, mushrooms, meatballs, or sausage; pasta with meat sauce; penne amatriciana and other piquantly-sauced pastas; steak, lamb chops, and other grilled meats; winter stews; braised boar and other game meats; hard cheeses like Pecorino and Parmigiano-Reggiano

 Locally Lusty

Pork roast with sage and rosemary; arancini (fried rice balls); eggplant, peppers, and tomatoes; capers and olives; anchovies

 Spend the Night Together

Though it doesn't sound immediately appealing, the "tarry" quality ascribed to some Nero d'Avolas adds a dark, resinous dimension to the wine. Find yourself some shoe polish and see if you notice any similar (but far subtler) scents in a tasting of Neros.

31 PETITE SIRAH

Dark and Intense as a Dominatrix's Boot

"CUT! IT'S PRONOUNCED 'Pah-soe Roh-*bulls*.'"

I was in California's Paso Robles, serving as head judge for the PBS television series *The Winemakers* when the filming came to an abrupt halt after I mangled the pronunciation of the very wine region where the series was based. I had assumed it was uttered as the elegant, Spanish-inflected "Rrroh-blays," not the clunky, Americanized "Roh-bulls," which sounds more like a piece of farm equipment than it does a vinous *appellation*. ("Billy, set that Robles over by the tractor.") But when locals on the set rushed to correct the errors of my tongue, I got the message.

My inability to pronounce it notwithstanding, Paso Robles—located on California's Central Coast about midway between San Francisco and Los Angeles—is one of the great emerging wine regions and a primary source for Petite Sirah. Like Paso itself, Petite Sirah is hearty, bold, and slightly rough around the edges—an impassioned fist-pump of a wine known for its plump frame and blueberry richness, sometimes coupled with traces of spice, pine needles, or melted chocolate. Not the same grape as Syrah though the wines share a similar flavor profile, Petite Sirah is typified by an inky-black color and jabs of tannic astringency. It's a high-alcohol bruiser, dark and intense as a dominatrix's boot.

Just as the passion for patent leather inspires a cultish follow-ing, so does Petite Sirah, although as far as I know the two aren't necessarily pursued at the same time by the same people. Petite Sirah, like its fellow Californian grape Zinfandel, even has its own advocacy organization, P.S. I Love You, which organizes events such as "Dark and Delicious" and a "Blue Tooth Tour."

The similarity between the two grapes doesn't end there, as both are rich, robust affairs that often come from old vines.

Petite Sirah can sometimes have tannins that shade to the aggressive. This puckering dryness is not necessarily a negative, as it's the primary reason why the variety can sometimes improve in the bottle for ten years or more, shedding some bitterness and gaining greater complexity. You can diminish its rambunctiousness by letting it breathe in a wide-rimmed decanter for an hour or more.

Petite Sirah's pronounced tannins are also the reason why the wine will obediently say "yes, Mistress" in the company of hard cheeses and robust meats. Two contestants in the food-pairing episode of *The Winemakers* proved this point brilliantly, pairing a bottle of Petite Sirah from Paso with succulent, fatty ribs from a local rib joint; the meat's proteins and fat took the wine's tannic intensity down a few notches, making the wine more flavorful and pleasurable. Another toothsome match is dark chocolate, its bitter undertones complementing the richness and sometimes chocolaty character of the wine.

BRAVEHEARTS ON *Petite Sirah*

"Petite Sirah is similar to Syrah—they are both deep in color, often inky black, and have dark berry flavors and firm tannins, but Petite Sirah can be even darker, blacker, and deeper in flavor."
—*Mollie Battenhouse, sommelier and wine director, Maslow 6, New York, NY*

"McManis Petite Sirah is great. The most recent vintage was rich and jammy and finishes lighter than you'd expect and has soft tannins as it fades. At about $12, it's great value for the coin."
—*Bruce Greenwood, actor,* Star Trek *(2009)*

"I love Petite Sirah and will decant it overnight. I make my own Chiarello Family Roux Old Vine Petite Sirah and buy others as well."
—*Michael Chiarello, vintner and host, Food Network's* Easy Entertaining with Michael Chiarello

"I find that I'm drawn to a full-bodied, earthy flavor. I love all varietals from Sonoma's Truett-Hurst Winery and their Burning Man Petite Sirah from the North Coast is one I drink most often."

—*Hilary Swank, actress*

PETITE SIRAH

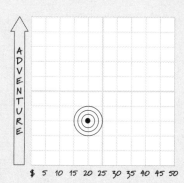

ADVENTURE

$ 5 10 15 20 25 30 35 40 45 50

 Audacious Alternative To
Syrah, Cabernet Sauvignon, Zinfandel

Enthusiasts Also Like
Aglianico, Cahors, Priorat, classic Cabernet, reds from Washington State

 Weight
Full

 Price
Medium ($12 to $40+)

 Cheat Sheet
Grown primarily in California, Petite Sirah offers a potent shot of mouth-filling black fruit and tannins that you can almost chew, joined by hints of earth, chocolate, or pepper.

 Label Logic
Petite Sirah is a grape.

 Bravely Said
Petite Sirah   *Peh-TEET Sih-RAH*

 Mark's Picks
Big House "The Prodigal Son"
Bogle
Chiarello Family
Concannon
Domani
EOS Estate
Foppiano
Four Vines "The Heretic"
Guenoc
Jaffurs
Rosenblum
Turley
Vinum Cellars

 Poosh It!
Further support of my suspicion that there exists a "Secret Society to Confuse Wine Drinkers" (Chapter 29). Petite Sirah is sometimes wrongly spelled Petite Syrah, even though Petite Sirah and Syrah are different grapes. Making matters worse, the French have a variant of the Syrah grape they call "Petite."

On the subject of footwear, the term "heeltap" is used to refer to the bit of wine left in a glass, and thus the toast "no heeltaps" wisely advises fellow diners to drain their glasses completely.

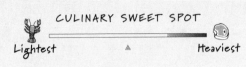 CULINARY SWEET SPOT

Lightest ▲ Heaviest

 Locally Lusty

Mexican-American food, especially with cheese, meat, or mushrooms

A Lovable Feast

Rich and/or grilled meats like leg of lamb, ribs, steak, especially au poivre, hamburgers; hard or sharp cheeses; venison, boar, and other game; dishes with mushrooms, black olives, and other earthy fare; dark chocolate

Spend the Night Together

Petite Sirah is another good wine with which to test Laurent's Law (Chapter 24). Open a bottle, and if it is too tannic, pour it into a decanter, let it aerate overnight, and try it the next evening.

32 PRIORAT

The Unslim Slatey

"I COULD BRING you back a piece of slate to lick, or you could try a bottle of Priorat wine. They are wines that taste of place."

So said Victor Gallegos, winemaker at Santa Barbara's famed Pinot producer Sea Smoke Cellars, but also the force behind Melis Vineyards in Spain's Priorat region. When he recently poured me some of his Priorat, I was struck by its palate-coating press of black plums, hints of herbs, and, indeed, a pleasantly minerally dynamic, which Gallegos says derives in part from the region's slatey soils. He described how in the 1990s ambitious young winemakers with modern winemaking methods completely resurrected this ancient vinous region of northeastern Spain, located southwest of Barcelona near the Mediterranean. With great conviction, he emphasized that the area is now capable of world-class wine, despite its isolated location, tractor-resistant hills, and inhospitable slate-laced soils.

If you set this comeback story to music, I got to thinking, what better choice is there than the equally fervid rapper Eminem, a.k.a. Slim Shady, and his famous declaration of rebirth: "Guess who's back? Shady's back!" Only here, given the Priorat's full body and graphite bite, we might revise the moniker to "Unslim Slatey." It gets this way not just because of the region's rocky terrain, where vines are forced to burrow deep into the slatey soils, but also due to the region's abundance of old vines, some even octogenarians, along with plentiful sunshine, and an unusual mix of grapes, the most prevalent of which are Garnacha (Grenache) and Cariñena (Carignan).

Often entering life with drawn daggers of tannins and acidity, Priorat doesn't have a bashful bone in its body, and thus can benefit from five years or more of aging in the bottle. Spanish cheeses like Manchego can also help put it in its place, as can the kind of rich fare for which its native Catalonia is famous. Got goat? Priorat wants some, too, or lamb or beef, best if it's stewed and flavored with *picada* (ground garlic, nuts, and parsley) or another hearty sauce. Grilled vegetables are also welcome in Priorat's world, especially if they are of an earthy sort, such as those of the parsnip or potato persuasion. The winemaker Gallegos told me that one of his best meals ever was Priorat served with nothing more than wild mushrooms lightly salted and roasted outside in local Arbequina olive oil.

Somebody's got to fund all of the hand-harvesting happening on the vertiginous slopes of Priorat (not to mention the trendy reputation of this wine), so it usually takes $25 or more to snag a good bottle. The "Les Terrasses" bottling from Alavaro Palacios, one of the region's pioneers, provides a solid introduction, as do Mas Igneus and Buil & Giné. If you're celebrating, swing for the fences with Clos Mogador, Clos Erasmus, or the Palacios "L'Ermita" or "Finca Dofi," the latter being the first wine I ever laid down to age, happily, to great effect.

BRAVEHEARTS ON *Priorat*

"Priorat is old-school Spain. Not the Guggenheim in Bilbao, but the real deal. Donkeys and humans laboring on wicked slopes in the Mediterranean sun. Wind-battered hermitages surveying deeply terraced valleys of improbable vineyards."

—*Victor Gallegos, general manager and viticulturist, Sea Smoke Cellars, Santa Barbara, CA*

"Priorat: buckets of ink, intense, tannic, but with incredibly interesting notes in the intensity."

—*Corie Brown, co-founder, food site ZesterDaily.com and former* Los Angeles Times *wine columnist*

"If you're a drinker of Châteauneuf-du-Pape, Zinfandel, or Syrah, this is definitely a wine you should put into your Rolodex of reds.

"Driving up the Priorat's side-winding roads with no guardrails, I was thinking: 'I'm going to die.' The vineyards are incredibly steep and rocky, and produce wine that is just as intriguing and intense, with the kind of minerality, acidity, and tannin that really cuts through the fat of suckling pig, lamb, and harder sheep's milk cheeses."

—*Fred Dexheimer, master sommelier and wine consultant, New York, NY*

"Because I'm a patriot, I love a wide variety of Spanish wines, from Rioja to Ribera del Duero to the difficult terrain of Priorat, which creates wine of great depth and dimension.

"A mature Priorat reminds me of what Zorro ends up as. He begins young, unpolished—like a young, alive, fruity wine such as a Rioja crianza. At the end, he's polished and educated—older, deeper, complex, like an aged Priorat."

—*Antonio Banderas, actor and star of* The Legend of Zorro

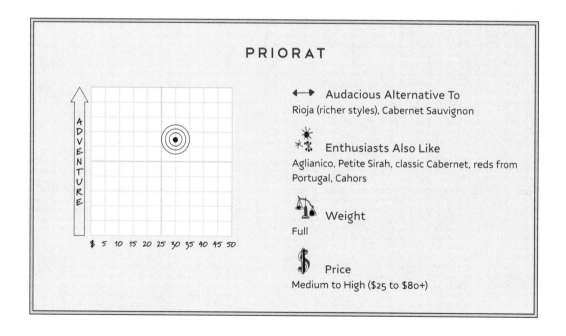

Cheat Sheet

A wine reborn that is as compelling as it is fashionable, Priorat marries abundant fruit with muscular tannins, yielding a Spaniard of minerality, intensity, and complexity.

 ### Label Logic

Priorat is a region. The wine is made with Grenache and/or Carignan, among other grapes.

 ### Bravely Said

Arbequina	Ar-be-KEEN-ah
Cariñena	Cah-ree-NYEH-nah
Finca Dofi	FING-cuh Doe-FEE
Garnacha	Gar-NAH-cha
Picada	Pee-CAH-dah
Priorat	Pree-or-RAHT
Rioja	Ree-OH-hah

Mark's Picks

Alvaro Palacios	AHL-bar-row Pah-LAH-thee-os
Buil & Giné	BOO-eel ey GEE-nay
Cims de Porrera	Sims day Poh-REYR-ah
Clos Erasmus	Clow Air-AHS-moose
Clos Mogador	Clow Moh-gah-DOOR
Laurel	
Mas Igneus	Mahs Ig-NAY-oos
Melis	MEL-is
Torres	TOE-ress

 ### Poosh It!

You say "Proriat," I say "Priorat"—both are correct, the first being Catalan and the name usually used on labels and the other being Spanish.

Priorat packs the kind of potency that Hemingway had in mind when he declared in *Death in the Afternoon* that "No one goes to bed in Madrid unless they have killed the night."

 ## CULINARY SWEET SPOT

Lightest ▲ Heaviest

 ### A Lovable Feast

Lamb, beef, other heavier meats; cassoulet and other stews; grilled vegetables; garlic, red pepper, eggplant, and other rustic Mediterranean flavors; olives and olive oil; Manchego, Gruyère, other firm cheeses; blue cheeses

 ### Locally Lusty

Richer meats flavored with *picada* (Catalan sauce); *rovellones del Monsant* (wild mushrooms); *calçotada* (onions)

Spend the Night Together

Old-school, formidable pour that it is, Priorat is the kind of wine that makes you want to run with the bulls, so open a bottle and watch the 1957 film adaptation of Hemingway's *The Sun Also Rises*, which is famous for its depiction of a Pamplona bullfight.

33 REDS FROM PORTUGAL

Richness and Distinction, by the Foot

QUESTION: WHAT DO you get with fifteen men gathered in a shallow concrete basin, stomping, singing, and slapping each other silly?

Answer: A fine Portuguese red, the grapes of which are often crushed with "the *pisar*," or treading by foot—an antiquated, hygienically-suspect method that seems more suited to Desilu than Ducru-Beaucaillou.

Miguel Roquette, owner of Portugal's Quinta do Crasto estate and self-proclaimed "Douro Boy," explained to me that such footwork is easier on the grapes than mechanical crushing, adding that any foot-borne impurities are destroyed by the resulting alcohol (let's hope). He said that grape stomping was also performed to "keep long-lived customs alive," which, tellingly, reflects the desire to retain a degree of tradition and personality in winemaking as many Portuguese wineries push to modernize. This is especially true in the Douro region of northeastern Portugal, which, like other high-potential wine zones around the world, is attracting a flood of new investment and talent. The Douro has long been famous for Port production (Chapter 43), but with sales of that sweet dessert wine stagnating, vintners there are focusing on creating dry red wine that can compete with the world's best.

An ambitious goal, but not far-fetched—since the Douro is blessed with prime volcanic soils, hot days with markedly cooler nights, and vertiginous hillsides—all serious boons to quality winemaking. It is also home to scores of indigenous, mostly unpronounceable grapes, blends of which form the basis of most wine from the region, though single-grape bottlings, such as that of the prestigious Touriga Nacional grape, also exist. Although styles vary, Douro reds are usually full-bodied, plummy, and smoky—not unlike a Cabernet Sauvignon or Syrah—but often with a certain distinctiveness that proves it no Cab copycat. This *gout de terroir* can manifest itself in a minerally edge, mocha flavors, surges of tannin, or all of the above.

While the most complex, *terroir*-driven bottlings of the Douro require a commitment of $40 or more, there are plenty of solid offerings below $25. Be on the lookout for Quinta do Crasto, Quinta do Vallado, and J. & F. Lurton. Just south of the Douro lies an even newer viticultural hotspot, the Dão, which is an even greater source of values. Casal de Tonda, Sogrape, Quinta de Cabriz are three of the Dão estates that can pull through for less than $15.

When I contemplate food pairings, I recall the spread friends and I had in the Ironbound section of Newark, New Jersey—a.k.a. "Little Portugal"—when we were there to celebrate the mayoral victory of Cory Booker. While sprightly Vinho Verde (Chapter 8) started things nicely with the frenzy of clams, mussels, and crab legs circulating around the table, a flurry of Portuguese reds provided the ideal irrigation for roast suckling pig, charcoal-broiled rack of lamb, and steak sautéed with prosciutto and potatoes. It was a victory both for New Jersey *and* for the palate.

BRAVEHEARTS ON *Reds from Portugal*

"Reds from Portugal are one of the most underrated categories in the world. Hard to pronounce names and grapes, and probably too-high prices, have kept them hidden from American consumers, but recently a slew of more inexpensive Douro wines have been imported, with better labels and just all-around better marketing."

—*Heather Willens, importer and owner, HW Wines, Buenos Aires, Argentina*

"With reds from Portugal, I like *sopa da pedra*, or stone soup: a broth with beans and a lot of Portuguese sausages. When it's very cold outside, the soup and wine make you very warm."

—*Diogo Campilho, winemaker, Quinta da Lagoalva, Ribatejo, Portugal*

"An exciting category just getting on its feet. Its dark, big fruits can pop like a California red. The finish on this wine can bring out all kinds of crazy flavors such as burnt honey and rose petal."

—Dana Farner, beverage director, CUT: Wolfgang Puck, Los Angeles, CA

"Portuguese reds are 'friend-makers.' Take one to a party and watch the bottle empty faster than the others on the table. Then kick yourself for not buying two bottles."

—Ross Outon, winner, first season of The Winemakers on PBS and beverage consultant, Austin, TX

REDS FROM PORTUGAL

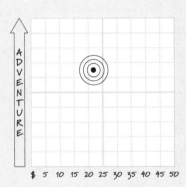

$ 5 10 15 20 25 30 35 40 45 50

 Audacious Alternative To
Cabernet Sauvignon, Syrah

 Enthusiasts Also Like
Classic Cabernet, reds from Washington State, Aglianico, Priorat, Cahors

Weight
Full

 Price
Medium ($15 to $50+)

 Cheat Sheet
Powered by indigenous grapes and the dedication of a new generation of winemakers, Portugal's dry reds are proving themselves robust, spicy, and able to convey a personality all their own.

 Label Logic
Douro and Dão are regions.

 Bravely Said

Bica de queijo	BEE-cah day KAY-jo
Cabrito	Ca-BREE-To
Dão	Dow
Douro	DOH-roo
Pisar	Pee-ZAHR
Touriga Nacional	Too-REE-gah Nah-see-oh-NAL

Mark's Picks

Casal de Tonda (Dão)	*Cah-SAHL day TON-da*
J. & F. Lurton (Douro)	
Poças Junior (Douro)	*POH-sahs ZHOO-nyor*
Quinta Cabriz (Dão)	*Keen-tah Kah-BHREEZ*
Quinta do Crasto (Douro)	*Keen-tah do Crash-toe*
Quinta do Portal (Douro)	*POUR-tow*
Quinta do Vallado (Douro)	*Vah-LAH-do*
Sogrape (Dão)	*So-GRAH-pee*

Poosh It!

The movement to make dry table wine of first rank is being led by a group of ambitious winemakers calling themselves the Douro Boys. Together, these men (and one woman) travel the world and evangelize on behalf of the Douro.

 CULINARY SWEET SPOT

Lightest   ▲   Heaviest

A Lovable Feast

Substantial meats, especially beef and lamb; stew; hard and blue-veined cheeses

Locally Lusty

Cabrito (roasted goat); roast suckling pig; *sopa da pedra* (hearty bean soup); cheeses such as the buttery *bica de queijo*

Spend the Night Together

Transform your place into a Portuguese wine center by serving a trifecta of Portuguese pours: Vinho Verde (Chapter 8) to start, a Duoro red with the main course, and Tawny Port (Chapter 43) or Madeira (Chapter 41) after dinner.

34 REDS FROM WASHINGTON STATE

Regally Robust

CONSIDER THE LAMB CHOP. This succulent wedge of flavor is fancy enough to be served in the finest restaurants, often in the form of the elegantly named "French cut." At the same time, it stirs the molecules of your inner barbarian, its robust taste and minerally edge never failing to deliver primal satisfaction. I can start with a knife and fork, but by the end of the meal I'm gnawing the bone for tasty bits like a crazed pinscher. And what other cut of meat is so beloved that it qualifies as a term of endearment? You might call your lover a "lamb chop," but probably not a "rib-eye."

Such is how I conceptualize the rich reds from Washington State. Derived mostly from Cabernet Sauvignon, Merlot, or, increasingly, Syrah grapes, these wines, at their best, manage to have major concentration and flavor while refraining from walloping you with overripe fruit and bitter tannins. Such elegance is in part due to the fact that much of Washington State's major growing areas are at about the same latitude as those of the Bordeaux region of France. This relatively cool climate yields wine of balanced ripeness and more refreshing acidity than equivalent wines from warmer regions.

As northerly as their grapes are situated, Washington wines are hardly a victim of the Pacific Northwest's infamous sogginess. Most of the state's vineyards are located in eastern Washington, where the Cascade Mountains run interference on the rain and the days are long and reliably sunny. This means that the reds often have plenty of the blackberry lushness that enthusiasts prize. Cabernet Sauvignon, in particular, is an unqualified success, a study in robust black fruit, telltale notes of cedar and mocha, and palatably restrained tannins. Even as it's become somewhat less popular as a stand-alone variety, Merlot is another forte of the Evergreen State, able to achieve more complexity and structure than is commonly seen in wine from this maligned grape (Chapter 28). Though not as common as the first two grapes, Syrah from Washington State is fast becoming a star of its own, capable of achieving some of the the peppery, olivey, smoky dynamic that makes France's Rhône wines (Chapter 26) so intriguing.

Hedonistic juice like this begs for similarly indulgent victuals. Our beloved lamb chops, of course, will light up your sensory dashboard, as will other robust meats, even better if they have grill marks or are scooped from a slow cooker. Earthier vegetables also take to these wines, particularly sweet Walla Walla onions, which are so good that they carry the title of state vegetable.

It's difficult not to find Washington State reds endearing. With its major regions—Columbia Valley, Yakima, and Walla Walla—emerging on international radar screens only in the 1990s, many of the wineries are still folksy, small-scale affairs, bastions of flannel-clad earnestness crafting big reds that can compete with the best of them. Leading lights include Leonetti, Quilceda, Cayuse, and K Vintners at the over-$50 high-end; L'Ecole No. 41, Januik, and Dunham Cellars in the midrange; and Hayman & Hill and Charles Smith below $20. Even the state's mass-market wineries inspire affection for offering consistent quality at remarkable levels of affordability and availability. Chateau Ste. Michelle and Columbia Crest, both owned by the same parent company, and Hogue Cellars, take the title for the United States's most prolific producers of dependably tasty wine under $20.

BRAVEHEARTS ON *Reds from Washington State*

"Eastern Washington and Walla Walla in particular is great because there's very diverse soil. It has great *terroir*. And it's far enough north so there are long hot days but cool nights. The grapes get a lot of vine time and develop into good ripe fruit.

"I was with Walla Walla winemaker Eric Dunham, and we brought a $70 Chardonnay to lunch at a taco truck and opened the wine with a little fishing knife and poured it into paper cups. I asked Eric, 'You don't mind pouring it in paper cups?' And he deadpanned: 'Well, it's already in glass.'" —*Drew Bledsoe, football great, New England Patriots*

"Eric Dunham is an extraordinary winemaker and Dunham's Lewis Vineyard Cabernet is one of his best. Tasting what Eric can do was a big part of the reason I asked him to collaborate with me on my Cabernet, Pursued by Bear.

"I stumbled onto Wineglass Cellar's Elerding Vineyard Cabernet when I was at the very beginning of my interest in wines from Washington State. This Cabernet made me sit up and take notice! David Lowe makes a superb example of what Washington State *terroir* is all about." —*Kyle MacLachlan, actor*

"Owen Roe Abbot's Table red wine needs more air time than most, but once it breathes, it's a taste you remember."

—*Matthew McConaughey, actor*

"L'Ecole No. 41's colorful label looks like it was made by a hippy lady who lives at the beach. But the wine is stupendous—very Bordeaux-like." —*Courtney Taylor-Taylor, lead singer and guitarist, The Dandy Warhols*

"I'm a huge fan of wines from Walla Walla—they make wines so powerful upfront but then are really clean. It gives you everything you need in a wine without being so heavy afterward that you want to go nap." —*Jason Priestley, actor*

"My daughter Annabel and her husband, Eduardo, recently introduced me to 'House Wine' from the Magnificent Wine Company. It's a warm and totally yummy blend of Cabernet Sauvignon, Merlot, Syrah, Sangiovese, Malbec, and Cabernet Franc from the Columbia Valley. I'm completely hooked on its flavor and very reasonable price. Fantastic with steak, lamb, pasta." —*Lynn Redgrave, the late actress*

"My real corruption with wine began with Steve Cropper, the guitarist for the Blues Brothers band. Friday nights we went over to his place for dinner. He had an extensive wine cellar, mainly Napa and Washington State reds—and he began to educate me on the deeper, richer, most beautiful reds."

—*Dan Aykroyd, actor*

DAN AYKROYD ON MOVIE CHARACTERS' PREFERENCES

- Elwood Blues (*The Blues Brothers*): "Stones Green Ginger wine is his beverage."

- Louis Winthorpe III (*Trading Places*): "Château Margaux 1990."

- Randolph and Mortimer Duke (*Trading Places*): "Mid-'90s Château Pétrus in jeroboams and magnums."

- The Ghostbuster guys (*Ghostbusters*): "Solidly into your bargain-priced Napa—$11.99 from Vaughn's supermarket."

- Dr. Peter Venkman (*Ghostbusters*): "If he's going on a date with a girl, he might spring for a nice mystery white—and ask the clerk to 'give me a nice white for a lady'—a Sauvignon Blanc or Chardonnay."

- Doctor Detroit (*Doctor Detroit*): "In pimp mode, he'd have a Boone's Farm peach wine; in his professorial mode, he'd be a Chardonnay man."

REDS FROM WASHINGTON STATE

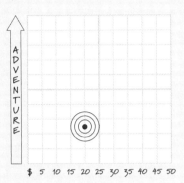

ADVENTURE

$ 5 10 15 20 25 30 35 40 45 50

 Audacious Alternative To
Cabernet Sauvignon, Merlot, Syrah (the overall categories); Zinfandel

 Enthusiasts Also Like
Classic Cabernet, (good) Merlot, bargain Bordeaux, Côtes du Rhône, Malbec, reds from Portugal, Petite Sirah

 Weight
Full

 Price
Low to Medium ($15 to $50+)

 Cheat Sheet
Powerful but balanced, Washington State reds are emerging wines of compelling richness, proportion, and value.

 Label Logic
Cabernet Sauvignon, Merlot, and Syrah are grapes.

Bravely Said

Syrah	Sih-RAH
Yakima	*YAH-kih-mah*

 Mark's Picks
Charles Smith Wines
Chateau Ste. Michelle
Columbia Crest
Dunham Cellars
Hayman & Hill
Januik   *JAH-nuck*
K Vintners
L'Ecole No. 41
Leonetti
Quilceda   *Kwill-see-da*
Waterbrook Winery
Woodward Canyon

 Poosh It!
Master sommelier Larry Stone told me he is a serious admirer of Washington State Syrahs, which he deems "ripe and luscious and complex"; among his favorites are Three Rivers, McCrea, Cayuse, and Columbia Lake Series.

 CULINARY SWEET SPOT

 Lightest ▲ Heaviest

 A Lovable Feast
Lamb chops and other heavier meats, including wild game; pepper and pepper sauces; grilled foods; stews; dry Jack and other hard cheeses; blue-veined cheeses

Locally Lusty
Walla Walla onions; local artisan cheese such as smoked Cheddar

SHOCK AND AWE

"Fellow daredevil Ryan Dunn and I had an eight-hour layover to Romania at London Heathrow Airport. It was my birthday and so we kept drinking wine until the flight. We wound up on the ground pouring condiments all over each other. Police with machine-guns walked us to the flight to make sure we left the country." —*Bam Margera, professional skateboarder, daredevil, and actor*

"Cook them potatoes in duck fat."
—*Ariane Daguin, owner and co-founder, D'Artagnan, on how to convert vegetarians to eating meat*

"I started in wine as a college student drinking Manischewitz at the 'Purple Jesus' parties—where the tongue turns purple the next morning and you're praying to Jesus that you never drink again." —*Dan Aykroyd, actor*

"When my friend director and actor John Huston, who had a terrific wine collection, died, I wrote his daughter Anjelica Huston and tried to buy his collection. A letter came back that said, 'Don't worry, we will drink the wines. Signed, Anjelica Huston and Jack Nicholson.'" —*Julio Iglesias, music legend*

"'I feel like I just bought a car in this S.O.B. today but I'm not driving out in it.'"
—*Christopher Ycaza, wine director and general manager, Galatoire's, New Orleans, LA, on what a regular said after he splurged on three bottles of the fabled Romanée-Conti*

"Bandmate Geddy Lee and I went to California's Turley Wine Cellars in late September of 1998 to spend a few days working the harvest. We pulled all of the leaves and spiders and all that stuff out of the bins, and so we were covered head-to-toe in grape juice. Later, Ged and I stopped at this restaurant for lunch. Our shirts and fingers were all purple—we were so proud! People were like, 'Yeah, you guys are locals, aren't you? We'll get you some service right away, sir.'"
—*Alex Lifeson, lead guitarist, Rush*

"My grandfather was a wine merchant, so I was exposed to good wines at the earliest possible age! I suppose I can blame my grandparents for getting me 'hooked.'"
—*Zac Posen, fashion designer*

"The former owner of my farm on Maui must have been a party animal back in the '70s. You go into the food cupboard and there's a hidden door that leads to a secret room from which there is no exit. I store wine in it now. God knows what used to go on in there, but you could imagine."
—*Mick Fleetwood, drummer and namesake, Fleetwood Mac*

"I had a secret door built for my wine cellar—it's in a medieval style, with dark wood walls, diamond-shaped bins, and stained glass lit from behind."
—*Courtney Taylor-Taylor, lead singer and guitarist, The Dandy Warhols*

"Occasionally when I don't have a corkscrew, I'll smash the top of a bottle. Do I worry about drinking glass? It's all part of the *terroir*."
—*Paul Grieco, wine director and co-owner, Hearth, New York*

"When I first met my wife Gwen [Stefani]'s big family, I brought six bottles of wine to dinner. Now I'm always the one who provides the wine. It's quite Pavlovian—my arrival signals good wine."
—*Gavin Rossdale, solo artist and former vocalist and guitarist, Bush*

"A year before I married, I carried home from Paris the most expensive bottle I'd ever bought: a Musigny 1961 from Comte de Vogüê. But what occasion would be noble enough to drink it? Three months after my wedding, my wife was in the kitchen, making my favorite dish for my birthday—*brandade de moreau*, garlicky ragout of salt cod and potato. She was making it in an old Provençal baking dish of mine. Suddenly, there was a crash from the kitchen. I raced in and there was the meal, along with the dish, scattered over the kitchen floor. Susan was in tears. 'This calls for the best bottle in the house,' I said. And so we drank the Musigny '61 with cheese, bread, and salad. It couldn't have been a better occasion."

—*Peter Hellman, wine writer and former wine columnist,* The New York Sun

"The specialized knowledge required in wine is irresistible to the nerd—and that is me."

—*David Chan, concertmaster and violinist, Metropolitan Opera Orchestra, New York, NY*

"I was in D.C. with about ten food and wine media people, at a highly regarded Italian restaurant that is no longer with us. We asked the very imperious sommelier for a light red. He responded by trying to sell us an enormous Barolo in the $300 range. He was haughty, arrogant, and dismissive—it was awesome. I loved this experience because it defined exactly what was wrong with wine service in the U.S. back in the bad old days of the '50s and '60s. Had I not known better, I might very well have felt the sense of humiliation, intimidation, and extortion that I think so many Americans may *still* believe they're going to receive. It's just the kind of barrier that the wine business has been laboring for years to move beyond."

—*Ted Allen, food writer and host, Food Network's* Chopped

"Tori Amos and I were writing a song together in the late 1980s. At dinner, she was with her boyfriend and I was with a girlfriend. We drank an amazing amount of wine—Tori was fine but I think her boyfriend collapsed."

—*Al Stewart, on schooling singer-songwriter Tori Amos in wine*

"We had just wrapped *A Guide to Recognizing Your Saints* produced by Trudie Styler, and we were celebrating with Trudie and her husband, who is, of course, Sting. Sting, who is really knowledgeable on wine, orders a Super Tuscan, a rich red from Italy—it was great food and wine and laughter."

—*Chazz Palminteri, actor and writer,* A Bronx Tale

"After Hurricane Katrina, we invited guests to go up to the wine room and pay what they thought was fair for the wine remaining in Restaurant August. No one really abused this opportunity. And if the wine wasn't up to snuff, you could send it back and we'd drink it in the kitchen."

—*John Besh, chef and restaurateur, Restaurant August, New Orleans, LA*

"When I was a banquet captain at the Rainbow Room, someone held a 1985-vintage vertical Champagne tasting of all *tete de cuvées* [elite Champagnes]. There were a lot of bubbles left over and the other server and I cleaned up, punched out, and turned off the lights—we sat under the table and polished off all the bottles!"

—*Gillian Ballance, former wine director, PlumpJack Group, San Francisco, CA*

"I was with two Washington State shellfish farmers at one A.M.—lowest tide—on the mudflats of Totten Inlet in south Puget Sound, Washington. We each wore a headlamp and carried an oyster knife and a real wineglass. We had a bottle of Willamette Valley Vineyards Pinot Gris and were there until four A.M., grabbing Olympias, Pacifics, and Totten Inlet Virginicas—whatever our headlamps fell on—and shucking them on the spot. Horse clams kept squirting us and sea lions made freaky snorting sounds just off-shore."

—*Rowan Jacobsen, author of* A Geography of Oysters

"Although I don't drink so much white wine, I do have a particular penchant for Corton-Charlemagne [white Burgundy]. It seems to have a desirable effect every time I'm lucky enough to encounter a bottle, so on tour we often have a Latour detour."

—*Nick Rhodes, keyboardist, Duran Duran*

BUBBLY

BUBBLY: ADVENTURE & PRICE AT A GLANCE

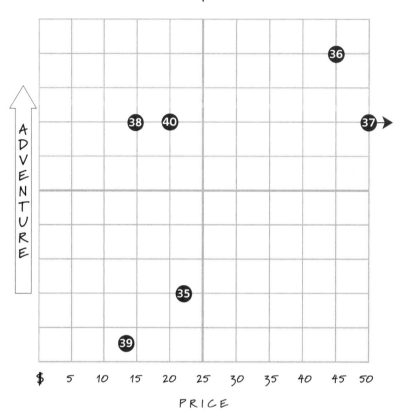

35. American Sparkling Wine
36. Grower Champagne
37. Rosé Champagne
38. Lambrusco
39. Prosecco
40. Sparkling Shiraz

35 AMERICAN SPARKLING WINE

Federal Fizz

ONE OF THE MOST fulfilling ways of prefacing your next vacation is to execute a PHBR. It works like this: while rolling to your hotel in your rental car, keep your eyes peeled for any establishment that sells wine. Once you find one, your job is to buy a bottle of bubbly for every day of your holiday. Stocking up like this is easier than you think: the bellman will retrieve the bottles with your suitcases (and secretly wonder when the party is), and your room's mini-fridge, once relieved of its tonic and Toblerone, will fit at least a few bottles for the coming consumption. That's all there is to the Pre-Hotel Bubbly Run: my foolproof way of circumventing the pecuniary injustice of alcohol markups in hotels.

When I conduct a PHBR, my wine of choice is American sparkling wine—not only because it tends to be available everywhere in the United States—even at the lonely, twenty-four-hour, serial-killer-attracting Sunset Strip bodegas I resorted to on a recent trip to Los Angeles—but because you'd be hard-pressed to find better bubbles at lower cost.

Because "American sparkling wine" is a mouthful, I nickname it "Federal Fizz," though that moniker is admittedly not as commanding as that of "Champagne," the eponymous region of northeastern France. Champagne, of course, has earned its gilded reputation, as its chalky soil, mercurial weather, and centuries-old winemaking techniques can deliver a combination of nuanced flavor and creamy pinpoint bubbles that is unrivaled. Even so, American bubbly is reliably respectable, and often downright delicious. Derived from grapes that get more sun than their French counterparts, it is generally more evocative of ripe fruit—hints of apple, lemon, or even passion fruit. Best of all, it is simple enough to be enjoyed informally—on the beach, before dinner, or in a midnight Jacuzzi.

Though there are excellent special-occasion cuvées topping $40—notably, Schramsberg's "J. Schram" and J Vineyard's "Vintage Brut"—most hover between $15 and $30. So with domestic sparklers you'll pay half the price of basic-level Champagne, even though many are made in the same labor-intensive, *méthode champenoise* process, where bubbles are induced in each bottle instead of in one big tank. But because you're not paying for Champagne's mystique or its vast marketing expenditures, the savings is significant.

American bubbly, like all sparkling wine, is famously friendly with food. Dry versions—whether "brut" (totally dry) or "extra dry" (a tinge of sweetness)—can handle almost anything your taste buds desire, with the exception of the heaviest of meats and the sweetest of desserts. If you're ever stumped about what to serve, simply visualize an eggroll with hot sauce, as this appetizer symbolizes so many of bubbly's natural affinities: all that is salty, fried, spicy, and eggy. But don't hesitate to serve American sparklers *throughout* a meal, too; refreshing and versatile, they can handle the job with the kind of alacrity for which Americans are famous.

BRAVEHEARTS ON *American Sparkling Wine*

"If you go to a wine store with twenty dollars, you're best off with bubbly, whether it's American sparkling wine, Cava, or Prosecco."
—*Ming Tsai, chef and restaurateur, Blue Ginger, Boston, MA*

"Some American sparklers try very hard to emulate Champagne and do a great job with their toasty, yeasty notes. They are delicious with roasted chicken and garlic. My favorites include Tobin James 'Dreamweaver,' Gruet Blanc de Noirs, and Iron Horse 'Wedding Cuvée.'" —*Inez Ribustello, sommelier and co-owner, On the Square, Tarboro, NC*

"American sparkling wines are some of the finest in the world. The biggest way these wines differ from their French counterparts is their lower level of minerality. Oysters and other shellfish are classic with it, but there really is nothing better than good potato chips, too."

—Anjoleena Griffin-Holst, wine director, Borgata Hotel Casino & Spa, Atlantic City, NJ

"For those who aren't crazy about Champagne, here's a trick—put a cube of ice in your glass. The fizz diminishes and you can taste what's behind the bubbles."

—Gavin Rossdale, solo artist and former vocalist and guitarist, Bush

"The Italians have an expression: *Bollicini prima, durante e dopo la cena* (Bubbles before, during, and after a meal)."

—Liz Willette, owner and importer, Willette Wines, New York, NY

AMERICAN SPARKLING WINE

ADVENTURE

$ 5 10 15 20 25 30 35 40 45 50

Weight
Medium

Price
Low to Medium ($15 to $30)

Cheat Sheet
Often obscured by the kingly shadow of Champagne, American sparkling wine is a more affordable, fruit-forward alternative to French bubbles.

↔ **Audacious Alternative To**
Champagne, Chardonnay

✳ **Enthusiasts Also Like**
Prosecco, grower Champagne, low/no oak Chardonnay, big wine

Bravely Said
champenoise   *shahn-puhn-wahz*

Mark's Picks

Argyle (Oregon)
Domaine Carneros
   (California)
Domaine Chandon
   (California)
Domaine Ste. Michelle
   (Washington State)
Gruet (New Mexico)   *Grew-aye*
Iron Horse (California)
J Vineyards (California)
Mumm Napa (California)
Piper Sonoma
   (California)
Roederer Estate   *ROH-duh-rer*
   (California)
Schramsberg (California)

Poosh It!

From the improbable locale of New Mexico comes Gruet, a dependably delicious, $15 bubbly whose French-inspired label makes it a winning gift.

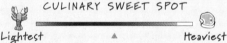

CULINARY SWEET SPOT

Lightest   Heaviest

A Lovable Feast

As an aperitif or with a broad range of foods including tortilla chips, popcorn, parmesan bread sticks, and other salty nibbles; seafood and lighter meats; fried chicken, calamari, egg rolls, and other fried foods; mayonnaise-based dishes and sauces; tempura, sushi, miso soup, and other Japanese fare; moderately spicy creations; most cheeses, including fresh, acidic types like goat and feta and gooey varieties like Brie and Camembert.

Locally Lusty

American celebrations such as Thanksgiving, Independence Day, and Super Bowl Sunday; brunch foods, especially eggy creations

Spend the Night Together

Do a taste-off between American sparkling wine and equivalent bottles of Champagne. Compare the level of fruit and yeasty, baked-bread aromas in the two.

Give your bubbly an extra kick by adding a bit of cognac, creating the cocktail called the "French 75," named after the powerful French 75mm Howitzer tank gun of World War I. The building blocks of a French 75 also make for a memorable wedding gift: send the couple a bottle of bubbly, a bottle of cognac, and two fluted glasses.

36 GROWER CHAMPAGNE

Farmer Fizz, Brewed by the Boss

I KNEW HE was The Boss. Pewter-gray coat. Haughty, wide-set Gallic eyes. Patrolled the Champagne estate like he owned the place. Resonant, guttural meow.

Meow? Okay, so it was a cat—namely, Lisou, the resident feline of Champagne Ledru, a small grower-producer in the esteemed Champagne village of Ambonnay. Lisou the Cat, for me, represents the honest, homespun allure of grower Champagne. Unlike the big-name, or *grand marque*, houses that garner all of the attention, grower Champagne estates are small, indie producers overseen not by a detached board of directors but by mom and pop, or, occasionally, mom and cat. At Champagne Ledru, you encounter not the slick tasting rooms and gleaming stainless-steel monstrosities of corporate Champagne houses, but Bea-Arthurian *vigneronne* Marie-Noëlle Ledru herself tending to a room of primitive vats and rustic, Rube Goldbergian vinification contraptions.

Unlike the big houses, which source their grapes from dozens of outside growers, artisanal producers like Ledru grow their own grapes on their own land. This is why such so-called "farmer fizz" is said to manifest a sense of *terroir*, or unique personality, as it reflects not a collage of different vineyard sites but the quirky subtleties of just one or a few individual patches of the Champagne region. Grower Champagne, then, can be more distinctive than its big-batch counterparts, which tend to surprise the palate less often, however well made they are. With many bottles priced in the $35 to $50 range, that frisson often comes at a discount relative to the prices of comparable bottles of big-house Champagne, as your dollars don't go to subsidizing

Gucci-grade branding campaigns, though they *may* help purchase sacks of Le Meow Mix.

While grower Champagne remains more of a rarity, its influence on critics and retail presence has grown considerably in the last decade. A favorite of sommeliers, it almost always occupies at least a few places on wine lists of restaurants favored by foodies. Don't fixate on finding a particular name, as I've found that the quality is reasonably reliable across different producers, though disappointments do happen. That said, if you encounter bottles of Egly-Ouriet or Jacques Selosse and your balance sheet can weather their higher tariffs, you should pounce immediately. Quality-obsessed importer Terry Theise's name on the back label is also a good marker.

Grower Champagne makes for an outstanding gift, especially if the recipient is a collector who thinks he's seen it all—or a future connoisseur newly arrived into the world. Inspired by Champagne legend Rémi Krug, who once told me that all Krugs "receive a few drops of Champagne after birth and before mother's milk," and by grower-producer Benoît Tarlant, who also administered what he calls a "Champagne baptism" to his two children, I slid my friends Samer and Alison bottles of Tarlant "Cuvée Louis" Brut Prestige for the two times Alison delivered. I'm pleased to report that within seconds of the stork's arrival, both Steve and Ted had their lips moistened with this elixir, priming them for a lifetime of stylish imbibing.

BRAVEHEARTS ON *Grower Champagne*

"Growers are so proud of their vineyards. They want you to taste the minerality, the earthiness, of their wine, just as any other small producer would. The growers celebrate vintage differences and don't need their wine to be a cookie-cutter luxury product."

—Liz Willette, owner and importer, Willette Wines, New York, NY

"My French grandmother passed this tip down to me osmotically: you should always have a 'just-in-case' bottle of Champagne on hand waiting around. In case of joy, you can pull it out."

—Bill Nye, PBS's "Science Guy"

"Grower Champagnes have a ton of character and uniqueness, and are some of the best examples of Champagne *terroir*. Though not cheap, they represent huge values over the big names."

—Joe Campanale, beverage director and co-owner, dell'anima, New York, NY

"Bubbles are inherently celebratory—they are a mood elevator and a spirit lifter. I enjoy them with everything from shellfish to meat."

—Brian Duncan, owner and wine director BIN 36, Chicago, IL

"I love Champagne, in fact I love anything carbonated, though not soda. We do a lot of carbonation in the restaurant. I think Champagne pairs really well with food, and not necessarily just at the start or end of a meal, though I do always prefer it with dessert over a dessert wine. The vast spectrum of sweet to dry Champagnes allows you to place it anywhere on a tasting menu."

—Wylie Dufresne, chef and owner, wd-50, New York, NY

"I usually recommend Champagne with oysters, because it makes everybody happy. And the bubbles are very good at scouring the palate. (Same reason beer works.) I go for a crisp, appley *blanc de blancs*—lighter style—but recently had Serveaux's Blanc de Noirs, which had a whole different profile—100% Pinot Meunier—and was the best oyster Champagne I've had."

—Rowan Jacobsen, author of A Geography of Oysters

"Scholium Project is animated by a similar spirit as that of Champagne growers. We both strive for wine of complexity and difference. I turn to Grower Champagne for inspiration and pleasure.

"We celebrate bottling our wine with Egly Ouriet Brut 'Les Vignes de Vrigny,' an unusual Champagne made entirely from Pinot Meunier. I also love Pierre Peters, Vilmart, and the exciting and strange Champagne from Jacques Selosse."

—Abe Schoener, founder and winemaker, Scholium Project, Suisun Valley, CA

SCHOLIUM PROJECT: SEEKING SINGULARITY

Few wineries embrace this book's spirit of drinking bravely as dramatically as Scholium (Skoh-lee-um) Project, a boutique operation thirty miles east of Napa in California's Suisun Valley. It's the brainchild of Abe Schoener, a philosophy-professor-turned-vintner whose futuristic glasses and impassioned manner give him the appearance of a Devo dude with a doctorate.

During a recent visit, Schoener spent a good two hours darting from barrel to barrel, ladling out samples of different wines with the zeal of a mad scientist. One could say that is exactly what he is, with the fermentation room his lab and wine barrels his test tubes, on a mission to craft wines with individual personality without worrying too much about their commercial appeal.

"Rather than erase the differences in wine, we try to multiply them," Schoener explained. "Making interesting wine is paramount."

Schoener achieves this complexity by way of relentless experimentation. He showed us wine he stores in stainless steel containers and contrasted it with the same juice kept in oak barrels. He let us taste the same wine stored in barrels of varying wood types, ages, and fill levels. He then had us taste white wine made like red wine with extended contact with grape skins. Got mold? Some of Schoener's barrels do, to impart what he calls a "complex micro-biology" to the wine. A portion of his grape harvest is crushed by machine, but much of it is stomped by him and his friends, often jubilantly, in giant, double-sized barrels called puncheons.

The upshot is wine that is often delicious, sometimes disconcerting, but rarely a snore. The fanciful names he gives them mirror their unconventional flavors and speak to his time in the academy; among them are Riquewihr (Gewürztraminer), the Gardens of Babylon (Petite Sirah), and the Prince in His Caves (Sauvignon Blanc).

It is no surprise that wines from Scholium Project have become something of a cult favorite among in-the-know sommeliers and other wine hipsters. Given the winery's small production runs, your best bet for tracking down bottles is a resourceful merchant or the Internet. Bottles are also finding their way into select restaurants, especially those with wine programs unafraid to embrace the singular.

GROWER CHAMPAGNE

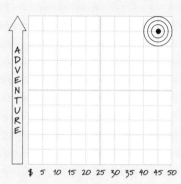

ADVENTURE

$ 5 10 15 20 25 30 35 40 45 50

 Audacious Alternative To

Champagne (big name)

 Enthusiasts Also Like

Rosé Champagne, American sparkling wine, old wine, low/no oak Chardonnay

 Weight

Medium

 Price

Medium to Expensive ($35 to $60+)

 Cheat Sheet

Coming from small, private owner-producers who grow their own grapes, grower Champagnes are prized for their insider status and individuality.

Label Logic

Champagne is a region in northeastern France and gives its name to bubbly made from the Chardonnay, Pinot Noir, and/or the little-known Pinot Meunier grape.

 Bravely Said

Ambonnay	*Om-bon-nay*
Champagne	*Sham-PAIN*
Gougère	*Goo-zhayr*
Pinot Meunier	*Pee-no Moon-yay*
Récoltant-Manipulant	*Ray-col-than Man-ee-pew-lahn*
Terroir	*Te-wahr*
Vigeronne	*Vee-nyuh-rhone*

 Mark's Picks

Egly-Ouriet	*Egg-lee Oo-ree-ay*
Guy Larmandier	*Lahr-mahn-dyay*
Jacques Selosse	*Suh-los*
Larmandier-Bernier	*Behr-nyay*
Paul Bara	
Pierre Gimonnet	*Jhee-mow-neh*
Pierre Peters	*Peh-TEHR*
René Geoffroy	*Jho-frwah*
Tarlant	*Tahr-lohn*
Vilmart	*Veel-mahr*

 Poosh It!

To confirm that a bottle is indeed a grower Champagne, look for the initials RM (short for *Récoltant-Manipulant*, or Harvester-Handler) introducing the tiny license number on the edge of a Champagne label; larger, *grand marque* producers will instead have an NM, meaning *Négociant-Manipulant* (Merchant-Handler).

 CULINARY SWEET SPOT

Lightest ▲ Heaviest

A Lovable Feast

As an aperitif or with oysters; sushi; caviar; smoked-salmon triangles and other hors d'oeuvres; seafood of all kinds, especially fresh trout, fillet of sole, and turbot; béarnaise, hollandaise, and other rich sauces; risotto, lobster bisque, and other creamy concoctions; eggy creations such as omelets, frittatas, and eggs Benedict; foie gras; truffles; dishes with mushrooms; most cheeses except stink bombs like Limburger and Roquefort.

 ### Locally Lusty

Gougères (crispy cheese balls); *Langres* (soft cow's milk cheese); *Maroilles* (semi-hard cow's milk cheese); *andouillettes* (pungent tripe sausages); white asparagus

 ### Spend the Night Together

Try drinking bubbly in a regular wineglass instead of a flute; though the latter is usually used to maximize the carbonation, several insiders—including Dom Pérignon's chief winemaker Richard Geoffrey—prefer a standard wineglass because its wider bowl makes it easier to nose the wine and, as Geoffrey told me, "It allows your mouth to touch and caress the Champagne better."

37 ROSÉ CHAMPAGNE

Lustworthy in Pink

A PRACTICE SAID to have originated with Napoleon's cavalrymen, *sabrer la bouteillé* involves running a knife up the neck of a Champagne bottle in order to decapitate its top. Because it combines a greatest-hits of don't-try-this-at-home features—a sharp knife, contents under extreme pressure, glass breakage, and a flying projectile—I couldn't resist trying it at home. My sabering style, however, was anything but courageous, as I donned yellow safety glasses, orange workman gloves, and a facial expression approximating Edvard Munch's *The Scream*.

The experiment was somehow a success, as the bottle split cleanly at the neck and a bit of bubbly frothed up in a celebratory geyser. My sparkler of choice was rosé Champagne, because if any libation deserves a death-defying ritual, it is this regal pick, despite the tendency of casual drinkers to misperceive pink bubbles as the province of hot-sheet motels and socialite dog purses. Insiders, however, know better, coveting rosé Champagne for its vibrant color (ranging from salmon to onionskin to Rizzo-pink), red-berry fruit, and luxurious creaminess.

Although fine examples of rosé bubbly are found throughout the world—including blushing versions of Prosecco, cava, and American sparkling wine—it reaches its apotheosis in the chalky soils of France's Champagne region. Rosé Champagne is usually made by blending a bit of red wine with a base of white before the secondary fermentation, though some producers use the *saignée* method common in the production of non-bubbly rosé wine (Chapter 16). Either way, this extra step, as well as the additional time it needs in the barrel and its small production runs, means that rosé Champagne will be more expensive than its non-pink counterpart, with prices starting at $45 and vaulting skyward from there.

Those extra greenbacks are worth it when it brings the rapturous highs that fine versions can deliver, like the unforgettably elegant Taittinger Comtes de Champagne Rosé I broke out for a celebration last year. A more economical pick is from the medium-sized house Billecart-Salmon, whose rosé is so coveted by wine pros that I'd suspect the existence of some sort of Billecart-Salmon-Rosé-Lovers Cartel if I didn't also lust for it. Find a magnum of it (Chapter 44) or another rosé Champagne and you'll feel as if you've donned epaulettes and an imperial sash. Grower Champagne producers (Chapter 36) are also a relatively affordable route to the pink sparkle.

Because of the influence of red grapes, rosé Champagne tends to be richer than its non-pink equivalent and thus ratchets the bubbly's famous food friendliness up to new heights. Not only does it shine in the presence of lighter foods—particularly pink picks like smoked salmon, raw tuna, and ham—but it can handle heartier fare like veal, heavy pasta, and lamb. Not long ago I was at a summer cookout where a bon vivant broke out a bottle of Dom Pérignon rosé to go with a platter of baby back ribs, and it was one of those high-low combinations, like denim and diamonds or a Warhol soup can, that shouldn't work but does so memorably.

BRAVEHEARTS ON *Rosé Champagne*

"Forget about your preconceptions, close your eyes, think bubbles, red berries, complexity and long, pleasant aftertaste as you taste one of the great treats of the last three centuries. Early in my career, I had dinner with my husband at Les Crayères, the top restaurant and hotel in Champagne, and had squab with rosé at the sommelier's recommendation. Having grown up drinking red Burgundy with my dad's pigeons, this was a new experience which opened doors to my love for rosé Champagne."

—*Mireille Guiliano, author,* French Women Don't Get Fat *and former CEO, Clicquot, Inc.*

"I love rosé Champagne because it's sexy and special and is often more complex than standard Champagne."

—David Burke, chef and restaurateur, David Burke Townhouse, New York, NY

"My wife and I find ourselves drinking Billecart-Salmon rosé more than any other kind of Champagne. The fine bubbles have a texture that you can almost chew. It works with almost any food—it's light enough for caviar before a meal but rich enough for an entree."

—John Besh, chef and restaurateur, Restaurant August, New Orleans, LA

"Dom Pérignon is a study in precision, flavor, and finesse, and the most profound example of this is their rosé. It offers real delicacy, complexity, and sex appeal all at the same time."

—Gordon Ramsay, restaurateur and television chef, London, England

"There's nothing frivolous about how we make rosé Champagne. It is the tension of Pinot Noir and Chardonnay together—very Pinot Noir in that the fruit is not sweet, yet it's very creamy and not tannic at all from the influence of Chardonnay grapes. There's an intriguing, contradictory quality to it—and contradiction is always an interesting state of attention.

"There's debate about this among professionals in Champagne about whether one should swirl before tasting. Personally, I do swirl. I'm cautious enough not to lose all of the carbonation. But I need to swirl to enhance the aromas in the Champagne."

—Richard Geoffrey, chief winemaker, Dom Pérignon, Champagne, France

"I love, love, love rosé Champagne. I hate that it's become popular because I like to think I have minority tastes. On the other hand, if that means there will be more of it around, I'm happy to share."

—Lettie Teague, wine columnist, The Wall Street Journal, and former executive wine editor, Food & Wine magazine

"I drink more Champagne than any other wine type. I start every party with it, and end every party with it."

—Abe Schoener, founder and winemaker, Scholium Project, Suisun Valley, CA

"Once at the Superbowl, I sabered open a bottle of Dom Pérignon with only a butter knife—and my friends were amazed. My wife came by and asked, 'What are you doing?' And I told her: 'I'm kicking off the Superbowl, baby!'"

—Guy Fieri, chef and television host

ROSÉ CHAMPAGNE

ADVENTURE

$ 5 10 15 20 25 30 35 40 45 50

⟷ Audacious Alternative To
Champagne (non-pink)

✳ Enthusiasts Also Like
Rosé, grower Champagne, big wine, old wine

⚖ Weight
Medium

💲 Price
Expensive ($45 to $200+)

☑ Cheat Sheet
Underestimated because of its hue, rosé Champagne remains one of winedom's treasures, showing dry, red-berry notes, spice, and an affinity for food and special occasions.

💡 Label Logic
Champagne is a region in eastern France. The wine is made from Chardonnay, Pinot Noir, and/or Pinot Meunier grapes.

🗨 Bravely Said

Biscuits rosé de Reims	*Bee-Skwee ro-zay duh Rahnz*
oeil de perdrix	*oid-pair-DREE*
rosé Champagne	*ro-zay Sham-pain*
Sabrer la Bouteille	*Sah-bray lah Boo-tay*

🍷 Mark's Picks

Alfred Gratien	*Grah-tyahn*
Billecart-Salmon	*Bee-kahr Sahl-mohn*
Delamotte	*Duh-lah-mote*
Dom Pérignon	*Dom Pay-ree-NYON*
Gosset	*Go-seh*
Krug	*Krewg*
Louis Roederer	*Loo-wee Roe-duh-rehr*
Perrier-Jouët	*PEH-hryay Zhew-EHT*
Pol Roger	*Pawl roe-ZHAY*
Taittinger	*Tay-tahn-ZHAY*
Tarlant	*Tahr-lohn*
Veuve Clicquot	*Vuhv-klee-KOE*
Vilmart	*Veel-mahr*

Poosh It!

With rosé Champagne, look not for the "eye of the tiger" but for the "eye of the partridge," or *oeil de perdrix*, a tasting term that refers to the pale, salmony tint you sometimes see in rosé Champagne.

 CULINARY SWEET SPOT

Lightest ▲ Heaviest

 A Lovable Feast

As an aperitif; with shrimp and other shellfish; raw tuna; smoked salmon; caviar; pasta dishes of all kinds; sausages, ham, and other pink meats; spareribs; mildly spicy fare; fresh, acidic cheese like feta and goat; Brie, Camembert, and other soft cheeses; for Valentine's Day, Mother's Day, anniversaries, or birthdays

 Locally Lusty

Pickled shoulder of ham; squab; steak tartare; mustard; potatoes dauphinoise (thinly sliced with cheese and cream); *biscuits roses de Reims*

 Spend the Night Together

Casanova will have nothing on you if you celebrate Valentine's Day with flower petals and a bottle of Perrier-Jouët "Fleur de Champagne" rosé, whose bottle is ornamented with an arabesque design of pink anemones.

Use the Internet to track down *biscuits roses de Reims*—crunchy, powdery, cookies designed for dipping into Champagne during the dessert course.

38 LAMBRUSCO

Violet Elixir, Integrity Intact

"I BET FEW people pick this," I said to the bartender after I ordered a glass of Lambrusco to drink with a pulled pork sandwich at New York's Gramercy Tavern.

"Yes, true," she said. "But once one person orders it, everyone else wants it."

Such is the plight of Lambrusco. Like pigs-in-blankets, Dobermans, and my native New Jersey, it has an enduring image problem, which, in its case, is born of those incessant "Riunite on Ice" ads of the 1970s, wedged as they were between segments of *The Mary Tyler Moore Show*, forever freezing its status as something no better than a candied wine cooler and no hipper than Ron Burgundy's mustache. While this reputation is well deserved for sweet, mass-market confections like Riunite, it doesn't do justice to the dry, artisanal Lambruscos increasingly winning over the libationally audacious.

But even when you locate quality Lambrusco, it often takes a few times before you can catch its drift, because it is a red *with fizz*, and, like revenge, should be served cold. Eventually, however, it becomes difficult to resist its violet foam and ripe, refreshing taste. Imagine treating your mouth to a fistful of chilled black cherries. Now picture the juice from those cherries tickling your palate with brisk acidity and a light sparkle. This is the essence of good Lambrusco, whose irrepressible fruitiness is often kept honest by a tilled-soil earthiness and a tongue-coating sensation of dryness.

Though commercial Lambrusco abounds, finding the good stuff takes some resourcefulness. Intrepid eateries, especially those with an appreciation for Lambrusco's native Emilia-Romagna region of Italy, are starting to offer it. When I recently had a bottle at New York's Otto Enoteca, it was one of the least expensive options on the list and the perfect sidecar with the pizza *quattro formaggi*. With quantities in short supply on these shores, don't stress about finding a specific producer, as a good merchant will be able to steer you to a well-made bottle or track one down. That said, Cantine Ceci's "La Luna" is a nifty pick, as not only does it bring the ruckus at only about $16—about average for small-production Lambrusco—but it makes an impression with a muzzle of string covering its cork.

Lambrusco's sprightly charm and dry taste make it so versatile that the famously food-passionate locals of Modena depend on it like Linus cleaves to his blanket. While they would tell you that it goes with everything (and justifiably so), it has superpowers of irrigation with the rich and oily, including the locally prized prosciutto di Parma and other *salumi*, cheeses like homespun Parmigano-Reggiano (extra points if it is drizzled with traditional balsamic vinegar from Modena), any pasta in a cream or *Bolognese* sauce, and—emphatically—pizza. You can even cross cultures and go Indian or Chinese, as Lambrusco's low alcohol and fruity ebullience make peace with spicy food. My favorite use for Lambrusco, however, is *after* dinner, on a sultry summer night, preferably with bowls of chilled strawberries or cherries—the perfect setting for you and yours to exult in the seductively purple powers of this uncomplicated elixir.

BRAVEHEARTS ON *Lambrusco*

"*Real* Lambrusco is young, fresh, sometimes earthy, and almost never sweet. The difference between sweet, commercial Lambrusco and the real kind is like the difference between a Budweiser and a microbrew. The Budweiser goes down, but it's crap."

—*William Mattiello, chef and owner, Via Emilia, New York, NY*

"Lambruscos have been misrepresented by industrial versions that have the soda pop flavor they think Americans want, but real, dry

Lambrusco goes so well with the fatty foods of the region—the acidity and the bubbles *really* cleanse the palate."

—*Lidia Bastianich, chef and and host of PBS's* Lidia's Italy

"A fantastic food wine, Lambrusco has deep aromas of cherries, stones, spice, and a savory note that somehow just says 'Italy.' These are the ones to reach for the next time you indulge in a rich lasagna or Bolognese-sauced pasta."

—*Mollie Battenhouse, sommelier and wine director, Maslow 6, New York, NY*

"Lambrusco often shows an *amaro*—slightly bitter—character that Italians like in their wine. It is wine without residual sugar, so that savory, *amaro* character often comes to the fore."

—*Lou Amdur, owner, Lou's Wine Bar, Los Angeles, CA*

"I love Lambrusco because it's not an obvious choice. It's great to drink something purple, frothy, refreshing, but not sweet. I *always* feel like drinking it at the beginning of an evening—even before white wine.

"I'm so into Lambrusco that Scholium Project is even making its own barrel of Lambrusco [the barrel is called "Lamby" at the winery]."

—*Abe Schoener, founder and winemaker, Scholium Project, Suisun Valley, CA*

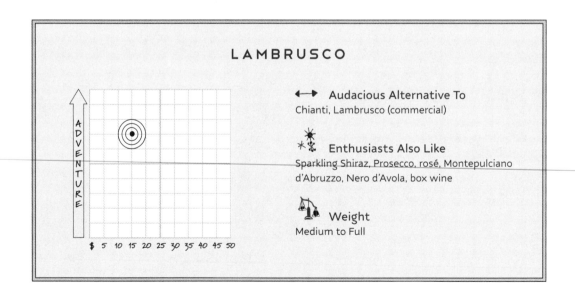

LAMBRUSCO

←→ **Audacious Alternative To**
Chianti, Lambrusco (commercial)

Enthusiasts Also Like
Sparkling Shiraz, Prosecco, rosé, Montepulciano d'Abruzzo, Nero d'Avola, box wine

Weight
Medium to Full

ADVENTURE

$ 5 10 15 20 25 30 35 40 45 50

Price
Low ($10 to $20)

Cheat Sheet
Lambrusco redeems itself with dry, small-batch versions whose foamy and fruity personality pairs perfectly with cured meats, pizza, and other casual fare.

Label Logic
Lambrusco is a grape.

Bravely Said
Emilia-Romagna	Ay-MEE-lee-ya Roh-MAN-ya
Lambrusco	Lahm-BRUCE-coe
Modena	MOD-en-ah
Taleggio	Tah-LAY-jo

Mark's Picks
Ariola
Ca' de' Medici
Cantine Ceci — *CHAY-chee*
Lini "Corrigia" — *LEE-nee Core-EE-jya*
Manicardi
Saetti — *Sah-EH-tee*
Villa di Carlo
Vittorio Graziano — *Vee-TOH-ryo Grahts-yah-noh*

Poosh It!
According to Lambrusco expert and importer William Mattiello, producer Vittorio Graziano gives strict instructions to buck tradition and drink his Lambrusco at room temperature to appreciate its special complexity. "You can drink it any way you want," Graziano is reportedly fond of saying. "Just don't drink it cold."

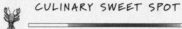

CULINARY SWEET SPOT

Lightest ▲ Heaviest

A Lovable Feast
Vastly versatile as an aperitif, with brunch, or with pork chops, whole-roasted pig, and other porcine preparations; hamburgers, hot dogs, fried chicken, and other cookout food; red fruit such as strawberries and cherries; richly-flavored leftovers

Locally Lusty
Prosciutto di Parma (preferably thinly sliced), mortadella, and other *salumi*; Parmigano-Reggiano (preferably in chunks), Taleggio, Ricotta most other cheeses; balsamic vinegar; pizza of all kinds; lasagna, tortellini in cream sauce, and other rich pastas; tomato bruschetta

Spend the Night Together
Given Lambrusco's stunning affinity with Italian meats like mortadella and cheese such as Parmigiano-Reggiano, host an antipasto party with a selection of Lambruscos and a selection of savory treats. Remember to serve a bowl of aged balsamic vinegar for dipping Parmigiano.

Host a "Vino Non Grata" night that features Lambrusco as well as other maligned types such as Soave, Chianti, Merlot, and sherry—all perfectly delicious when made by producers committed to quality.

39 PROSECCO

Italian Agent of Sprezzatura

OF ALL THE Brave New Pours I describe in this book, the one which requires the least amount of bravery on the part of a drinker is Prosecco. This is the easy Italian Prince, the gently-priced miracle worker that is so instantly likable and uplifting that I nickname it *Prozac*-co.

When I pour it at my parties, I often tell my guests that it is "Italian Champagne," even though only bubbly from France's Champagne region is supposed to officially carry that label. No matter: the term gets the point across that this is an agent of European sprightliness and charm. I like to think of Prosecco as the liquid embodiment of the Italian concept of *sprezzatura*: stylishly carefree and primed for fun.

And why shouldn't it be? It hails from an area northwest of the dreamscape that is Venice, where Prosecco grapes are fermented and then bubbles are added through a tank carbonation process that makes it far less expensive to produce than the usual labor-intensive means of making traditional Champagne. This means that you can often get your bubble fix from Prosecco for $15 or less, versus thrice that or more for Champagne and its equivalents throughout the world.

While Prosecco will not have the baked-bread nuances and ultra-creamy texture of the finest Champagne, what it lacks in refinement it makes up for in sunny charm. This is an August afternoon sipper, its subtle citrus and melon personality a perfect fit for outdoor lollygagging. It comes dry (labeled "sec") or sometimes a bit sweet (marked "extra dry"), which is the counterinituive labeling that afflicts most kinds of bubbly. I tell my students to think of Prosecco as "7UP that gets you soused"—a pleasure potion that you can stock like soda.

Speaking of easy sips, because Prosecco is inexpensive and uncomplicated, it has gained fame as a terrific base for certain mixed drinks. Foremost among them is the Bellini, a confection of peach purée and Prosecco made famous at Harry's Bar in Venice. Another toothsome concoction is the Sgroppino, where Prosecco combines with lemon sorbet and chilled vodka, topped by a few mint leaves.

But Prosecco's mixological prowess doesn't diminish its brilliant affinity for food. It complements virtually the entire gastronomic spectrum, from the fried and salty to the creamy and tangy. Its versatility and charm has become so admired that I wouldn't be surprised if the word "Prosecco" is pre-printed on the paper some restaurants use for their wine lists. And these aren't just watering holes: according to a recent article in the *New York Times*, Prosecco outsells Champagne by two-to-one at New York's acclaimed Union Square Cafe.

So here's your homework assignment: dispense with the killjoys who dismiss Prosecco as the simpleton of bubblies, and order a bottle the next time you see it on a wine list. Not only will it be one of the restaurant's least expensive bottles, but your fellow diners will eye the bottle, then its glinty ice bucket, and ask enviously: "What are *they* celebrating?"

BRAVEHEARTS ON *Prosecco*

"Prosecco really does bring cheer. It is also one of the great mixers, whether it's with blueberries, strawberries, or pomegranate juice. . . . If someone refuses a glass of bubbly, they should probably not be at the party to begin with."

—*Ming Tsai, chef and restaurateur, Blue Ginger, Boston, MA*

"At CUT we made a cocktail with vodka and peach purée shaken, served up in a martini glass, and topped with Prosecco. We call it a *Bellinissima*."

—*Dana Farner, beverage director, CUT: Wolfgang Puck, Los Angeles, CA*

"Prosecco is an excellent sparkling wine in its own right, but also a fantastic introductory wine for those who think they don't like Champagne. It can ease anyone into a peaceful, satiated Sunday."

—*Elizabeth Harcourt, sommelier, Corton, New York, NY*

"Although it is generally simple and refreshing, some Prosecco is as complex and delicious as Champagne—at half the price. I have used it for many toasts at various events (including weddings), and it is festive and delicious enough."

—*Heather Willens, importer and owner, HW Wines, Buenos Aires, Argentina*

"The more you sip, the more fluid your Italian will become."

—*Anjoleena Griffin-Holst, wine director, Borgata Hotel Casino & Spa, Atlantic City, NJ*

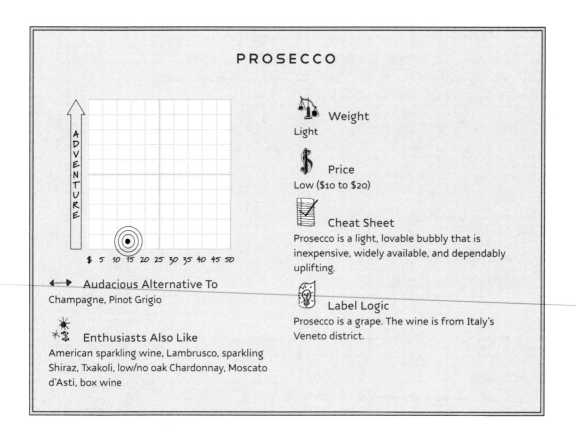

PROSECCO

ADVENTURE

$ 5 10 15 20 25 30 35 40 45 50

Weight
Light

Price
Low ($10 to $20)

Cheat Sheet
Prosecco is a light, lovable bubbly that is inexpensive, widely available, and dependably uplifting.

Audacious Alternative To
Champagne, Pinot Grigio

Enthusiasts Also Like
American sparkling wine, Lambrusco, sparkling Shiraz, Txakoli, low/no oak Chardonnay, Moscato d'Asti, box wine

Label Logic
Prosecco is a grape. The wine is from Italy's Veneto district.

Bravely Said

Conegliano	*Konay-lee-ano*
Prosecco	*Pro-SEHK-koh*
Sgroppino	*Gro-PEE-no*
sprezzatura	*SPRETT-sa-toor-ah*
Valdobbiadene	*Val-do-bi-ad-en-ay*
Veneto	*Vehn-eh-toe*

 Mark's Picks

Bisol "Crede"	*BEE-sol CREH-dah*
Carpene Malvoti	*Cahr-peh-NEH Mahl-VOHL-tee*
Collalto	*Kohl-LAHL-to*
Jeio	*Jay-oh*
La Marca	*Lah Mahr-kah*
Mionetto	*Mee-oh-neh-TOE*
Nino Franco	*NEE-noe FRANH-koe*
Ruggeri	*Rooj-JEH-ree*
Villa Sandi	*SAHN-dree*
Zardetto	*Zar-DAY-toe*

 Poosh It!

If the label includes the tongue-twisters "Conegliano" or "Valdobbiadene," these are the two major grape-growing towns for Prosecco in the Veneto.

The combined Conegliano-Valdobbiadene zone, which insiders proudly call "Prosecco land," is a tip-off to the highest-quality vineyards.

 CULINARY SWEET SPOT

Lightest ▲ Heaviest

 A Lovable Feast

As an aperitif or with almost anything; lighter finger foods like poached shrimp; salty snacks such as nuts and pretzels; casual seafood preparations; creamy pasta sauces; fried food such as calamari, *frites*, fried chicken; spicy ethnic food such as Chinese and Thai; most cheeses except the mega-stinky (e.g., Gorgonzola)

 Locally Lusty

Tramezzini (finger sandwiches with crusts removed) with fillings such as tuna with black olive pesto or chicken salad; tomato bruschetta; panini of all kinds; antipasto such as prosciutto-wrapped melon, lentil fritters, or pickled vegetables

 Spend the Night Together

Prosecco also mixes well with pomegranate juice or with saba, the Italian condiment made from reduced grape must.

According to the *New York Times Magazine*, designer Philippe Starck's house cocktail in summertime combines Champagne with lime juice, fresh ginger (peeled and passed through a juicer), and fresh mint (lightly crushed). To economize, substitute Prosecco for the Champagne.

40 SPARKLING SHIRAZ

Purple Fizz, All in Your Head

SHHH. LOOK CLOSELY. Do you see it? Notice its crimson flush, fruity musk, and scurry of motion? We're stalking exotic game now—and its name is sparkling Shiraz.

This is an animal of a completely different sort—a bubbly red. Just writing that phrase sets off alarm bells of cognitive dissonance. Quality red wine is not supposed to sparkle any more than Anthony Bourdain is supposed to bury his head in a plate of Tempeh bacon.

Well, we're in Australia now, where experimentation is embraced, and in the case of sparkling Shiraz, it sometimes triumphs. To be sure, bubbly reds exist elsewhere, particularly in Italy as Lambrusco (Chapter 38), but it achieves a special kind of foamy fun in Oz.

Pour yourself a swig—and a swig is really what it is, being so casual and foamy—and you'll spy a cola-colored sip, topped by a froth that tickles your upper lip. Its flavors are similar to those of a non-sparkling Shiraz, with plenty of plush black cherries and plums, along with traces of chocolate or licorice or earth. A good version can have undertones of sweetness from oak-barrel aging or ripe fruit, but mostly it will be dry, sometimes with a tug of tannin on your tongue—a sensation that at first may seem odd in a bubbly. After several sips, however, many folks get over its unexpected effervescence and start to cotton to its plummy exuberance.

Beloved in its native Australia where the locals call it "spurgle," sparkling Shiraz remains a rara avis on American shores. Better retailers should carry at least one version, but it will take an Internet search to track down specific producers. Bottles hover around the $20 mark, and occasionally clock in at $30 or more.

Sparkling Shiraz's cleansing fizz and berry charm make it a toothsome partner for a multiplicity of foods and occasions. Dark-meat poultry is a natural match, so much so that one of my wine-wise friends always seems to have a bottle in tow when we feast on Peking duck. Pork dishes are also sublime, as demonstrated by the deliriously happy diners irrigating their pork buns and pork sausage lettuce-wraps with it at New York's porcine palace Momofuku Ssäm Bar. Its hint of sweetness gives it an undeniable affinity with brunch foods, particularly those topped with fresh fruit or syrup, so you might consider popping a bottle during your next sit-down with Aunt Jemima.

We should also gain inspiration from the Ozzie tradition of serving it with Christmas turkey by including it in our own turkeyfests, where it will not only flatter the bird and its accompanying kaleidoscope of yam and berry flavors, but it will be an object of curiosity, excitement, and most important—bubble-borne distraction—at the Thanksgiving table.

BRAVEHEARTS ON *Sparkling Shiraz*

"Sparkling Shiraz is the drinking man's beer."
> —*Reid Bosward, winemaker, Kaesler Vineyards, Barossa Valley, Australia*

"Two weeks ago, I was in Texas, where it was over one hundred degrees. If you like red wine, sparkling Shiraz is perfect for hot weather. You can throw it in an ice bucket.

"Sparkling Shiraz works well with pork and duck and sweet glazes over meat. Because it is a celebratory wine that matches well with turkey, it is a great Thanksgiving wine."
> —*Ben Riggs, veteran winemaking consultant, McLaren Vale, Australia*

"These wines are quite diverse, from big and rich to sweeter commercial styles with most sharing a lush spicy character. D'Arenberg's sparkling red, the "Peppermint Paddock," is quite different because it is predominately from the grape Chambourcin with a bit of Shiraz and a touch of fortified Shiraz."

—*Chester Osborn, winemaker, d'Arenberg, McLaren Vale, South Australia*

"Sparkling Shiraz is a great party starter served with 'devils on horseback,' smoked oysters wrapped in bacon secured with a toothpick and grilled.

"When made from old, low-yielding Shiraz vines by the *méthode champenoise* process together with a couple of years on yeast lees, these wines can be astonishing."

—*Andrew Wigan, chief winemaker, Peter Lehmann Wines, Tanunda, Australia*

"Sparkling Shiraz reminds me of what I love about Australians—their straightforwardness and exuberance. There's not an unhappy bone in this wine.

"I was introduced to Sparkling Shiraz by the late Sir Noel Power, an Australian, an absolute bon vivant, and the former chief justice of Hong Kong's Supreme Court. We were at a late-morning reception in Southern Australia and he and everyone else started drinking it. The weather was hot and the wine was strong, and soon I said to myself, 'God, this is just great stuff.' So I bought tons of it and brought it back to the States. I still bring it out every Christmas."

—*Bart Araujo, owner, Araujo Estate Wines, Napa, CA*

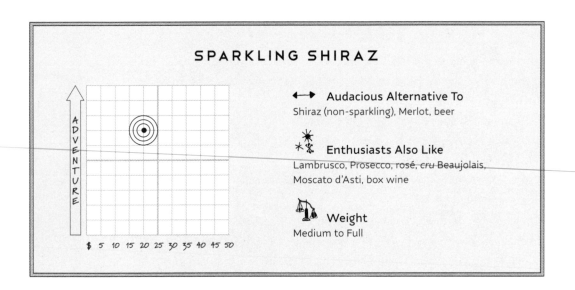

SPARKLING SHIRAZ

ADVENTURE

$ 5 10 15 20 25 30 35 40 45 50

◄—► **Audacious Alternative To**
Shiraz (non-sparkling), Merlot, beer

✳ **Enthusiasts Also Like**
Lambrusco, Prosecco, rosé, ~~cru~~ Beaujolais, Moscato d'Asti, box wine

⚖ **Weight**
Medium to Full

Price

Medium ($18 to $30)

 Cheat Sheet

Discombobulating but delicious, sparkling Shiraz is red, fizzy, and festive.

 Label Logic

Shiraz is a grape, known outside of Australia as Syrah.

 Bravely Said

Brachetto d'Aqui	*Brah-KEHT-to DAH-kwe*
Shiraz	*She-raz*

 Mark's Picks

Chook
d'Arenberg "Peppermint Paddock"
Fox Creek
Hill of Content
Paringa
Reilly's
Seppelt
Wyndham Estate "Bin 555"

 Poosh It!

"Chook" is Australian slang for chicken or hen. Some say that it was originally inspired by the clucking sound that chickens make; an apt gift for a saucy lass in your life is Fox Creek's "Vixen" sparkling Shiraz.

 CULINARY SWEET SPOT

Lightest ▲ Heaviest

 A Lovable Feast

As an aperitif, with brunch, or with poultry, especially Thanksgiving turkey and dark meat such as roast duck; pork dishes; cured and smoked meats; barbecue fare such as ribs, hamburgers, and hot dogs; moderately spicy Asian and Mexican food; leftovers, especially cold steak sandwiches

 Locally Lusty

Christmas turkey; meat pies; Vegemite (dark, yeasty spread) on toast; macadamia nuts

 Spend the Morning Together

Whether you're brunching with fruit tarts, French toast with fruit, or just a bowl of Froot Loops, do it with sparkling Shiraz and see how the wine's flavors provide a bridge to the fruity foods.

LIBATION AS INSPIRATION

"Any place where there's a concentration of good musicians you're going to find a lot of people who love wine.

"With wine, you go places. Wines stimulates the imagination, allows you to travel geographically and explore things that are otherwise not obvious."

—*David Chan, concertmaster and violinist, Metropolitan Opera Orchestra, New York, NY*

"Musicians are pleasure junkies. Wine, like music, surrounds you and gets inside your head. It *sends* you. It is pure hedonism."

—*Courtney Taylor-Taylor, lead singer and guitarist, The Dandy Warhols*

"When you drink wine after a long day, it automatically puts you in a state to be more reflective. Wine forces you to sit. To me, it means sitting down and relaxing."

—*Chazz Palminteri, actor and writer,* A Bronx Tale

"I don't recommend this, and I don't know why, but I tend to be more lyrical—more on the ball musically—if I have a hangover.

"Wine makes me dream . . . I dreamt the chorus to my song 'Post World War Two Blues.' I've also dreamt the same album about three times. Although I never made it, I still remember the chord shapes . . . I'm more imaginative with wine."

—*Al Stewart, folk-rock musician "Year of the Cat"*

"Wine encourages expression in a nice, ambient way. It is a helping hand, a titillation. Wine is very gradual and relaxing. It allows you to pause for thought. It doesn't demand for you to have your mind made up."

—Mick Fleetwood, drummer and namesake, Fleetwood Mac

"In 1972, I was drinking red Bordeaux—I think it was Château Lynch Bages— and I heard this song in my head. So I sat down at my baby grand piano in my drawing room and out came the song 'Isn't Life Strange.'"

—John Lodge, singer and bass guitarist, The Moody Blues

"Ninety percent of my music came out of a nice bottle, with a nice buzz. It's magic. I write music in the evening, when everything is quiet and relaxed. It's when I say, 'I got this great &%##@&# idea.'

"I didn't write the hit 'I Can't Drive 55' with wine, of course."

—Sammy Hagar, vocalist, Chickenfoot, former vocalist, Van Halen

DESSERT WINES

DESSERT WINES: ADVENTURE & PRICE AT A GLANCE

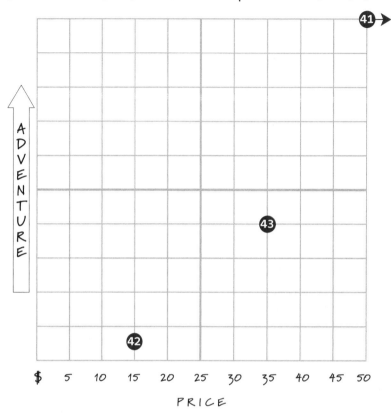

41. Madeira
42. Moscato d'Asti
43. Tawny Port

41 MADEIRA

Caramelly Time-Traveler, Ouija Optional

THOUGH NO ONE in my family qualifies as an adherent of the occult—the occasional La Toya Jackson Psychic Network commercial notwithstanding—my mother recently convinced my sister and me to join her in trying to channel her long-deceased mother during a stay at an allegedly haunted hotel in Massachusetts. So my sister invested in a Ouija board, and I, of course, volunteered to bring a séance-worthy sipper, a 1969 Madeira that we drank clandestinely from paper cups due to hotel's draconian no-alcohol policy.

While the jury's out as to whether we actually communicated with my grandmother, I think we all connected with the Madeira, as the wine's haunting and utterly unique taste of burned caramel and old-fashioned, stenciled-letter bottle made it the perfect prop for a supernatural exercise.

It wasn't just Madeira's flavor and appearance that made it so appropriate, but the fact that it is a wine with its own history to tell, one reaching back hundreds of years when it enjoyed massive popularity in the States. American colonists had a major jones for it, so much so that the founding fathers raised a glass of it to toast the signing of the Declaration of Independence, no matter that it actually springs from foreign soils—specifically, the volcanic island of Madeira, a Portuguese protectorate off the coast of Morocco.

Though Prohibition and quality problems eventually undercut its popularity, today there are compelling reasons why the casual drinker should give Madeira—vintage-dated and other fine versions, not the bulk type used for cooking—a close look. First, of course, is its taste, which is as exotic as the subtropical island from which it originates: tangy and nutty in its drier styles and a complex mix of caramel and molasses, balanced by zippy acidity, in its sweeter manifestations.

Next, you need not worry about Madeira spoiling before you can finish the bottle, as it is the most long-lived of any wine type. Like the famous Samsonite bag, it has been through the ringer before it ever reaches you, fortified as it is with brandy during fermentation and then exposed to both high heat and oxidization, both of which are normally wine's assassins. Here, however, they prove the adage that what doesn't kill you makes you stronger, creating a wine of near indestructibility—lasting centuries when sealed and several months when opened. Heat and oxidation, in fact, are the conditions under which the wine was originally found to thrive. Sea captains of the seventeenth century, using barrels of Madeira as ballast, discovered that long, hot, jarring ocean voyages actually improved the taste.

Rarity that it is, fine Madeira is a wine for special occasions: perfectly patriotic on Independence Day or Thanksgiving, or, because its sweet-sour character harmonizes with the flavors of pumpkin, on Halloween. Drier styles of Madeira have a special affinity with soup, beef-based consommé being a classic match. Sweeter Madeira has an easy way with caramelized desserts or a wedge of Stilton.

Opening a bottle to *create* a special occasion is another fine use for Madeira. Even at $50 to $250 or more a bottle, it is actually one of the least expensive ways of tasting wine of significant age (Chapter 46). I recently built a small party around an unused bottle of the 1969 Madeira we drank for the séance, which rang up at $70, a fraction of what a top Bordeaux or Burgundy with that much age would cost. Given Madeira's interminable life-span and that a little bit goes a long way (about twelve to fifteen pours per bottle), if you divide its price by the number of times you can drink it, it becomes that much more cost effective as a means of imbibing history.

BRAVEHEARTS ON *Madeira*

"The notion of an elixir comes to mind when I think of drinking Madeira. It is a world-class wine that has such an interesting history, discovered by accident. It lasts forever after opening. I always feel better when I drink some."

—*Karen King, former wine director, The Modern at MoMA, New York, NY*

"Madeira doesn't taste like Port or Sherry—its palate is uniquely blessed by powerful acidity, which amplifies every flavor and dramatically frames the wine's honeyed richness.

"From the dawn of colonial times until after the Civil War, few important works—commercial, political, or artistic—were planned without a decanter of Madeira to inspire the imagination. And any family who could afford it purchased a pipe [a barrel containing about six hundred bottles], of Madeira, yearly, cherished as an heirloom, passed down from generation to generation."

—*Mannie Berk, Madeira expert and proprietor, Rare Wine Company, Sonoma, CA*

"Of all mature wines to buy, Madeira probably offers the least risk of being spoiled because the wine is so famously durable."

—*Richard Brierley, former head of North American wine sales, Christie's*

"I got into Madeira a while ago. I have a bunch that came from a English cellar, including bottles from the royal wedding of Charles and Diana in 1981 and the investiture of the Prince of Wales, July 1969.

"I prefer the Bual—sweeter, richer, more caramelly style—over the drier Verdelho style. Madeira is more acidic than Port, and that's why you store it standing up—or the acid will eventually eat the cork."

—*Alex Lifeson, lead guitarist, Rush*

"My New Year's resolution is to organize my life so I drink more aged Madeira. You can open your wallet wide and shake it and *never* be sorry with it. A four-hundred-dollar bottle will last a year or serve a dinner party of twelve people.

"Many people have only had ordinary cooking Madeira, and so I love watching their eyes light up when they have fine, aged Madeira. Its unique *rancio*, or oxidized, flavor profile takes people to a groovy frontier. In just a few sips they'll be tasting the kind of wine that Thomas Jefferson used to drink all of the time."

—*Lou Amdur, owner, Lou's Wine Bar, Los Angeles, CA*

"Always unique, mysterious, intense: an unforgettable experience!"

—*Rémi Krug, owner, Champagne Krug, Champagne, France*

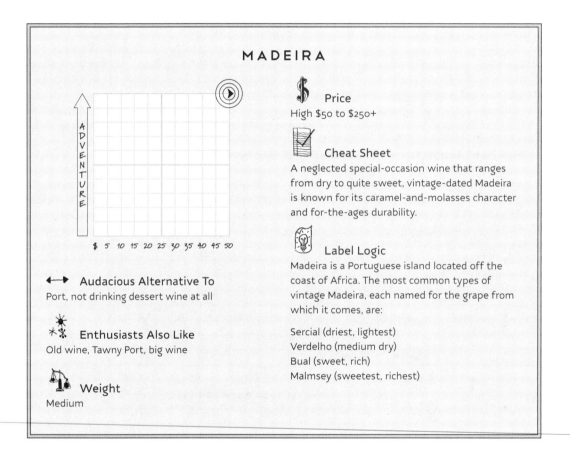

MADEIRA

ADVENTURE

$ 5 10 15 20 25 30 35 40 45 50

Audacious Alternative To
Port, not drinking dessert wine at all

Enthusiasts Also Like
Old wine, Tawny Port, big wine

Weight
Medium

Price
High $50 to $250+

Cheat Sheet
A neglected special-occasion wine that ranges from dry to quite sweet, vintage-dated Madeira is known for its caramel-and-molasses character and for-the-ages durability.

Label Logic
Madeira is a Portuguese island located off the coast of Africa. The most common types of vintage Madeira, each named for the grape from which it comes, are:

Sercial (driest, lightest)
Verdelho (medium dry)
Bual (sweet, rich)
Malmsey (sweetest, richest)

Bravely Said

Madeira	Me-DEER-ah
Sercial	Sehr-see-AHL
Verhelho	Vehr-DEH-lyoh

 Mark's Picks

Barbeito	Bahr-BAY-too
Blandy's	
Broadbent	
D'Oliveiras	Dah-lee-VAY-ras
Henriques & Henriques	
Leacock's	

 Poosh It!

During its ocean voyages of centuries ago, the best Madeiras were of the *vinho da roda* (or "round trip") variety, meaning that the longer and hotter the trip was, the better the Madeira became.

CULINARY SWEET SPOT

Drier versions

Lightest ▲ Heaviest

Sweeter versions

Lightest ▲ Heaviest

 A Lovable Feast

Drier versions: as an aperitif; almonds and other salty nuts; tapas; soups such as consomme, corn chowder, and oxtail; mushrooms; roasted red peppers; salads

Sweeter versions: by itself or with caramelized desserts; pumpkin; chocolate; nuts such as almonds and pecans; strawberries with balsamic vinaigrette; Stilton and other blue-veined cheeses; for Thanksgiving, Independence Day, and birthdays

 Spend the Night Together

Celebrate the repeal of Prohibition with Madeira from its year (1933). I did this after tracking down a bottle of 1933 Justino Henriques Malmsey Madeira.

A more affordable introduction to the pleasures of Madeira comes from the Historic Series of Sonoma's Rare Wine Co. (www.RareWineCo .com). Each bottling named for an American city in which a particular Madeira style was popular centuries ago, they include the dry, nutty Charleston Serical and the sweet, toffee-like New York Malmsey, each blends of several years and about $50 a bottle.

42 MOSCATO D'ASTI

Wine of Mass Seduction

I'M ALWAYS DISMAYED at how many people announce they don't drink dessert wine with the finality of someone declaring their political affiliation or directional dexterity. It's as if they've convinced themselves that they lack the proper gene for it.

The solution is straightforward: they must try Moscato d'Asti, which I consider the official dessert wine of those who don't like dessert wine. Based on the preferences of my wine-pro friends, it also seems to be the official dessert wine of those who *do* like dessert wine.

Originating from the Muscat grape, Moscato d'Asti acquires its universal likeability from its peach-and-orange-blossom aromatics and lightly sweet taste. A world apart from the syrupy confections that besmirch the reputation of dessert wine, Moscato d'Asti's hedonistic qualities are counterbalanced by a vein of lemony crispness and a light sparkle. It is also low in alcohol, a mere 6% or so, because winemakers stop fermentation early, preventing some of the grape sugar from converting into alcohol. This is a Brave New Pour so widely adored that its fan base ranges from Corie Brown, the former *Los Angeles Times* wine columnist, to Lil' Kim, the bawdy hip-hop queen. Lil' Kim rhymes about sipping "Mescotto" in Brazil in her song "Lighters Up."

Moscato's greatest loyalists, of course, are the citizens of its native Asti, a village located in the Piedmont region of northwestern Italy. More than anyone else they know that no matter how rich their tagliatelle gets, there is always room postprandially for a few glasses of feathery-light Moscato d'Asti. It makes for a nectarous sendoff by itself, or is ideal with fresh fruit or fruit-based concoctions such as fruit tarts and baked apples. You can follow the locals' cue and splash a bit on a bowl of fresh fruit. It is also perfectly suited to the fruity and sweet complexion of brunch foods—a refreshing change-up from the same old mimosa. With its gentle sweetness and low alcohol, there's just no reason not to break it out with a spicy dinner if you so desire.

Moscato d'Asti couldn't be easier to source, as stores stock it readily and restaurants often make it a permanent part of their dessert-wine list. You'll rarely pay more than $20 for Moscato d'Asti, and most bottles seem to hover around $15. It doesn't get any better with age, so look for the youngest bottles available. Drink it cold from regular wineglasses.

Finally, if the name "Asti" seems familiar, you're probably thinking of Asti Spumante, another Muscat-based wine from this Piedmont village. Although the "spumante" has been officially dropped from its name, it still lives up to the meaning of that word, being fully foamy. It is also sweeter and more alcoholic, and thus not particularly respected by insiders.

BRAVEHEARTS ON *Moscato d'Asti*

"Moscato d'Asti is my favorite dessert wine. It may be the perfect pairing with wedding cake. If I ever get married again I'm going to make sure that I serve Moscato. (I didn't the first time and maybe that's why it didn't take!)"

—*Lettie Teague, wine columnist,* The Wall Street Journal, *and former executive wine editor,* Food & Wine *magazine*

"Since my husband and I started drinking lightly off-dry wine like Moscato with dessert, we haven't touched many of the heavier dessert wines we have in our cellar.

"Moscato d'Asti is that rare wine that is unpretentious yet chic."

—*Corie Brown, former* Los Angeles Times *wine columnist*

"I enjoy the fact that people are constantly still discovering Moscato d'Asti. Consumers always come into the store describing some fabulous revelation they had with this festive little wine."

—*Debbie Zachareas, co-owner, Ferry Plaza Wine Merchants, San Francisco, CA*

"I had just gotten the wine column for *GQ* magazine in the mid-eighties and was in the office of Robert Chadderdon, a famous and feared importer known for quality and inaccessibility. After I interviewed him, he opened a wine he said was undiscovered by Americans and poured a glass for me to taste blind. 'What do you think of that?' he asked. I sipped and said, 'Oh, yes, Moscato d'Asti. I quite like it.' Come to think of it, I don't believe I've ever again guessed a wine correctly when the pressure was on."   —*Alan Richman, food and wine writer*

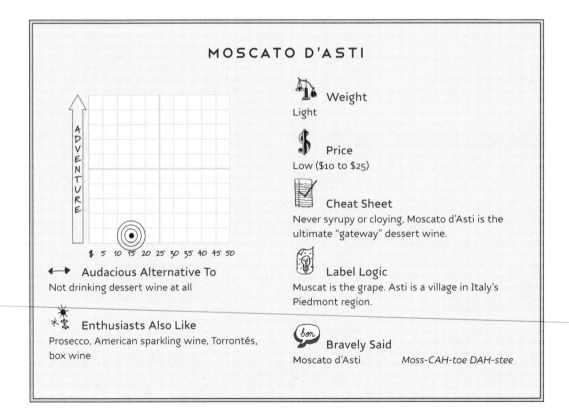

MOSCATO D'ASTI

ADVENTURE

$ 5 10 15 20 25 30 35 40 45 50

⟷ Audacious Alternative To
Not drinking dessert wine at all

Enthusiasts Also Like
Prosecco, American sparkling wine, Torrontés, box wine

Weight
Light

Price
Low ($10 to $25)

Cheat Sheet
Never syrupy or cloying, Moscato d'Asti is the ultimate "gateway" dessert wine.

Label Logic
Muscat is the grape. Asti is a village in Italy's Piedmont region.

Bravely Said
Moscato d'Asti   *Moss-CAH-toe DAH-stee*

Mark's Picks

Ceretto	Cher-REHT-toe
"Santo Stefano"	STEH-fah-no
Coppo	KOP-po
La Spinetta	Lah Spuh-NET-ah
Michele Chiarlo	Mee-KEH-leh KYAR-low
"Nivole"	
Prunotto	Proo-NOH-toe
Rivetti	Ruh-vet-tee
Saracco	Sah-RAH-Koe
Vietti	VYEHT-Tee

 Poosh It!

Moscato's lightness is its liberation: its light effervescence frees its cork from having to be muzzled by a Champagne-style cage or drunk in a fluted glass, and its lightly sweet taste allows it to be enjoyed at any time of the day.

A good name to know in Moscato d'Asti is Paolo Saracco, a quality-obsessed producer whose bottlings are considered among the finest in Piedmont.

CULINARY SWEET SPOT

Lightest ▲ Heaviest

 A Lovable Feast

By itself as dessert or with fresh fruit; sorbets; pound cake, crème brulée; meringue; shortbread; ginger-flavored creations; cookies; chocolate truffles; wedding cake; spicy fare; for brunch or Mother's Day

 Locally Lusty

Panettone (fruit-filled Italian sweet bread); tiramisù; gelato, especially peach; biscotti; poured over fresh fruit

 Spend the Night Together

Freeze some Moscato d'Asti in an ice tray, and then chop it up, which essentially creates a simple form of *granite*, or flavored flakes of ice. Sprinkle the iced bits over fruit and serve it with glasses of Moscato d'Asti on the side.

Official Dessert Wine of Those Who Don't like and do Dessert Wine

43 TAWNY PORT

Low Maintenance, High Performance

SOME OF MY fondest wine-saturated memories involve vintage Port, the fortified dessert wine of renown and tradition. Its drawback, however, is that it's more demanding than a diva at the zenith of her popularity. Not only does it require you to pay dearly for its performance, but it takes forever to coax out of its metaphorical dressing room, requiring at least a good ten years of bottle age before it even approaches drinkability, a glacial slog that has been likened in literature to a "grim struggle." Add the fact that decanting is sometimes needed to remove its age-rendered sediment, and you've got a finger-wagging, wine equivalent of Patti LaBelle on your hands.

Enter aged Tawny Port, the other "serious Port," a springy-limbed people-pleaser to vintage Port's difficult diva. It is a low-maintenance, Cameron Diaz of a wine that can be a relatively cheap date, requires no special handling, and is ready when you are. On the last point, fine Tawny Port is immediately drinkable because vintners in its native Portugal do all of the aging for you. After it is fortified with brandy and fermentation ends, the Port is aged in oak barrels for as long as forty years, as indicated on the bottle by its ten, twenty, thirty, or forty-year labeling. These numbers represent an approximation, as Tawnies are a blend of several different vintages.

During the aging process, the barrel's permeability exposes the wine to a bit of oxygen, which gradually transforms it from a ruby-hued agent of astringency into a nut-brown (i.e., tawny) smooth operator, evocative of roasted walnuts, toffee, or dried fruit. It might also bring to mind such exotica as brown sugar, cocoa dust, or orange peel. Though styles vary by producer, particular blend of grapes (all native Portuguese varieties), and duration of aging, it is often lighter and more nuanced than the fruit-driven power of vintage Port. Except for a rare style called Colheitas, aged Tawny Port is not associated with a particular vintage year (i.e., it is "nonvintage"), giving a Port house the freedom to blend in wine from different years and thus maintain a consistent style from year to year.

Like Madeira (Chapter 41), the fact that a Tawny has already seen its fair share of aging at the winery means that an opened bottle can generally keep for several weeks. This, again, stands in stark contrast to vintage Port, which doesn't get nearly the oxidative workout before release and thus fades a day or two after opening.

Though specimens with thirty or forty years of maturity can exceed $60, many with ten years of age cost less than half as much and are still perfectly delicious, even if they lack the haunting essence of older port. Warre's ten-year "Otima," Tawny bottled in modern, clear glass, is a good starting point. Quality is strong across producers, though lately I find myself gravitating most often to Ramos-Pinto, Warre's, Delaforce, and Niepoort. Regardless of the maker, people like to drink Tawnies with a bit of a chill to make them brighter and more refreshing.

Aged Tawny Port is tempting year-round, but there's something about the brisk, wood-smoke-infused air of autumn and winter that demands its liberal use. It has an affinity with roasted nuts, as it does with the salty goodness of Stilton cheese and foie gras. Tawnies take no prisoners with desserts, especially those of the chocolate, caramel, or apple persuasion; sipping it with pumpkin pie at the end of a Thanksgiving feast is also a masterstroke. Of course, you'll never err enjoying a Tawny in lieu of dessert, preferably on a sheepskin rug in front of a crackling fire—a winter restorative nonpareil.

BRAVEHEARTS ON *Tawny Port*

"Old Tawnies are staples of the Port producers themselves who always drink them lightly chilled. They are sublime, nutty, with a hint of caramel and orange. I rarely pass an evening without having a glass of chilled Tawny after dinner."

—*Dominic Symington, director, Symington Family Estates, Douro, Portugal*

"I'll sip a nutty ten-year, spicy twenty-year, or decadent single-vintage Colheitas over just about any dessert. In fact, my idea of food porn is the juxtaposition of sweet and salty. Try a Tawny Port alongside a plate of almonds, Parmigiano-Reggiano, and a dab of high-quality honey."
—*Leslie Sbrocco, wine consultant and author*

"Try Tawny Port with peanut brittle for a whole new meaning of life."
—*Inez Ribustello, sommelier and co-owner, On the Square, Tarboro, NC*

"Vintage Port may be king but Tawny Port is the president, having won by election."

—*Dirk Niepoort, family proprietor, Niepoort, Douro, Portugal,*
on Tawny Port's popularity

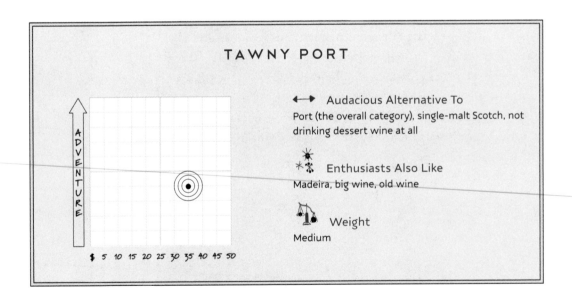

TAWNY PORT

ADVENTURE

$ 5 10 15 20 25 30 35 40 45 50

←→ Audacious Alternative To
Port (the overall category), single-malt Scotch, not drinking dessert wine at all

✳🍸 Enthusiasts Also Like
Madeira, big wine, old wine

⚖ Weight
Medium

Price

Medium to High ($25 to $100+)

 Cheat Sheet

User friendly, widely loved, and easily sourced, aged Tawny port is an ideal on-ramp to the pleasures of fine Port.

 Label Logic

Port is named for Oporto, a city in northern Portugal. Port is made from a blend of native grape varieties, the most important of which is Touriga Nacional.

 Bravely Said

Colheitas	*Kool-YAY-tahs*
Oporto	*Oh-POOR-toe*

 Mark's Picks

Cockburn	*Coh-burn*
Delaforce	
Dow's	
Niepoort	*NEE-port*
Quinta do Vesuvio	*KEEN-tah doh Veh-ZUH-vyoh*
Ramos-Pinto	*RAHN-moos PEEN-too*
Taylor Fladgate	
Warre's	

 Poosh It!

The poetic term "angels' share" (or, in French, "*la part des anges*") describes the small amount of wine that evaporates through the wooden cask as Tawny Port and other wines age; it has also been used to refer to the wisp of vapor released when Champagne is opened.

 CULINARY SWEET SPOT

 Lightest ▲ Heaviest

 A Lovable Feast

By itself; with salty nuts such as almonds and cashews; with desserts featuring chocolate, apples, or other fruit, nuts, caramel; pumpkin pie, especially at Thanksgiving; figs or dates; peanut brittle; crème brulée; blue-veined cheeses like Stilton or Roquefort; English Cheddar, Parmigiano-Reggiano, and other hard cheeses; foie gras

Spend the Night Together

To illustrate how food-and-wine opposites sometimes attract, try a Tawny with salty cheese. Many people find that a sodium-rich, blue-veined cheese like Stilton or Roquefort is a pleasing contrast to the sweetness of Port. The same goes for enjoying Port with the savoriness of foie gras.

On the Square's Inez Ribustello swears by Tawny with peanut brittle from North Carolina's Rusty's Peanut Brittle (www.RustysPeanutBrittle .com).

THE LINGERING FAREWELL

"My cousins and I used to fight to see who could sit in Grandpa's lap, and whoever did got to finish his last little bit of wine. We'd fight for 'lap position.'"

—Joe Montana, football legend

"We had a fantastic '96 Masseto, a famous Merlot from the producer Tenuta dell'Ornellaia, given to us as a gift that was so good we ended up sitting at the table almost worshipping the bottle after the wine was gone."

—Bruce Greenwood, actor, Star Trek (2009)

"You know a wine is special when you get to the last little bit in a bottle and don't want it to end. You think to yourself, 'Now *this* wine is different.'"

—Chazz Palminteri, actor and writer, A Bronx Tale

"My last meal would be my mother's gravy with pasta—and a Chianti, in a straw basket."
—Tom Colicchio, chef and restaurateur, Craft, New York, NY

"In addition to being a Boston police officer for thirty-five years, my dad is a true oenophile. When I turned twenty-one, he left a joking note on the cellar door that read 'Happy Birthday, son. Someday, *none* of this will be yours!'"

—Jeff Corwin, host and executive producer, Animal Planet's "The Jeff Corwin Experience"

"I was dining with actor Danny DeVito and our two families were together at a restaurant at a twelfth-century cottage in Rome's countryside. We started at three A.M.—they kept the restaurant open for Danny. There were eight courses. You actually saw the lady making the pasta fresh for us with flour and eggs. The wine—a Brunello di Montalcino, a rich red from Tuscany—was so great that Danny asked the restaurant if he could buy a case, but the owner said, 'Mr. DeVito, one bottle is all we have left.' So we ordered it and once it was gone, it was time to go. It was just one of those great moments—it transcended everything." —*Malcolm McDowell, actor*

"My daughter sometimes says, 'Julio, you can't drink wine *every* day.' And I tell her, "Daughter, you can take anything from me, but not my wine."

—*Julio Iglesias, music legend*

"My dining room has an old barn-wood floor from Amish country and a fifteen-foot table—at dinner, my friends, family, and I look like Knights of the Roundtable. After dinner, in leather chairs, drinking wine and just talking is a real moment for me—swirling the wine, tasting its creaminess. I love the whole euphoric feeling of it. —*Guy Fieri, chef and television host*

"I don't usually categorize specific bottles of wine by their remarkable vintage, or indeed by their delicate aroma of exotic raspberry fruit or blueberries. It isn't necessarily an exquisite accompanying meal that captures my imagination, or the perfect view, where a distant skyline of cypress trees melts gently into the evening sunset. It is something rather more simple, which inevitably settles in my memory most; that is whom I shared the experience with. I feel a great bottle of wine should never be sacrificed without some conversation. It is the sound of the cork popping that announces the third and final act of the day, this is often where the real drama unfolds; the exchange of opinions, sharing information and airing of views, perhaps a secret revealed. Not even a masterful sommelier's elaborate routine can distract me from the great pleasure of communication."

—*Nick Rhodes, keyboardist, Duran Duran*

THREE FOR
THE ROAD

THREE FOR THE ROAD:
ADVENTURE & PRICE AT A GLANCE

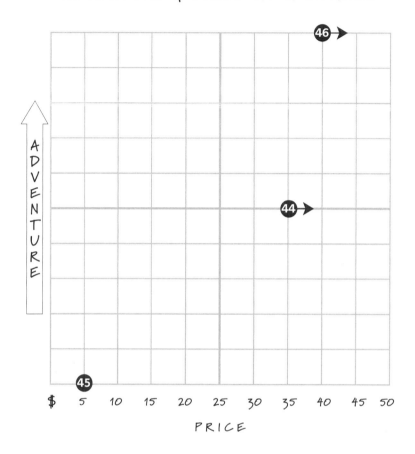

44. Big Wine

45. Box Wine

46. Old Wine

44 BIG WINE

Success in Excess

WHEN MY FRIEND Burt quietly produced a six-liter bottle of Château d'Yquem 1989 at a large gathering, a collective gasp emanated from those of us who knew that this golden nectar was the world's most coveted dessert wine. Surreally large like Underdog on Thanksgiving, the bottle attracted the attention of even those indifferent to wine. Soon scores of captivated souls were moving toward the bottle like zombies marching to Michael Jackson in the *Thriller* video. After Burt asked me to open this monstrosity, the flimsy corkscrew I had and my own inexperience with bottles this colossal had me on my knees, desperately trying to pry free its uncooperative cork, twisting and struggling as if I were wrestling a crocodile. If it weren't for the help of another pair of hands, the thirsty throng would have would have treated me to a stoning on the order of that in Shirley Jackson's *The Lottery*.

Therein resides the magic of so-called large-format bottles. Their visual impressiveness and relative scarcity make them the extroverts of oenophilia, objects of fascination and flamboyance that transfix observers like a supermodel in IMAX. There is a synergistic effect: the impact of a big bottle exceeds the sum of its equivalent in standard bottles. There's also an optical illusion at work in that these bottles appear to contain more wine than they actually do. And they send the message that the owner has achieved some degree of connoisseurship: think of all of the steakhouses that display big bottles like trophies, conveying the message that "we're in the big leagues, just like these bottles."

Big bottles also speak volumes about a drinker's expansiveness of spirit. Like keeping a large summer house, owning oversized bottles suggests that the drinker made a purchasing decision with the intention to share. They also flatter one's guests, giving them the sense that they are important enough to partake in such a special bottle.

Celebrations and parties are, of course, the natural habitat for these behemoths. They've helped me up the ante at many a holiday and family affair, such as the magnum of Veuve Clicquot Yellow Label Champagne I brought to a recent Mother's Day celebration. Big bottles also provide a unique excuse for hosting a party—how many magnum soirees have you attended? When at least two couples are involved, I like to tote along a magnum to BYOB-friendly restaurants. Not only will a server sometimes charge only a single corkage fee for what is the equivalent of multiple bottles, but with all of that extra wine, there's ample opportunity to give your server a taste, which can make the pesky corkage fee evaporate altogether.

Happily, you don't need to spring for Yquem or the equivalent to experience the glorious excess and synergy that come with big bottles. Large-format versions of moderately priced wine can often be found in larger shops, be they Cabernet Sauvignon, bargain Bordeaux (Chapter 23), non-vintage Champagne, or Riesling; I recently picked up a magnum of Gruet sparkling wine for $35. That said, many of the large bottles you'll see contain special-occasion, age-worthy juice and are priced accordingly. Not only does an oversized bottle inject a measure of frisson into experiencing a fine wine, but because it has a lower ratio of air to liquid, wine in larger bottles matures more slowly, not unlike the average male when compared to the fairer sex.

BRAVEHEARTS ON *Big Wine*

"There's something communal I value about a big bottle. It's the wine counterpart to breaking bread, and it also commands a presence on the table."

—*Neil DeGrasse Tyson, astrophysicist and director, Hayden Planetarium,
New York, NY*

"I choose jeroboams for special events—they make a big statement that you were thinking of serving a lot of people a decent amount of wine. It's amazing how far one 'jero' can go at a party.

"At our wedding, we shared Krug Grande Cuvée and Roulot Meursault 'Tessons' 1999 out of jeroboams with our closest friends and family.   —*Robert Bohr, wine director and partner, Cru, New York, NY*

"I love elaborate, long, big dinners with music, noise, kids—chaos! A few magnums of Bordeaux go along with these kinds of dinners. Big bottles are good fun and good theater."

—*Gavin Rossdale, solo artist and former vocalist and guitarist, Bush*

"I love cracking open a big format and walking around and giving people pours. It's like a victory you and your friends can share together. There's nothing better than a gigantic seafood tower, then a big, salt-roasted prime rib, and drinking from big bottles. The bottles sit there as a representation of what a special night it is."

—*Guy Fieri, chef and television host*

"Starring in *A Clockwork Orange* gave me my first serious money and I was thinking of buying an Edward Burra painting at London's Agnew Gallery on Old Bond Street. Some Sotheby's wine specialists came to the gallery, and we all ended up having lunch upstairs. Afterward, they brought a huge jeroboam of brandy from 1815—which is the date of the Battle of Waterloo. Two people were needed to pour it. It didn't taste anything like brandy, it was utterly delicious—so good that I decided that I would *not* drive home."   —*Malcolm McDowell, actor*

BIG WINE

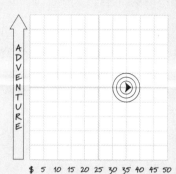

 Audacious Alternative To

Standard 750-ml bottles

 Enthusiasts Also Like

Old wine, rosé Champagne, classic Cabernet, (good) Merlot, Madeira, bargain Bordeaux

 Cheat Sheet

A surefire way to enthrall your guests or gift recipients, large-format bottles add a heady, über-generous element to the wine experience.

 Label Logic

Large-format bottle sizes (regular, non-sparkling wine) (size names for Champagne bottles are somewhat different):

Magnum (2 bottles)
Double Magnum
    (4 bottles)
Jeroboam (6 bottles)   *Jer-oh-bow-uhm*
Imperiale (8 bottles)
Salmanazar (12 bottles)   *Sal-mahn-ah-zar*
Balthazar (16 bottles)
Nebuchadnezzar   *Neb-uh-kuhd-NEZ-uhr*
    (20 bottles)

 Poosh It!

The rare occurrence of three regular bottles in one is called a "Marie-Jeanne" for regular wine and a "tregnum" or "tappet hen" for Port.

 Spend the Night Together

Host your own BYOM (Bring Your Own Magnum) party.

After you finish a larger bottle, have every guest sign it with a permanent marker.

If possible, compare an older version of the same wine in standard and large format. Which one seems to have matured more quickly?

To create an extra-special birthday present, buy magnums of affordable bubbly and create a custom label for it. For my friend Hernie's fortieth birthday, I purchased three magnums of Gruet sparkling wine online, and with the help of Photoshop and a mischievous heart, I customized the label of each with suitably compromising photos from our college days.

45 BOX WINE

Bespigotted, but Punch Line No More

IF SEDUCTION IS your game, the only thing more soul crushing than serving wine-in-box to the object of your affections is doing that *and* then referring to it by one of its alternative names—a "bladder pack." If I ran the world, I'd impose a twelve-hour waiting period on using the term "bladder pack" after any conversation involving the phrase "slip into something more comfortable."

But what about serving boxed wine with take-out or at a beach-side cookout or another informal setting? This is now an attractive option, as not all box wine is the vinous approximation of a beer helmet or Wonder Bread dots. Though there are still plenty of mass-produced box wines filled with nasty, third-rate juice, shelves are increasingly seeing more examples of the oxymoronically-named "premium box wine," these versions representing a significant improvement over the processed, flavorless dreck that most of us expect from a cardboard enclosure.

As they did with screw caps, box wine is something that other countries embraced early on, as imbibers in Australia, New Zealand, and even France found little ignominy in keeping a box in their fridges for casual drinking. It's been a harder sell in our wine-romanticizing culture, but discerning drinkers in the United States are starting to warm to the category as they recognize its many virtues.

Price, of course, is box wine's claim to fame, the average 3-liter box selling for $18 to $25, which, factoring in its 4-bottle equivalence, translates to a wallet-preserving $4 to $6 a bottle. Better boxes aren't this cheap due to inferior grapes, but because they avoid the high costs of bottling and have far lower storage and transportation expenses. It is for this reason that wine boxes are considered a "greener" alternative to bottles, as they impose significantly fewer carbon emissions than their glass counterparts.

"Wine box" isn't entirely accurate as these contraptions actually comprise a bag-in-box, or, to be even more precise, the box houses a self-sealing pouch that deflates as you draw a pour from its plastic spigot. Highly effective at keeping out oxygen, its design preserves wine for up to a month, which is ideal for the "house wines" meant for everyday consumption—that is, the vast majority of all wine. Moreover, its corkless design eliminates the scourge of cork taint, the mildewy smell afflicting an estimated 10% of all cork-bottled wines.

The most common sizes you'll see are 3-liter (the equivalent of 4 standard-sized bottles) and 5-liter (about 6.5 bottles). Also gaining favor is the 1-liter Tetra Pak, an angular box curiously reminiscent of one of those Juicy Juice cartons that are as much a part of the school cafeteria experience as are mean girls and linebacker-like lunch ladies. The producer Yellow+Blue is especially fond of using the Tetra Pak, as its light weight fits with the company's eco-friendly image, as does its name (combining yellow and blue makes green).

BRAVEHEARTS ON *Box Wine*

"Bottles are desperately inefficient: they're heavy and fragile and let in damaging light. For people who drink modest wine regularly, box wines are a godsend. The laws of economics suggest to me that if buyers have access to the same quality product for half the price in a more efficient and space-saving package, eventually they'll catch on."   —*Marnie Old, author,* Wine Secrets, *and wine educator*

"I keep returning to VRAC Chardonnay from the Mâcon-Villages region in France. The label tells us "VRAC follow a centuries-old European tradition where villagers buy their wine in bulk [or] 'en VRAC.' It comes directly from the winemaker's barrels, ensuring that they are drinking their favorite wine at the most affordable price." It's rich and tasty and a little fruity! Heaven."

—*Lynn Redgrave, the late actress*

"I am a huge believer in box wine. I like its appeal outside of wine's normal sense of formality—and of course that it's more eco-friendly and long-lasting. The packaging also lends itself to really interesting graphic design.

"While I'm all for the beauty of corks, I love not having to put wine in a bottle. I'm currently enclosing some of my wine in tanks to be served on tap at restaurants, and the beauty of it is that the tanks come back to me—nothing gets thrown away."

—*Abe Schoener, founder and winemaker, Scholium Project, Suisun Valley, CA*

"Bag-in-boxes are an extension of the French tradition of going to the vineyard with a jug to get some wine for the week. Previously, the only box wines in the United States were commercial, cheap wine. It all seemed rather contradictory, since Americans have been open to other 'new' packaging such as screw caps and synthetic corks. I wanted to bring a high-quality box wine to the United States—it is at once economical and ecological, and the vacuum seal keeps it good for a month once opened."

—*Jenny Lefcourt, co-owner, Jenny & François Selections and importer of*
"From the Tank" box wines

"I lived in France and we'd sit around and drink from jugs and boxes at lunch and dinner. The college kids there weren't doing it to get smashed—they handled it with much more maturity."

—*Guy Fieri, chef and television host*

"Just out of college and working as young chefs, a friend and I were stranded out in Greenwich, Connecticut. So we bought a big wooden cask of Beaujolais Nouveau and put it next to the Christmas tree in our living room. We thought it would last, but by New Year's, we had to go buy a case and fill the cask back up with different reds."

—*David Burke, chef and restaurateur, David Burke Townhouse, New York, NY*

"The tradition of putting three-quarters of a liter in a glass bottle is so *twentieth century*. It doesn't necessarily provide the drinker with a better product because bottles with corks can be chipped, corked, and oxidized.

"When a large group at DBGB orders a box wine, we usually pour it into a decanter, but sometimes we just let the box sit on the table. If there's any left, it's easy to take home and pop in your refrigerator.

"I call box wines 'soft double magnums.'"

—*Colin Averas, sommelier, DBGB Kitchen and Bar, New York, NY*

BOX WINE

ADVENTURE

$ 5 10 15 20 25 30 35 40 45 50

←→ **Audacious Alternative To**
Bottled wine

✳✶ **Enthusiasts Also Like**
Côtes du Rhône, Vinho Verde, Moscato d'Asti, Moschofilero, Vermentino, rosé, *cru* Beaujolais, sparkling Shiraz, Lambrusco, Prosecco

⚖ **Weight**
Varies

$ **Price**
$4 to $6/bottle equivalent

☑ **Cheat Sheet**
Compromised aesthetics notwithstanding, box wine offers rising quality in a package that is undeniably affordable, convenient, durable, and eco-friendly.

Mark's Picks

White

Black Box Chardonnay (California)

Bota Box Pinot Grigio (California)

Killer Juice Chardonnay (California)

Wine Cube Chardonnay and Sauvignon Blanc (California)

Würtz Riesling Trocken (Germany)

Yellow+Blue Torrontés (Argentina)

Red

Andes Peaks Cabernet Sauvignon (California)

Black Box Cabernet Sauvignon (California)

Bota Box Cabernet Sauvignon or Shiraz (California)

Domaine d'Estezargues, "From the Tank" Côtes du Rhône (France) *deh-stay-ZAR-gwoy*

Domaine le Garrigon Côtes du Rhône (France), in a wooden box

Domaine Grand Veneur Côtes du Rhône (France) *Vuh-nuhr*

VRAC Côtes du Rhône (France)

Wine Cube Cabernet Sauvignon–Shiraz or Cabernet Sauvignon (California)

Yellow+Blue Malbec (Argentina)

 Poosh It!

When appearances count, follow the lead of some restaurants and serve your wine in a glass decanter, while keeping the box far out of view. If your designs are romantic, candlelight and rose petals can provide further distraction.

 Spend the Night Together

To fully experience the convenience that box wines offer, contrast the space that a 3-liter box requires in your refrigerator against the room needed for four bottles. If the space saved doesn't convince you, try dropping the box to the floor, followed by the four bottles. You'll have plenty of wine from the box to drink while sweeping up the glass from the bottles.

46 OLD WINE

Complexity and Ceremony

ONE OF MY favorite stories about old wine came when I was at the Toronto home of Alex Lifeson, the lead guitarist for the legendary power trio Rush. He told me about how his wife was once hurrying to a bachelorette party and accidentally grabbed (and later guzzled) his prized bottle of '73 Stag's Leap Cabernet Sauvignon—one of the American wines that triumphed at the storied Judgment of Paris competition that put California on the world's wine map. Alex pointed me to a shelf in his cellar where he now keeps everyday wines specifically for his wife, who isn't the connoisseur that he is. Inspired by Alex's ingenuity, I now advise collectors to build in their own cellars what I call a "Lifeson Ledge"—that is, an area from which family and friends can pull bottles without disturbing the collector's fine, old treasures.

Don't get the wrong idea: you needn't be a rock star or a connoisseur to enjoy age-worthy wine. More than ever before, opportunities exist to acquire such wine for a reasonable price and appreciate the unique fragrances and flavors that age can impart.

To be sure, almost all wine is made for immediate consumption; contrary to common conception, a scant 2% or so of the world's wine actually tastes *better* after aging in the bottle. But when it does, the payoff can be immense. After ten years or more, a young red's astringent tannins and disjointed flavors can eventually be supplanted by a smoother texture and enticing secondary aromas and flavors such as mushrooms, leather, and earth. An even tinier proportion of white wine and Champagne can benefit from aging, but again, when it does, its acidity can slowly diminish to reveal intriguing hints of things like hazelnuts, dried fruit, or, in the case of Riesling, petroleum or "petrol." Rarefied examples of dessert wine can also gain a wonderful complexity over the years (Chapter 41).

Although there is no intuitive way to know which (and for how long) wines are ageable, I have listed below wines with a reputation for being built for the long haul, especially when they come from top producers in exceptional years. Tasting notes of professional wine critics and bloggers make general predictions as to when to "drink" or "hold" particular bottles of wine, as do the users of community Web sites such as CellarTracker.com. Note that ageable wine in large-format bottles like magnums (Chapter 44) tend to mature more slowly, as their ratio of air to wine is considerably smaller, so less air (and thus oxidation) makes it to the wine.

It isn't just its physical transformations that make mature wine so alluring but also the sense of ceremony conferred by wine from a particular year. Instead of commemorating an anniversary or birthday in a Carvel cake's frosting, you'll multiply a special day's impact by doing it with a bottle of wine from the relevant vintage. "Vintage" is simply the year in which a wine's grapes were grown; better years occur when a region's weather was good enough for the grapes to ripen evenly and achieve balanced levels of acidity. An Internet search—starting with a visit to the vintage chart (covering 1970 and later) at RobertParker.com—will tell you how a particular vintage year fared in a given region of the world.

Hunting down mature wine—and especially that of a specific vintage—isn't as daunting as it seems. Fine merchants such as California's K&L and New York's Sherry-Lehmann tend to have inventories of well-aged wine on hand, especially those from a region's better vintages. If you have a specific producer and/or year in mind, the trusty database at Wine-Searcher.com can indicate which retailers have the wine in stock. Moreover, some wineries will periodically release older or "library" selections of age-worthy wine—so you can always email your favorite producer to see if they are releasing any library vintages.

If you can't find the right bottle in a shop or a winery, you might investigate auctions, whether online or live. Online auctions such as WineBid.com are easy to search and useful for sourcing single bottles, such as the red Bordeaux from 1971 I just purchased for a good buddy's birthday. Regular auctions—Zachys, Christie's, Acker Merrall, and the like—often require a purchase of multiple bottles but offer the added assurance that professionals have vetted the condition and provenance of the bottles. Many of their sites allow you to search for a particular year, producer, or region—or download the auction catalog and search those categories in the index.

BRAVEHEARTS ON *Old Wine*

"One of my favorite dinners was when Joseph Phelps had a bunch of restaurateurs from San Francisco up to the winery. I sat with Phelps himself that night, and I took him a bottle of 1941 Sebastiani, the famous California Cabernet that I found at a distributor in Michigan. It was a gift for letting me work the harvest at the winery. He was like, 'Where did you find this? This is a piece of California winemaking history!' After Phelps insisted on opening it, everyone had a little sip, and it was fantastic."   —*Alex Lifeson, lead guitarist, Rush*

" 'Oh yeah, I took the Stag-something. It was great. The girls just loved it.' "   —*Alex Lifeson, on how his wife described the fate of his prized bottle of '73 Stag's Leap Cabernet that she accidentally swiped for a bachelorette party*

"You have to be open to different wine types, because if the specific year you're looking for wasn't good in traditional places like Bordeaux and Burgundy, you want to look to mature wine from places such as Champagne or Madeira."

—*Richard Brierley, former head of North American wine sales, Christie's*

"What kind of wine do I like? I believe it was Diogenes the Cynic who was first credited with the correct answer to this question: 'Other people's.' But let it be clear that Diogenes and I are referring specifically to those other people who have a case of Château Lafite Rothschild Pauillac 1982."   —*P. J. O'Rourke, writer and political satirist*

"I like a 1982 Mouton Rothschild when it's my birthday, to honor another year of life."
                                        —Busta Rhymes, hip-hop artist

"When my buddy turned forty I gave him a case of '66 Léoville–Las Cases. Buying birth-year-dated wine is a great thing to do for a friend."
                                        —Jason Priestley, actor

BRIERLEY'S GUILTY PLEASURE: MIXING WINE AND COKE

It's relieving to know that Richard Brierley, who has spent a career tasting some of the world's finest wines as Christie's head of wine sales for North America, has a guilty pleasure that is strikingly humble. Summertime finds him quaffing inexpensive red wine mixed with Coca-Cola, a Basque concoction that the locals call "Calimocho."

"I'm supposed to a purist, a fine wine guy. But in the summer, I like to drink a Calimocho. It's like an upscale sangria: it's got sweetness and fizz and is very refreshing. It is a great aperitif and readies your palate for something more serious."

He conceded: "I don't tell many people about this. I like the irony of it all."

INGREDIENTS

Coke (or Diet Coke)
Red wine (preferably simple and Spanish)
Ice

1) Mix together equal parts of Coke and red wine.
2) Add a generous amount of ice. (The ice will diminish the soda's fizz, while the soda makes the wine more quaffable.)
3) Drink liberally.

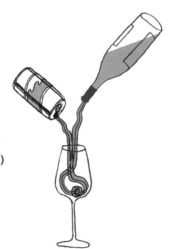

"We reflected on what happened over the century and who was President when the grapes were crushed."

—*Neil deGrasse Tyson, astrophysicist, on opening a bottle of 1900 Château Latour for the millennial New Year's dinner*

"I love the earthiness and sexy, animalistic smell and taste of Château Haut-Brion. There's a perfect harmony between the fruit—mostly dark berries—and the soul of the *terroir*. Must be an old vintage . . ."

—*Eric Ripert, executive chef and co-owner, Le Bernardin*

"I don't trip on it too much, but there's something psychological—even spiritual—about drinking wine from your birth year. And I was born in October, harvest season. You have the wine and ask yourself—'Is this what it tasted like, what it smelled like back then?' It is especially poignant after your second or third bottle."

—*Sammy Hagar, vocalist, Chickenfoot, and former vocalist, Van Halen*

"I recall a bottle of Ausone 1900. We were in our Paris home and had just finished our meat course with a bit of wine left when we decided to walk down the street to the Pont des Arts to watch the Eiffel Tower midnight illuminations while sipping the last few drops. It was magical."

—*Mireille Guiliano, author,* French Women Don't Get Fat *and former president, Clicquot, Inc.*

"In 1988, at Château Ausone in Bordeaux, we tasted back to 1831. It was magic, history, haunting bouquets and tastes, ethereal wines— and then walking out into the vineyards under a full moon. Sorry, but it is true!"

—*Serena Sutcliffe, head of Sotheby's international wine department, London, England*

"I went to Paris to publicize the movie *Time After Time*. The local Warner Brothers PR guy took me to lunch at Maxim's, which happened to be a great mistake because it was his birthday and I asked when he was born. He said 1947 and so I asked the waiter what they had in the vault from that year. The waiter brought a Château Ausone 1947, which was then the unheard of price of only six hundred dollars. It was the best bottle of wine I've ever had. It just tasted *different*. My God, it was so good that I took both the label and the menu and had them framed and hung them in my bathroom. I smile every time I think about that bottle."

—*Malcolm McDowell, actor*

"When I was twenty-six and opened my first restaurant, I hosted a luncheon for Angelo Gaja, who brought his winery's '78 Barbarescos as well as '61 Barbarescos, the latter of which was the final wine produced by his father. He left me a '61, which I still have in my cellar. I'll open it if the doctor says I have one day to live."

—*Todd English, chef and restaurateur, Olives, Charlestown, MA*

"My daughter was born in 1970 and so I bought a dozen bottles of 1970 Lynch-Bages, a red Bordeaux. We've enjoyed them throughout the years, including celebrating after she graduated from university and after she sailed around the world. We did the same with my son, who was born in 1972."

—*John Lodge, singer and bass guitarist, The Moody Blues*

"I'll never forget a tasting I attended in Dallas some years ago. It was a charity fundraiser and people paid one thousand dollars per person to attend. We tasted an 1870 Mouton Rothschild from a jeroboam, and then a 1970 Mouton Rothschild alongside a 1970 Mondavi Cabernet Sauvignon. It was a revelation to me that hundred-year-old wine could be so wonderful. It still had bouquet, the color was still there, and it had an old but still healthy character. The Mondavi 1970 wine showed beautifully beside the Mouton."

—*Robert Mondavi, the late pioneer of fine California wine*

OLD WINE

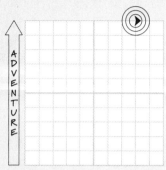

 Mark's Picks

AGEWORTHY WINE TYPES (mostly the finest versions in the best years)

Red
Aglianico
Barolo and Barbaresco
Brunello
California Cabernet Sauvignon
Châteauneuf-du-Pape
Italian super-Tuscans
Northern Rhône (Hermitage and Côte-Rôtie)
Petite Sirah
Priorat
Red Bordeaux
Red Burgundy

White and Bubbly
Gewürztraminer
Riesling
Champagne (mostly vintage-dated selections)
White Bordeaux
White Burgundy (Chablis, Puligny-Montrachet,
    Chassange-Montrachet, Meursault,
    Corton-Charlemagne)

Dessert
Sauternes from France and other fine
    Late-Harvest styles
Madeira (vintage)
Port (vintage)

Major U.S. Wine Auctioneers
Acker, Merrall, & Condit (New York)
Bonhams & Butterfields (San Francisco)
Chicago Wine Company (Chicago)
Christie's (Los Angeles and New York)
Hart Davis Hart (Chicago)
Morrell & Company (New York)
Sotheby's (New York)
Zachys (New York)

 Audacious Alternative To
Non-aged wine

 Price
Medium to High

 Cheat Sheet
Mature wine offers new taste sensations and a uniquely special way to commemorate life's anniversaries.

Label Logic
An older wine bottle with an unusually low level of wine, or "fill level"—such as that at or below the bottle's shoulder—may indicate that the bottle was improperly stored and has suffered excessive and irreparable oxidation.

Poosh It!

The French idiomatic expression "*avoir de la bouteille*" ("to have some bottle") refers to someone or something that gains wisdom or value with age. A man of surprisingly good taste, fictional serial-killer Hannibal Lecter, bestowed a birth-year bottle of the dessert wine Château d'Yquem on FBI agent Clarice Starling in recognition of her thirty-third birthday in the novel *Hannibal*.

 Spend the Night Together

Consider saving as souvenirs some of the empty bottles of aged wine you drink; collectors sometimes give them the poetic name of "dead soldiers," which presumably refers to their dutiful service slaking thirst and also to the fact that their spirits, literally, have departed.

A relatively affordable way of sampling several older wines at one time is to attend the pre-auction tastings that some auction houses hold the night before or morning of an auction; admission can be as low as $80. Alternatively, some houses offer free pours of mature wine to registered bidders at the auction itself.

Collectors may want to build a party around wine from a particular symbolic animal of Chinese years. So a "Year of the Tiger" tasting would include wine from any of the following vintages: 2010, 1999, 1987, 1975, 1963, 1951, and so forth.

APPENDICES

THE BRAVEHEARTS

Exclusive Insights from 146 Wine-Passionate Luminaries

Name and best-known *terroir*

ANDREW ADAM, *winemaker, Conway Family Vineyards, Rancho Arroyo, CA*

TED ALLEN, *food writer and host, Food Network's* Chopped

LOU AMDUR, *owner, Lou's Wine Bar, Los Angeles, CA*

TORI AMOS, *singer-songwriter*

JOSÉ ANDRÉS, *chef and restaurateur, The Bazaar by Jose Andrés, Los Angeles, CA*

BART ARAUJO, *owner, Araujo Estate Wines, Napa, CA*

ERIC ARNOLD, *author,* First Big Crush: The Down and Dirty on Making Great Wine Down Under

DONATELLA ARPAIA, *food/entertaining authority and restaurateur, Mia Dona, New York, NY*

KERIN AUTH, *co-owner, Tinto Fino Vinos de España, New York, NY*

COLIN AVERAS, *sommelier, DBGB Kitchen and Bar, New York, NY*

DAN AYKROYD, *actor*

KEVIN BACON, *actor*

GILLIAN BALLANCE, *former wine director, PlumpJack Group, San Francisco, CA*

ANTONIO BANDERAS, *actor*

LIDIA BASTIANICH, *chef and host, PBS's* Lidia's Italy

MARIO BATALI, *chef and restaurateur, Babbo, New York, NY*

MOLLIE BATTENHOUSE, *sommelier and wine director, Maslow 6, New York, NY*

PIERRE DE BENOIST, *winemaker, Domaine A. & P. Villaine, Burgundy, France*

MANNIE BERK, *Madeira expert and proprietor, Rare Wine Company, Sonoma, CA*

JOHN BESH, *chef and restaurateur, Restaurant August, New Orleans, LA*

DREW BLEDSOE, *football great, New England Patriots*

APRIL BLOOMFIELD, *chef and co-owner, The Spotted Pig, New York, NY*

ROBERT BOHR, *wine director and partner, Cru, New York, NY*

REID BOSWARD, *winemaker, Kaesler Vineyards, Barossa Valley, Australia*

RICHARD BRIERLEY, *former head of North American wine sales, Christie's, and head of fine wine, Vanquish Wine, London, England*

CORIE BROWN, *co-founder, food site ZesterDaily.com and former* Los Angeles Times *wine columnist*

JEFF BUNDSCHU, *president, Gundlach Bundschu, Sonoma, CA*

DAVID BURKE, *chef and restaurateur, David Burke Townhouse, New York, NY*

JOE CAMPANALE, *beverage director and co-owner, dell'anima, New York, NY*

DIOGO CAMPILHO, *winemaker, Quinta da Lagoalva, Ribatejo, Portugal*

JEAN-LOUIS CARBONNIER, *president, Carbonnier Communications, New York, NY*

FLOYD CARDOZ, *executive chef, Tabla, New York, NY*

DAVID CHAN, *violinist and concertmaster, Metropolitan Opera, New York, NY*

MICHAEL CHIARELLO, *vintner and host, Food Network's* Easy Entertaining with Michael Chiarello

MORGAN CLENDENEN, *winemaker and co-owner, Cold Heaven Cellars, Santa Rita Hills, CA*

TOM COLICCHIO, *chef and restaurateur, Craft, New York, NY*

JEFF CORWIN, *host and executive producer,* Animal Planet's *"The Jeff Corwin Experience"*

ARIANE DAGUIN, *co-founder and owner, D'Artagnan Newark, NJ*

FRED DEXHEIMER, *master sommelier and wine consultant, New York, NY*

ALAIN DUCASSE, *chef and restaurateur, Le Jules Verne, Paris, France*

WYLIE DUFRESNE, *chef and owner, wd-50, New York, NY*

BRIAN DUNCAN, *owner and wine director BIN 36, Chicago, IL*

TODD ENGLISH, *chef and restaurateur, Olives, Charlestown, MA*

DANA FARNER, *beverage director, CUT: Wolfgang Puck, Los Angeles*

GUY FIERI, *chef and television host*

MICK FLEETWOOD, *drummer and namesake, Fleetwood Mac*

DENNIS FOLEY, *wine consultant and auctioneer*

JODIE FOSTER, *actress*

DOUG FROST, *master sommelier and master of wine*

VICTOR GALLEGOS, *general manager and viticulturist, Sea Smoke Cellars, Santa Barbara, CA*

RICHARD GEOFFROY, *chief winemaker, Dom Pérignon, Epernay, France*

ANTHONY GIGLIO, *wine educator and author*

DEAN GOLD, *owner/chef, Dino, Washington, DC*

PETER GRANOFF, *master sommelier and co-owner, Ferry Plaza Wine Merchants, San Francisco, CA*

NIGEL GREENING, *owner, Felton Road Wines, Central Otago, New Zealand*

PAUL GRIECO, *wine director and co-owner, Hearth, New York, NY*

ANJOLEENA GRIFFIN-HOLST, *wine director, Borgata Hotel Casino & Spa, Atlantic City, NJ*

BRUCE GREENWOOD, *actor,* Star Trek (2009)

MIREILLE GUILIANO, *author,* French Women Don't Get Fat *and former president, Clicquot, Inc.*

DR. SANJAY GUPTA, *chief medical correspondent, CNN, and neurosurgeon*

SAMMY HAGAR, *vocalist, Chickenfoot, and former vocalist, Van Halen*

NICK HARMER, *bass guitarist, Death Cab for Cutie*

PETER HELLMAN, *wine writer and former wine columnist,* The New York Sun

ANDREW HOLT, *owner, Poonawatta Estate, Edna Valley, Australia*

LAURIE HOOK, *chief winemaker, Beringer Vineyards, Napa, CA*

ELIZABETH HARCOURT, *sommelier, Corton, New York, NY*

JULIO IGLESIAS, *music legend*

ROWAN JACOBSEN, *author,* A Geography of Oysters: The Connoisseur's Guide to Oyster Eating in North America

JOSH JENSEN, *winemaker and owner, Calera Wine Company, Hollister, CA*

HELEN JOHANNESEN, *wine director, Animal, Los Angeles, CA*

DANIEL JOHNNES, *wine director, Daniel Boulud's Dinex Group, New York, NY*

KEVIN JUDD, *winemaker and co-founder, Cloudy Bay Vineyards, New Zealand*

KAREN KING, *former wine director, The Modern at MoMA, New York, NY*

RÉMI KRUG, *president, Champagne Krug, Champagne, France*

MIKE "COACH K" KRZYZEWSKI, *head coach, Duke University men's basketball team and U.S. national team*

JENNY LEFCOURT, *co-owner and importer, Jenny & François Selections, New York, NY*

JOHN LEGUIZAMO, *actor*

ALEX LIFESON, *lead guitarist, Rush*

SHELLEY LINDGREN, *wine director and co-owner, A16, San Francisco, CA*

JOHN LITHGOW, *actor*

JOHN LODGE, *singer and bass guitarist, The Moody Blues*

MATTHEW MCCONAUGHEY, *actor*

MALCOLM MCDOWELL, *actor*

JAY MCINERNEY, *novelist and wine columnist,* The Wall Street Journal

KYLE MACLACHLAN, *actor*

VIRGINIA MADSEN, *actress*

BAM MARGERA, *daredevil, former professional skateboarder, and actor*

WILLIAM MATTIELLO, *chef and owner, Via Emilia, New York, NY*

ALLEN MEADOWS, *wine critic and publisher, Burghound.com*

CESAR MILLAN, *National Geographic Channel's "Dog Whisperer"*

ROBERT MONDAVI, *the late California wine legend*

JOE MONTANA, *football great*

CHRISTIAN MOREAU, *winemaker and owner, Domaine Christian Moreau Père & Fils, France*

BEBE NEUWIRTH, *actress*

DIRK NIEPOORT, *family proprietor, Niepoort, Douro, Portugal*

DREW NIEPORENT, *restaurateur, Tribeca Grill and Nobu, New York, NY*

BILL NYE, *PBS's "Science Guy"*

MARNIE OLD, *author,* Wine Secrets, *and wine educator*

P. J. O'ROURKE, *writer and political satirist*

KYLE ORTON, *pro football player*

CHESTER OSBORN, *winemaker, d'Arenberg, McLaren Vale, South Australia*

ROSS OUTON, *winner the of first season of* The Winemakers *on PBS and beverage consultant, Austin, TX*

CHAZZ PALMINTERI, *actor and writer,* A Bronx Tale

MONTE PITT, *owner, Patton Valley Vineyards, Willamette Valley, OR*

ALFRED PORTALE, *chef and co-owner, Gotham Bar and Grill, New York, NY*

ZAC POSEN, *fashion designer*

JASON PRIESTLEY, *actor*

NICKI PRUSS, *winemaker, Stag's Leap Wine Cellars, Napa, CA*

MICHAEL PSILAKIS, *chef and co-owner, Anthos, New York, NY*

GORDON RAMSAY, *restaurateur and television chef, London, England*

LYNN REDGRAVE, *the late actress*

NICK RHODES, *keyboardist, Duran Duran*

INEZ RIBUSTELLO, *sommelier and co-owner, On the Square, Tarboro, NC*

ALAN RICHMAN, *food and wine writer*

BEN RIGGS, *veteran winemaking consultant, McClaren Vale, Australia*

ERIC RIPERT, *chef and co-owner, Le Bernadin, New York, NY*

JOËL ROBUCHON, *chef and restaurateur, L'Atelier de Joël Robuchon, New York, NY*

GAVIN ROSSDALE, *solo artist and former vocalist and guitarist, Bush*

MIGUEL ROQUETTE, *owner, Quinta do Crasto, Douro, Portugal*

BUSTA RHYMES, *hip-hop artist*

MARCUS SAMUELSSON, *chef and co-owner, Aquavit, New York, NY*

LESLIE SBROCCO, *wine author and consultant*

ABE SCHOENER, *founder and winemaker, Scholium Project, Suisun Valley, CA*

NANCY SILVERTON, *baker and co-owner, Osteria Mozza, Los Angeles, CA*

AL STEWART, *folk-rock musician, "Year of the Cat"*

DAVE STEWART, *musician and co-founder, The Eurythmics*

LARRY STONE, *"dean of sommeliers" and general manager, Rubicon Estate, Napa, CA*

SERENA SUTCLIFFE, *head of international wine department, Sotheby's, London, England*

HILARY SWANK, *actress*

DOMINIC SYMINGTON, *director, Symington Family Estates, Douro, Portugal*

BENOIT TARLANT, *family proprietor, Champagne Tarlant, Champagne, France*

COURTNEY TAYLOR-TAYLOR, *lead singer and guitarist, The Dandy Warhols*

LETTIE TEAGUE, *wine columnist,* The Wall Street Journal, *and former executive wine editor,* Food & Wine *magazine*

TERRY THEISE, *wine importer, Bethesda, MD*

LAURENT TOURONDEL, *chef and restaurateur*

MING TSAI, *chef and restaurateur, Blue Ginger, Boston, MA*

YIANNIS TSELEPOS, *winemaker and co-owner, Domaine Tselepos*

NEIL DEGRASSE TYSON, *astrophysicist and director, Hayden Planetarium, New York, NY*

JEAN-GEORGES VONGERICHTEN, *chef and restaurateur, Jean-Georges, New York, NY*

YIANNIS VOYATZIS, *chief winemaker, Boutari, Naoussa, Greece*

DAVID WELSH, *lead guitarist, The Fray*

ANDREW WIGAN, *chief winemaker, Peter Lehmann Wines, Tanunda, Australia*

HEATHER WILLENS, *importer and owner, HW Wines, Buenos Aires, Argentina*

LIZ WILLETTE, *owner and importer, Willette Wines, New York, NY*

CHRISTOPHER YCAZA, *wine director and general manager, Galatoire's, New Orleans, LA*

DEBBIE ZACHAREAS, *co-owner, Ferry Plaza Wine Merchants, San Francisco, CA*

MARK'S VINOUS VOCABULARY

Billecart-Salmon-Rosé-Lovers-Cartel: the tendency of so many wine pros to love this rosé Champagne to the extent that they almost form an alliance

Downed Power line: Txakoli, for the way its lemony tang zips around your mouth

Drink Bravely: my cri de coeur encouraging the exploration beyond wine's usual suspects. As this book's opening quote shows, the French Renaissance writer François Rabelais actually used this very phrase in one of his sixteenth-century works.

Federal Fizz: nickname for American sparkling wine

Flaah-wehrz, Smells Like: *generally*—anything unequivocally worthwhile; *specifically*—Torrontés, for its ability to consistently give pleasure and for its explosively floral aromatics

Floral, Flinty Invigorator, The: Riesling from Austria, for its stone-fruit aromatics and minerally tang

Fresca Flask: a wine-filled soda bottle used for the purposes of smuggling (Chapter 14); *see also* Sprite-ing (a wine)

Gin & Tonic after a Diet and a Discount: Vinho Verde, for its tangy taste, light body, and low price

"Give It a Shock": a disarming way of asking a waiter to chill a bottle of red wine to focus its flavors; ideally, the wine is "shocked" for about ten minutes in an ice-filled wine bucket.

Maternal Cheek Pinch: Nero d'Avola, for its comforting black fruit, soft tannins, and floral perfume

Medieval on Your Tongue: the astringency often seen in Cahors and other highly tannic wines

Mosko, The: the nickname Greek vintners should adopt for Moschofilero to make it more accessible to consumers

Official Dessert Wine for People Who Don't Like Dessert Wine: Moscato d'Asti, for its universal appeal driven by ambrosial aromatics and a light, non-syrupy taste

Official Wine of *Fruits de Mer* Platters: Muscadet, for its affinity with shellfish

PHBR: Pre-Hotel Bubbly Run; used to circumvent the pecuniary injustice of alcohol markups at hotels; recommended with Federal Fizz (Chapter 35); *see Federal Fizz*

Pinot Grigio with Fangs: Sauvignon Blanc from New Zealand, for its brassy intensity

Pivot Noir: for Pinot Noir's ability to pivot between the foods we associate with white and red wines

Poosh It!: my general term for taking things to the next level; with wine, it refers to broadening your vinous horizons through new wine types, deeper knowledge, and memorable experiences. You are "pooshing it" by reading this book.

Prozac-co: Prosecco, for its uplifting effect

Rosé Rule of P: the idea that you can't go wrong with serving rosé with anything pink—ham, pork, shrimp, lobster—or with anything Provençal—bouillabaisse, salade Niçoise, or grilled sardines

Rosé Ruler: my homemade card featuring a row of Pantone-like color samples, created to demonstrate rosé's wide spectrum of hues

Seafoodie Wine, The Ultimate: Albariño, because of its simpatico with seafood and popularity among the food-obsessed

Secret Society to Confuse Wine Drinkers: the clandestine body responsible for the suspiciously large number of inconsistencies and contradictions in language of wine (see Chapter 29)

7UP That Gets You Soused: Prosecco, for its citrusy, casual, and quaffable character

Snore-low: Merlot that is cheap, characterless, and in dispiritingly abundant supply

Sprite-ing (a wine): pouring wine into a green-tinted soda bottle for clandestine imbibing; useful in movie theaters and sporting events (Chapter); *see also* Fresca Flask

Unslim Slatey, The: Priorat, for the wine's full-body and graphite bite and the eponymous region's rebirth as a world-class wine region

Vinous Penalty Box: imposing a time-out on—i.e., aerating—an astringent wine like Cahors to soften its tannic sensation

V-Spot: Viognier, for its sensual appeal

Wine Buyer's Amnesia: the tendency to forget that you actually paid for a wine bottle, especially when it happened more than three months ago. Its effect is to help a BYOB-er write off the wine purchase as a sunk cost, thereby making BYOB seem like an even better deal than it already is.

 For a free, multimedia companion to these concepts, including exclusive photos and video, please visit www.MarkOldman.com/companion.

"IF YOU LIKE THIS, YOU MAY LIKE THAT"

Ususal Suspect → Brave New Pour

Bubbly

USUAL SUSPECT:
Champagne

- American Sparkling Wine
- Grower Champagne
- Rosé Champagne
- Prosecco
- Txakoli

Whites

USUAL SUSPECT:
Chardonnay

- American Sparkling Wine
- Gewürztraminer
- Low/No Oak Chardonnay
- Viognier

USUAL SUSPECT:
Pinot Grigio

- Grüner Veltliner
- Low/No Oak Chardonnay
- Moschofilero
- Muscadet
- Prosecco
- Torrontés
- Vermentino

USUAL SUSPECT:
Riesling

- Gewürztraminer
- Moschofilero
- Riesling from Australia
- Riesling from Austria
- Torrontés
- Viognier

USUAL SUSPECT:
Sauvignon Blanc

- Albariño
- Grüner Veltliner
- Low/No Oak Chardonnay
- Moschofilero
- Riesling from Australia
- Rueda
- Sauvignon Blanc from New Zealand
- Txakoli
- Vermentino
- Vinho Verde

Reds

USUAL SUSPECT:
Cabernet Sauvignon

Aglianico
Bargain Bordeaux
Cahors
Classic Cabernet
Côtes du Rhône
Malbec
(Good) Merlot
Petite Sirah
Priorat
Reds from Portugal
Reds from Washington State

USUAL SUSPECT:
Merlot

Bargain Bordeaux
Classic Cabernet
Malbec
(Good) Merlot
Montepulciano d'Abruzzo
Reds from the Loire
Reds from Washington State

USUAL SUSPECT:
Pinot Noir

Bargain Burgundy
Cru Beaujolais
Pinot Noir from New Zealand
Pinot Noir from Oregon
Reds from the Loire
Rosé

Other Usual Suspects

USUAL SUSPECT:
Beaujolais Nouveau

Cru Beaujolais
Rosé

USUAL SUSPECT:
Beer

Lambrusco
Sparkling Shiraz
Txakoli
Vinho Verde

USUAL SUSPECT:
Chianti

Montepulciano d'Abruzzo
Nero d'Avola
Lambrusco

USUAL SUSPECT:
Gin or Vodka and Tonic

Txakoli
Vinho Verde

USUAL SUSPECT:
Lambrusco (Commercial)

Lambrusco (dry, small-batch)
Sparkling Shiraz

USUAL SUSPECT:
Red Bordeaux

Bargain Bordeaux
(Good) Merlot
Reds from the Loire

USUAL SUSPECT:
Red Burgundy

Bargain Burgundy
Pinot Noir from Oregon
Pinot Noir from New Zealand

USUAL SUSPECT:
Rioja

Côtes du Rhône
Malbec
Montepulciano d'Abruzzo
Nero d'Avola
Priorat
Reds from Washington State

USUAL SUSPECT:
Standard 750-ml bottles

Big Wine
Box Wine

USUAL SUSPECT:
Syrah

Cahors
Malbec
Nero d'Avola
Petite Sirah
Reds from Portugal
Sparkling Shiraz

USUAL SUSPECT:
White Zinfandel

Rosé
Moscato d'Asti
Sparkling Shiraz
Torrontés

USUAL SUSPECT:
Zinfandel

Aglianico
Côtes du Rhône
Nero d'Avola
Petite Sirah

With or After Dessert

USUAL SUSPECT:
No dessert wine at all

Madeira
Moscato d'Asti
Tawny Port

USUAL SUSPECT:
Port

Madeira
Tawny Port

USUAL SUSPECT:
Scotch

Madeira
Tawny Port

EXEMPLARS OF ECONOMY

(Many less than $15)

Box Wine

Côtes du Rhône

Cru Beaujolais

Lambrusco

Low/No Oak Chardonnay
 (excluding Chablis)

Malbec

Montepulciano d'Abruzzo

Moscato d'Asti

Moschofilero

Muscadet

Nero d'Avola

Prosecco

Riesling from Australia

Rosé

Rueda

Sauvignon Blanc from
 New Zealand

Torrontés

Vermentino

Vinho Verde

RELIABILITY ACROSS PRODUCERS VS. MINEFIELDS

Especially Reliable   Minefields: Choose Carefully

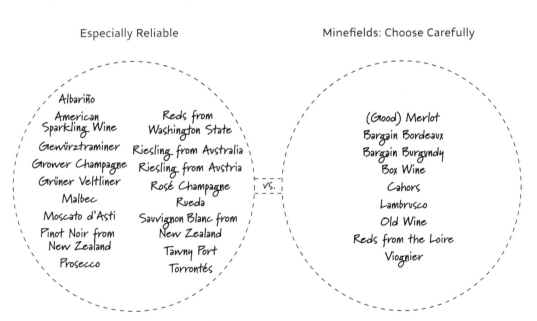

Albariño
American Sparkling Wine
Gewürztraminer
Grower Champagne
Grüner Veltliner
Malbec
Moscato d'Asti
Pinot Noir from New Zealand
Prosecco
Reds from Washington State
Riesling from Australia
Riesling from Austria
Rosé Champagne
Rueda
Sauvignon Blanc from New Zealand
Tawny Port
Torrontés

vs.

(Good) Merlot
Bargain Bordeaux
Bargain Burgundy
Box Wine
Cahors
Lambrusco
Old Wine
Reds from the Loire
Viognier

GULPABLE VS. INTELLECTUAL

Gulpable: Glug and Go

Intellectual: Contemplation
Required to Fully Appreciate

Albariño
Box Wine
Côtes du Rhône
Cru Beaujolais
Low/No Oak Chardonnay
Malbec
Moscato d'Asti
Moschofilero

Muscadet
Prosecco
Rosé
Sparkling Shiraz
Torrontés
Txakoli
Vermentino
Vinho Verde

vs.

Aglianico
Cahors
Grower Champagne
Grüner Veltliner
Low/No Oak Chardonnay (Chablis)
Madeira
Old Wine
Pinot Noir from New Zealand
Pinot Noir from Oregon
Priorat
Riesling from Austria

SHAGGY DOGS

(IMMEDIATELY LIKABLE)

Albariño
American Sparkling Wine
Big Wine
Côtes du Rhône
Cru Beaujolais
Low/No Oak Chardonnay
Malbec
Montepulciano d'Abruzzo
Moscato d'Asti

Nero d'Avola
Prosecco
Reds from Washington State
Rosé
Tawny Port
Torrontés
Vermentino
Vinho Verde

Snob Picks (a.k.a. Ascot Appeal)

Big Wine

Classic Cabernet

Low/No Oak Chardonnay
(Chablis)

Madeira

Old Wine

Rosé Champagne

The Inner Sanctum =
Snob Picks + Somm Sips

Big Wine

Old Wine

Rosé Champagne

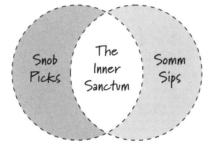

Somm Sips (Darlings of Wine Pros)

Aglianico

Albariño

Big Wine

Grower Champagne

Grüner Veltliner

Malbec

Moscato d'Asti

Old Wine

Pinot Noir from
New Zealand

Pinot Noir from Oregon

Priorat

Reds from Portugal

Riesling from Australia

Riesling from Austria

Rosé

Rosé Champagne

Rueda

Sauvignon Blanc from
New Zealand

Torrontés

Txakoli

Vermentino

EMBARISSTAS
(PERILOUS PRONUNCIATIONS)

Aglianico

Gewürztraminer

Grüner Veltliner

Montepulciano d'Abruzzo

Moschofilero

Rueda

Txakoli

Viognier

THE CURIOSITY SHOP
(STRIKING POURS)

Big Wine

Lambrusco

Madeira

Sparkling Shiraz

Txakoli

BUZZ MAKERS VS. DAY DRINKERS

Buzz Makers:
Especially High Alcohol
(Often over 14%)

Day Drinkers:
Especially Low Alcohol
(Often 12% or lower)

Aglianico
Classic Cabernet
Madeira
Petite Sirah
Priorat
Reds from Portugal
Tawny Port

VS.

Cru Beaujolais
Moscato d'Asti
Muscadet
Prosecco
Reds from the Loire
Vinho Verde

GASTRIC PROVOCATEURS
(APERITIFS)

(Ample acidity and light to medium weight)

Albariño

American Sparkling Wine

Grower Champagne

Grüner Veltliner

Lambrusco

Madeira (dry versions)

Moschofilero

Muscadet

Prosecco

Riesling from Australia

Rosé

Rosé Champagne

Rueda

Sparkling Shiraz

Torrontés

Txakoli

Vermentino

Vinho Verde

BORN TO BRUNCH

(Light, fruity, casual, and/or bubbly)

American Sparkling Wine

Cru Beaujolais

Lambrusco

Low/No Oak Chardonnay

Moscato d'Asti

Prosecco

Rosé

Sparkling Shiraz

Txakoli

FIT FOR FORAGERS
(VEGETARIAN FRIENDLY)

(Ample acidity, low/no tannin, low/no oak, low to medium weight, and/or herbal notes)

American Sparkling Wine

Bargain Burgundy

Cru Beaujolais

Grower Champagne

Low/No Oak Chardonnay

Madeira (dry versions)

Moschofilero

Pinot Noir from New Zealand

Pinot Noir from Oregon

Prosecco

Reds from the Loire

Reds from Washington State

Riesling from Australia

Riesling from Austria

Rosé

Rosé Champagne

Rueda

Sauvignon Blanc from
    New Zealand

Vermentino

MADE FOR MEAT EATERS

Aglianico
Bargain Bordeaux
Cahors
Classic Cabernet
Côtes du Rhône
Malbec
(Good) Merlot

Montepulciano d'Abruzzo
Nero d'Avola
Petite Sirah
Priorat
Reds from Portugal
Reds from Washington State

TAKEN WITH BACON

(Ample acidity, medium weight, and/or spicy)

Aglianico
Bargain Burgundy
Côtes du Rhône
Cru Beaujolais
Lambrusco

Pinot Noir from New Zealand
Pinot Noir from Oregon
Reds from the Loire
Rosé
Sparkling Shiraz

BLAZE BALMS
(SPICE FRIENDLY)

(Low to moderate alcohol, bubbly, casual, and/or off-dry)

American Sparkling Wine
Cru Beaujolais
Gewürztraminer
Grower Champagne
Grüner Veltliner
Lambrusco
Moscato d'Asti
Moschofilero
Pinot Noir from New Zealand
Pinot Noir from Oregon

Prosecco
Riesling from Australia
Riesling from Austria
Rosé
Rosé Champagne
Sparkling Shiraz
Torrontés
Vermentino
Viognier

Classic Pairings

Albariño	Shellfish and fish
Cahors	Cassoulet
Champagne	Caviar, *gougères* (crispy cheese balls)
Classic Cabernet	Steak
Cru Beaujolais	Charcuterie
Gewürztraminer	Muenster cheese, sausages, spicy fare
Grüner Veltliner	Vegetables (including asparagus)
Lambrusco	Mortadella
Low/No Oak Chardonnay (Chablis)	Fish (lighter types), oysters
Madeira (drier versions)	Consommé
Madeira (sweeter versions)	Caramelized and/or chocolate desserts, Stilton cheese
Malbec	Fire-grilled beef
Merlot	Beef tenderloin
Montepulciano d'Abruzzo	Rich pasta dishes
Nero d'Avola	Spaghetti and meatballs
Muscadet	Oysters and clams
Pinot Noir	Salmon, mushrooms, beets
Priorat	Manchego cheese
Prosecco	Mixed drinks
Red Bordeaux	Lamb
Red Burgundy	Roast chicken, Époisses de Bourgogne
Reds from the Loire	Bistro fare (e.g., coq au vin, steak frites), chévre
Rosé	Provençal fare (salade niçoise, black olive tapenade, bouillabaisse)
Rosé	Pink fare (e.g., lobster, shrimp, ham, pork)
Sauvignon Blanc from New Zealand	Goat cheese, Dishes with "green" tastes (e.g., herbs, spinach, green pepper, asparagus)
Sparkling Shiraz	Peking duck
Tawny Port	Salty nuts, chocolate
Txakoli	Tapas
Viognier	Spicy fare

FRISSON FELLOWS

Mark's Brave New Pairings

American Sparkling Wine	Hotel rooms, popcorn, Shrimp Po' Boys
Bargain Burgundy	Pepperoni pizza
Classic Cabernet	Red Vines Licorice
Côtes du Rhône	In-N-Out Burgers,™ lamb kabobs
Cru Beaujolais	Teriyaki dishes
Grüner Veltliner	Trout salad
Lambrusco	Chilled strawberries, pizza
Low/No Oak Chardonnay	Falafel
Madeira	Ouija boards
Malbec	Chili con carne
Merlot	Dark chocolate
Moscato d'Asti	Krispy Kreme doughnuts, spicy Asian food
Petite Sirah	Burritos
Prosecco	Fried chicken
Reds from the Loire	Thanksgiving dinner
Riesling from Australia	Fish tacos, salads and salad dressing
Riesling from Austria	Lobster tail and endive in cream sauce
Rosé	French fries dipped in béarnaise sauce, hot dogs
Rosé Champagne	Barbecued ribs
Sparkling Shiraz	Pork buns, Froot Loops
Torrontés	Dishes with *sriracha* (Thai chile sauce), lobster rolls
Txakoli	Fish and chips
Vermentino	Artichokes
Vinho Verde	Sliced tomatoes on bread

T-DAY (THANKSGIVING)

(Versatile, of moderate weight, festive, and/or crowd pleasing)

With dinner

American Sparkling Wine

Bargain Bordeaux

Bargain Burgundy

Big Wine

Cru Beaujolais

Gewürztraminer

(Good) Merlot

Pinot Noir from New Zealand

Pinot Noir from Oregon

Reds from the Loire

Rosé Champagne

Sparkling Shiraz

Viognier

After dinner

Madeira

Tawny Port

V-DAY (VALENTINE'S DAY)

(Fragrant, romantic, and/or regal)

American Sparkling Wine
(including Iron Horse's
"Wedding Cuvée")

Bargain Burgundy

Big Wine

Cru Beaujolais (especially
St.-Amour)

Grower Champagne

Old Wine

Pinot Noir from New Zealand
(including Wild Rock's
"Cupid's Arrow")

Pinot Noir from Oregon

Rosé

Rosé Champagne (including
Perrier-Jouët's "Fleur de
Champagne")

Torrontés

Viognier (including Jean Luc
Colombo's "Amor de Dieu"
Condrieu)

With dessert (especially chocolate)

Madeira

Tawny Port

I-DAY (INDEPENDENCE DAY)

(American, barbecue friendly, and good for groups)

American Sparkling Wine
Big Wine
Box Wine
Classic Cabernet
Madeira (for its historical
  significance)

(Good) Merlot
Petite Sirah
Reds from Washington State
Rosé

M-DAY (MOTHER'S DAY)

(Fragrant, floral, pink, and/or special)

American Sparkling Wine
Bargain Burgundy
Big Wine
Gewürztraminer
Grower Champagne
Moscato d'Asti

Pinot Noir from New Zealand
Pinot Noir from Oregon
Rosé
Rosé Champagne
Torrontés

B-DAY (BIRTHDAY)

(Celebratory, festive, and/or special)

American Sparkling Wine
Big Wine
Classic Cabernet
Grower Champagne
Madeira

Old Wine (especially from the
  relevant birth year)
Prosecco
Rosé Champagne
Txakoli

PG-13 POURS

Bleasdale "Uncle Dick" Sparkling Shiraz (Australia)
Desert Wind Chardonnay "Bare Naked" (Washington State)
Fox Creek Sparkling Shiraz "Vixen" NV (Australia)
Olssens Nipple Hill Pinot Noir (New Zealand)
Ra Nui "Sexy Rexy" Rosé (New Zealand)
Trevor Jones Chardonnay "Virgin" (Australia)
Wooing Tree Pinot Noir (New Zealand)

SIDEBARS

BRAVE NEW POURS
BY COUNTRY

ARGENTINA
Malbec, 175
Torrontés, 62

AUSTRALIA
Viognier, 105
Low/No Oak Chardonnay, 90
Riesling, 49
Sparkling Shiraz, 240

AUSTRIA
Riesling, 53
Grüner Veltliner, 86

CHILE
Gewürztraminer, 81
Merlot, 179
Viognier, 105

FRANCE
Bargain Bordeaux, 156
Bargain Burgundy, 127
Bourgeil, 143
Cahors, 161
Chablis, 92
Chinon, 143
Condrieu, 105
Côtes du Rhône, 170
Cru Beaujolais, 123
Gewürztraminer, 82
Grower Champagne, 221
Low/No Oak Chardonnay, 92

Malbec, 175
Merlot, 180
Muscadet, 45
Reds, 143
Rosé, 113
Rosé Champagne, 227
"Sancerre Rouge," 143
Vermentino, 100
Viognier, 105

GREECE
Moschofilero, 41

ITALY
Aglianico, 152
Lambrusco, 232
Merlot, 179
Montepulciano d'Abruzzo, 184
Moscato d'Asti, 254
Nero d'Avola, 189
Prosecco, 236
Rosé, 113
Vermentino, 100

MADEIRA
Madeira, 249

NEW ZEALAND
Low/No Oak Chardonnay, 90
Pinot Noir, 133
Sauvignon Blanc, 57

ACKNOWLEDGMENTS

A Tarzan chest pound for the extraordinary efforts of:

Amy Cherry: whose guidance sparkles as luminously as her name. She is the Platonic ideal of a nurturing and perspicacious editor. And to all Nortonians, whose fine work and kind support I appreciate deeply: Jeannie Luciano, Bill Rusin, Louise Brockett, Devon Zahn, Albert Tang, Steve Colca, Laura Romain, designer Chris Welch, and copyeditor Virginia McRae.

Stephanie Abou: whose sage and catalyzing counsel, whether in El Tigre or the 13th Arrondissement, is captured by her trademark exclamation, "Onward!" And all at Foundry Literary + Media.

Kate Neupert: director of Braveheart R&D, a paragon of professionalism, persistence, and marksmanship.

My Bravehearts: cool cats every one, for their extraordinary generosity, wit, and turn of phrase.

Amy Fletcher of A. E. Photography, cover photographer, whose eye rivals that of a bird of prey.

A 21-gun salute for the inspiration of:

Rob Schipano: longtime design shaman, who never fails to translate my crazy dreams into grand designs.

Gail Spangler: a beacon of savoir-faire, strategy, and deal-making.

Alex Sumner: Tom Ford on a long board and a maestro of the sartorial.

Burt and Deedee McMurtry: marvels of magnanimity and cosmopolitanism. Evan Lodes: whose age-to-palate ratio is without parallel, as well as Cathy McMurtry, and John and Janet McMurtry.

My *vieux amis* and co-conspirators: Samer "Meats, Breads, Cheeses" Hamadeh and Mark "Denim Romeo" Hernandez.

Jane Emery: my literary and Rexian hero, and source of the expression "We're not drunk; we're just exhilarated."

Sanctums of scribing: Paragraph NYC, Soho House, Norwood,

and Doma Café, where the Internet doesn't crackle but the brainwaves always do.

Other honorables and indomitables (in no particular order): Bobby and Jen Peters, Daniela and William Eggleston III, Mireille and Edward Guiliano, Kevin Whelan and cast and crew of *The Winemakers* on PBS, Joan Lane, Melanie Lazenby, Kevin Warsh and Jane Lauder, Judge Kirby and Lan Xue, James Crimmens, Eileen Foliente, Dillon Cohen, Alison Harmelin, Jim Canales, Heidi Roizen, Julie Waters, Laurent Vernhes, Barbara Romer, Tom "Nellie" Nelson, Andrea Hazen and Hazen Art Advisors, Daphne Park, Marnie Old, Wendy Munger, Ahovi Kponou, John "Size 40?" Abbott, Marty Higgins, Dick Christie, Leslie Sbrocco, Mallory Tipple, Hanna Lee, Stephanie Walczak, Michael Dorf, Craig Falkenhagen, Jo Maeder, El Tigre, Nascar C. Phillips, Bill Seeson, David Cashion, John Akeley, Leslie and George Hume, Barbara Stallins and the Stanford Wine Program, Guy Fieri, Lettie Teague, Pete Hellman, Maile Carpenter, Peggy Cecconi, Daniel Richman, Thomas Carrier, Ryan O'Hara, Tyler Colman, Ann Louise Oaklander, Nick Fauchald, Dana Cowin, Christina Grdovic Baltz, Corie Brown, Howard Wolf, Thomas Nutt, Lee Schrager, Patrick Jong, Devin Padgett, Woof Camp, Hillbillies wine lunch, Mike and Gwendolyn Osborn, Heather Willens, Thomas Novella, Birnham Wood Wine Camp, Amanda Casgar, Sibi Daniels, Natalie Thrall, Didier Depond, Kelly Addison, Dixon Robin, Mitchell Fenster, Richard Rubenstein, Dan Beltramo, Michel and Lori Nischan, M. Alexander Hoye, Peta Hartmann, Gene Sarcinello, RoseAnna and Jeremy Stanton, James Corl, Her Excellency Price Hicks, Gabby Bockhaus, Adrian Jasso, K. Don Cornwell, Kasia "Jan 5" Moreno, Lee and Cece Black, Alan Chin and Vanessa Rocco, Laura Locke, Marcy Lerner, Vicki Sant, Phil Melconian, Cathy and Bob Johnson, Jesse Kornbluth, Alexis Krase, Naomi Gabay, Lauren Gould, Chico Mitsui, Bethany Scherline, Brian von Dedenroth, Adam Plotkin, Rick Haelig, Kevin Hartz, Annick De Scriba and all at Editions Solar, Bill Weiss, Gillian Ballance, Amir Hemmat, Dan Fredman, Cam Steele, Caryl Chinn and Kate Williams and all at Karlitz, Tim McDonald, Debra Maddox, Lorie Ann Boyd, Dawn Rowan, Jessie Heron, Samantha Rouff, Josh Wesson, Jeff Rosenblum, Melanie Young, Ava Friedmann, Britt Sponzo, Elizabethe Hooker, Diella Koberstein, James Stegman ("Mojo Rescuer"), Steve Millington, Lauren Glassberg, John Ostahaus, Jee Won Park, Helen Bing, Bill Nancarrow, Carl and Mario at Villa Mosconi NYC, Radu

Moldovean, Leslie Hatamiya, Connie Hernandez and all Hernies, Matt Cashin, Jason Whitt, Matt Paige, John Arrillaga Jr., Natalie Hayes, Clara Ha, The Great Walton Ford, Gareth Conway, Leta Soza, Michael Dorf, Doug Frost, Lizzi Nuell, Alona Elkayam, Debbie Zachareas, Donna Swider, Alyssa Rapp, Teri Tsang Barrett, Elizabeth Fago, Elizabeth Hooker, J. B. Handley, Donna White, Jo Addy, Debra Maddox, Lisa Mattson, Jon and B. J. Blum, Pamela Mitchell, Adrienne Jamieson and Patrick Chamorel, Kendra Cole, Mario Bosquez, Joy Sohn, Mary Russell, Sissy Biggers, Ross Walker, William Tisherman, Joy Simmons, and Eric Waters.

And finally, my gratitude to the continuing encouragement and kindnesses of Mrs. Joan Saylor and all my family, especially Drs. Marilyn Oldman, Elizabeth Oldman, and Elliott Oldman.

"Poosh it."

INDEX

About Mark Oldman

Passionate about helping wine enthusiasts jostle the jaded and slay the snooty, Mark Oldman lectures and writes widely on wine. He is author of the best-selling *Oldman's Guide to Outsmarting Wine*, which was called "perfect" by *Wine Enthusiast*, "winespeak without the geek" by *Bon Appétit*, and "shortcuts to a connoisseur's confidence" by *BusinessWeek*. Currently in its eighth printing, Oldman's Guide won the Georges Duboeuf Best Wine Book of the Year Award, was a finalist at the World Food Media Awards, and is published in Japan, Belgium, and in four volumes in France.

One of the country's leading wine personalities, Mark is a main judge in the PBS television series *The Winemakers* and is filming the show's next season in France's Rhône Valley. He has written about wine for several lifestyle publications, including *Food & Wine*, *Departures*, and *Travel + Leisure*, and he chooses all of the wine picks for the 15 million annual readers of *Everyday with Rachael Ray* magazine. He also lectures at the country's top gastronomic festivals, including the Aspen Food & Wine Classic, the Boston Wine Expo, and the South Beach Food Network Wine & Food Festival.

Since graduating Phi Beta Kappa from Stanford University with a B.A., M.A., and J.D., Mark has long been keenly interested in innovating in the areas of education and consumer advocacy. Mark co-founded the career portal Vault.com in 1997 and served as the company's president through its successful sale in 2007 to a private equity firm. He has served on four major boards of Stanford, including the university's board of trustees, for which he was chairman of its committee on investment responsibility.

Visit Mark online:

URL: www.MarkOldman.com

Facebook: www.facebook.com/wetakem

Twitter at: twitter.com/markoldman